My friend Sandy L[...] 'ss few of will us ever confront. It is as if [...] e multiple demons— the ones that threa[...] that triumph is possible. No novelist would believe that her [...] ble. Not even a fiction writer would dare create a heroine of her beauty, resilience and generosity.

Some people are given burdens to bear that seem insupportable. Occasionally, a Sandra LeSourd not only bears them, but is strengthened by them and becomes a guide for others. This book is her searing story and a loving map for others who are looking for the way out.

—Diane Sawyer, ABC News

Thank you for sharing so honestly and helpfully in your new book...

—Mrs. Billy Graham

Sandy LeSourd's life and ministry attest to the fact that any compulsive/addictive behavior can be overcome by the power of the Holy Spirit. The solutions offered in *The Compulsive Woman* really work because they are based on the truth of God's Word.

—Joy Strang, Publisher of *SpiritLed Woman* Magazine

The Compulsive Woman is a wonderful self-help manual for those battling addictions or codependent issues. It teaches the importance of forgiveness and provides the tools for acquiring a healthy self-image. This book is a must-read for anyone dealing with compulsive behaviors.

—Don Colbert, M.D., Author of *Toxic Relief, Walking in Divine Health* and *The Bible Cure Series*

Finally, a book about emotional healing that is practical as well as biblically sound! Sandy LeSourd doesn't offer a sterile, clinical approach to overcoming addictive behavior. She writes candidly—revealing her own pain and celebrating the many victories she has achieved through trusting Christ. I believe you will experience similar victories when you read this important book.

—J. Lee Grady, Editor of *Charisma* Magazine

The Compulsive Woman is extremely well done. It will be a bestseller!

—Terry Kellogg, C.C.D.P., Author and Lecturer

Women who struggle with any form of hurtful, life-controlling behavior will find in Sandra LeSourd's book an extremely compassionate friend who can show them the way to freedom.

—Brenda Davis, Editor of *SpiritLed Woman* Magazine

Sandra LeSourd dives to uncharted depths in her exploration and experience of the human condition: one full of despair, woundedness, shame, terror, addiction, compulsion and unimaginable pain. She then soars to heights—ascended to only by divine intervention—in order to bring us to a place of solace, peace, comfort, victory and overcoming grace. *The Compulsive Woman* is a must in your library of recovery and healing, whether male or female. We all can gain from her sometimes humorous but life-changing insights.

—Jonathan Benz, Pastor at Covenant Centre International and President of Emissary International

Utterly vulnerable, spellbinding read! We are all crippled in different places, and Sandy promises that Jesus is always bigger. I loved it, and so did my thinker-husband!

—Ann Kiemel Anderson, Author of *First Love*

The Compulsive Woman is the most comprehensive and easy-to-read book regarding recovery from addictions of all kinds. It will be of value to you, no matter where you are in your own journey.

—Sally I. Kennedy, Songwriter and Author of *52 Little Parables from Ireland*

Sandra LeSourd has written a practical and inspiring book that is much needed in the Christian world today. So many compulsions are "too much of a good thing" and therefore do not appear to be bad. I'm grateful that Sandra is willing to share her own past problems to help other women today.

—Florence Littauer, Author of *Personality Plus*

Sandy LeSourd has a fascinating ability to share her life experiences, but more important than that, she shares what she has learned about conquering compulsions. We will definitely recommend her book in our conferences.

—Dr. Francis MacNutt, Author and Founder of Christian Healing Ministries

I have read books that outline problems and books that promise help. Here these two worlds are drawn together. In a practical, loving, detailed way, Sandra walks us through the depths of the valley to a place of peace and hope.

—SHEILA WALSH, AUTHOR, SINGER, SONGWRITER

Your book will be an inspiration to many people caught in the clutches of alcohol, drugs, etc., who need to find a realistic solution to their problems. I admire you for your courage in writing *The Compulsive Woman* so frankly and without blaming others for your problems…for I know others must have contributed to the defeats you suffered. I hope your book will be a bestseller and an inspiration to thousands of compulsive people.

—LENORA SLAUGHTER FRAPART, EXECUTIVE DIRECTOR, MISS AMERICA PAGEANT, 1935-1967

The Compulsive Woman challenged what I once believed—that Christians don't need addiction recovery or inner healing. As Sandy reveals her struggles with addictions and wounds from her past, you will gain precious insight into overcoming your "besetting sins" and how to truly help those you love. Warning: this book is hazardous to your traditional myths and sacred cows. I "double-dog" dare you to read it.

—MELINDA FISH, EDITOR OF *SPREAD THE FIRE* MAGAZINE AND AUTHOR OF *RESTORING THE WOUNDED WOMAN*

The Father's desire has always been to bring us into full freedom. Bless Sandy for sharing such a powerful and anointed message for the women of the new millennium. This book is a must read.

—CAROL ARNOTT, CO-PASTOR WITH HUSBAND, JOHN, OF TORONTO AIRPORT CHRISTIAN FELLOWSHIP

THE Compulsive WOMAN

SANDRA LeSOURD

CREATION
HOUSE PRESS

THE COMPULSIVE WOMAN by Sandra LeSourd
Published by Creation House Press
A part of Strang Communications Company
600 Rinehart Road
Lake Mary, Florida 32746
www.creationhouse.com

Scripture quotations marked KJV are from the King James Version of the Bible.

Scripture quotations marked NIV are from the Holy Bible, New International Version. Copyright © 1973, 1978, 1984, International Bible Society. Used by permission.

Scripture quotations marked NKJV are from the New King James Version of the Bible. Copyright © 1979, 1980, 1982 by Thomas Nelson, Inc., publishers. Used by permission.

Cover design by Karen Gonzalves
Interior design by Sallie Traynor

Library of Congress Catalog Card Number: 2002112467
International Standard Book Number: 0-88419-945-2

This book was previously published as *The Compulsive Woman*, ISBN 0-8007-9111-8, by Chosen Books, Fleming H. Revell Company, copyright © 1987.

Names and details in this book have been changed to protect the privacy of the individuals involved. Any similarities between persons mentioned in this book and persons known to the reader are coincidental and are not intentioned.

02 03 04 05 — 87654321
Printed in the United States of America

To

The

Great

Physician

How Can I Say Thanks...

The writing of *The Compulsive Woman* has been a long—and sometimes painful—journey. Without the loving care and concern of countless people, it could never have been birthed.

Without the sustaining love, support and direction of my late husband and editor, Leonard LeSourd, my story would never have been told. He believed in the face of my unbelief. He took my outpourings—always excessive, sometimes compulsive—and wove together a combination of personal stories, case histories and a vast collection of facts and figures. This life-changing, life-saving book is a tribute to God's amazing grace, His healing mercies and His life-giving freedom from our bondages. Len knew it all along…he knew my story had to be told.

My deepest thanks go to Elizabeth Sherrill for her penetrating analysis and sensitive editing of the manuscript. Also, I want to express my gratitude to Jane Campbell for her creativity in compiling research and for her steady enthusiasm for the project.

There were many along the way who encouraged me to record my story. I wasn't sure I wanted to. It was so private, so personal and so painful to tell. And all the parties were still alive. Standing in a dinner line at a weekend retreat in the mountains of Montana one July evening, I told my story to Dr. William Berg of Minneapolis, who was the retreat leader. His response was simple and direct: "Sandy, write a book and tell your story. It will ignite people's hope, give them faith to struggle on and assure them that no situation is too hopeless for the healing power of God."

A special thanks goes to Brennan Manning, whose tapes and books ministered hope and the reality of God's unconditional love and forgiveness to me in the early days of my recovery when I didn't feel lovable or forgiven.

Extra thanks go to the indomitable forces behind the production of this book: Regina Trollinger, Yvonne Burgan, Mary White, Virginia Payne, Ann Moran, Sondra Johnson, Elaine Brink, Jeanne Sevigny and Pat Dowell. Your willingness to serve and your caring hearts have been such a blessing to my life.

Very special thanks to the inexhaustible Alice Harrison, who went way past the extra mile revising and adding new material to this updated edition. You are a Godsend!

And to my wonderful family members, friends, doctors, counselors, pastors and fellow travelers, too many to list, whose love, dedication, prayers, time and sacrifice have been crucial factors in my journey to recovery…to you all, my everlasting love and gratitude.

TO GOD BE THE GLORY!

—SANDRA LeSOURD

FOREWORD

andy LeSourd has written a personal, frank and sometimes startling account of the inner journey of a woman who first discovered herself lost within her compulsive behaviors, but then, crying out to God, she found a full, abundant life, free of bondage. The line between the control of one's thoughts and actions, and abandonment to obsession and compulsion, may be a narrow one for all of us. This story of the former Miss Vermont's life realistically highlights a transcendence of that line.

Obsessions with alcohol, eating, sex, shopping—in every behavior imaginable—are counterproductive and destructive. Sandy found her obsessive behavior to be an enormous liability in her relationships with men, her children, society at large, herself and, most importantly, God. Many obsessions can frequently remain hidden socially or perhaps even be reinforced by the company that one keeps. When this happens, the compulsive individual is *helpless*.

This helplessness is mostly born of inner wounds. Sandy, for example, experienced abuse at the hands of an uncle at age five and grew up in the insecurity of a broken home. The sense of helplessness eventually festers into hostility and uncommon dependencies. Ultimately the ability to communicate and share adequately with *anyone* at all is diminished or destroyed. Such a life becomes empty and painful.

On the other hand, people who are truly disciplined exhibit a self-control that is characterized by inner peace and harmony. They are an asset and benefit to themselves, their loved ones and society. This control comes not from the outside, but from surrender to the leadership of Jesus Christ within through the Holy Spirit. It was only after surrendering her self-will and the determination to make things happen that Sandy was able to understand her powerlessness and to integrate acceptance and gratitude into her life. She learned to *feel* rather than just to act out symbolically.

We all suffer from an *unction dysfunction* when the Holy Spirit is not allowed to work perfectly within us. The Holy Spirit's functioning unction made manifest in us gives the vital discipline that a whole and productive life requires. The beauty in Sandy's story, as she tells it here, is found in her difficult journey from a dysfunctional life of compulsion to a functional, fulfilled life. Each of us must cry out to God daily, as Sandy did, to receive His unction and attendant discipline. Only then can we avoid the downward spiral of compulsion and uncontrolled self-indulgence that is so evident in our society today.

Sandy's life and this book show us the beauty of a lady, helplessly out of control, who came to know God's sovereignty and direction. May the Lord bless Sandy and her message as she turns the hearts of all who read this book to the Lord, the only One who should have control over our lives.

—James P. Gills, M.D.
Founder and Director of St. Luke's Cataract & Laser Institute
Tarpon Springs, Florida

Contents

Table of Contents

Table of Contents

Who Is the Compulsive Woman?

o you know her? Is she your relative, friend or neighbor? Is she you?

She's the woman whose life revolves around food. She eats too much—or too little. Junk food and sweets are often her downfall. She's the woman whose TV is on all day; perhaps she lives her life around soap operas. She's the cyberspace nut who spends most of her waking hours on the computer. She's the woman who volunteers for everything, who can't say *no*.

The compulsive woman is an exercise fanatic, jogging miles every day, rain or shine. She's the one who hits the mall hoping for a shopping high even though her credit cards are maxed out. She may be a chain-smoker or a closet alcoholic, hooked on prescription drugs or sex or dependent on male approval for her sense of worth.

The compulsive woman is easy prey for psychics, spiritists and cults of every kind. She's a perfectionist who never lives up to her own expectations. Her natural drive and energy have become distorted; her motor is running wild, and she doesn't know how to turn it off. She has an irrational need to do something over and over to the point where she has lost control.

In other words, the compulsive woman has a complicated problem, and the solution to her problem has to address more than her primary addiction or symptom.

1

The Compulsive Woman

According to a study in the February 1987 issue of *Ms.* magazine, "The patterns of dependence (for women) have been obscured by the tendency to look at individual addictions rather than the forces that create dependency." One of the significant features of the *MS.* survey was a precedent-setting demonstration that the compulsive personality expresses itself in more than one addiction. *Cross-addictions,* that is, multiple or reinforcing addictions, are a tremendous problem for the compulsive woman, and a cure is difficult as long as one tries to treat only the symptoms without getting at the root causes: fear, anger and—in particular—shame.

Whereas guilt has to do with our behavior, shame hits us where we live. "I'm not OK... I'm such a bad person no one loves me...I'm a mistake... My pain doesn't matter..."—a compulsive woman is born.

The compulsive woman is often addicted to love—toxic, destructive love. Or she may be dependent on men as the primary source of her value. And this pattern leads to lack of self-direction, self-control and self-esteem.

Doctors Connell Cowan and Melvyn Kinder state:

> Addicted people are willing to endure anything in order to reexperience that physical and psychological state of being, that compelling satisfaction they feel whenever they take in that substance, whatever it is—alcohol, drugs, nicotine, food, or a man's love. This hunger for love becomes obsession when it reaches such a proportion that the woman feels she needs it just to feel that life is worth living, just to maintain her everyday emotional balance.[1]

I was led to a study of compulsive behavior not out of any abstract interest, but through the desperate need to understand my own life and behavior. I had not one but all of the compulsions mentioned above. I was cross-addicted to almost *everything* at one time or another. The despair it caused led me at various times to try to kill myself. If you identify with my symptoms and misery, I hope that my pathway to recovery will also inspire and encourage you in your battle to gain mastery over yourself and your life that has gone out of control.

I have built this book from my own life struggles. As a result of my research into compulsivity, I have included in the back of the book self-assessment tests, information about compulsive/addictive behaviors and resources telling where you can find help.

Introduction

It is possible for the compulsive woman to break the patterns that control her, to recover her self-worth, and to lead a constructive and joyous life. That is the promise of this book.

—SANDRA LeSOURD

PART ONE

ILLNESS AND RECOVERY

MANY PEOPLE OPERATE in their daily lives as automatons, almost completely unaware that their nearly every action is dictated by compulsion, with little or no freedom of choice and with virtually no spontaneity. Many people don't know the difference between compulsion and choice... [They] are so overwhelmed and tyrannized by their compulsions that they must act out (do things) immediately, impulsively, without thought or consideration in order to overcome complete and utter paralysis.

—Theodore Isaac Rubin, M.D.
The Winner's Notebook

1

FACING OFF

As I walked up to the wooden gate of the camp sponsored by the Compulsivity Clinics of America, after having been dropped off in the parking lot by a friend, I felt my stomach knot in fear. *Don't be silly,* I told myself. *You're here to learn more about yourself—why you've been a compulsive person all your life. There is nothing to be afraid of.*

I had felt this way before—the first day of school...being dropped off at Girl Scout camp. But to have these feelings now was ridiculous. I was forty-eight years old!

Anxiously I looked about the crowded parking lot—doors slamming, men and women tugging suitcases and duffel bags from yawning car trunks. Were all these people as apprehensive as I was?

A ruddy-faced young man standing in the center of the parking lot pointed toward a gray wooden lodge half-hidden in the Minnesota woods. Falling oak leaves swirled about his head as he spoke. "You'll be staying up there at the end of the path. Down here," he gestured at a brown log building closer by, "is where you will be fed."

A comforting thought, being fed. Was I going to be preoccupied with food this week?

Only a month ago my interest had been perked by a telephone conversation with a vivacious young woman who had just "graduated" from this Compulsivity Clinic course. She had enrolled with serious food disorders, only to discover she was alcoholic as well.

I knew I had been an alcoholic—correction, was a recovering alcoholic—and that I had other compulsive behavior problems as well. It was time to subdue the rest of these monsters.

The advance information had fascinated me:

> The Compulsivity Clinic program offers you the opportunity to uncover the causes of your compulsive behaviors. It provides support to make lifestyle changes. You will learn about:
>
> - Addictive relationships
> - Managing change
> - Dealing with shame and guilt
> - Chemical dependencies
> - Sexual abuse and addiction
> - Suicide and depression
>
> Self-defeating lifestyle problems can include:
>
> - Workaholism
> - Relationship dependency
> - Eating disorders
> - Smoking
> - Gambling
> - Online dating/Internet porn

As I struggled up the walkway with my suitcase, I was filled with fresh resolve to uncover those hidden areas buried deep within myself. Dread and exhilaration—unlikely companions—coursed through my veins.

At the door of the lodge a staff member issued a green plastic three-ring notebook containing the week's schedule and other information; then with a warm smile she assigned me to a bed. All the staff people looked energetic, lean, disciplined and bright. I wondered how they viewed us.

What are these people going to find out about me?

More terrifyingly: *What am I going to find out about myself?*

The women's sleeping areas were separated by carpeted room dividers. I found my cubicle at the far end on the right side. Good. I would have some privacy here. Suddenly I wanted to protect myself from getting too close to these others.

Across the aisle I glimpsed a thin young woman solemnly unpacking an orange nylon duffel bag, methodically and mechanically sorting her personal belongings. A pile of paperback books slid onto the floor with a thud. As she dove to retrieve them, the words *child abuse* on one of the covers caught my eye. I could only speculate that my silent roommate across the way bore some invisible scars.

After tidying up my tiny cubicle, I looked it over with satisfaction. To counter harsh ceiling lights, I had brought my small gooseneck reading lamp. It now threw a comforting beam of light on my "security blanket"—a new blue down bathrobe, a recent purchase so I would not be cold in the Minnesota night air.

At five o'clock we all streamed back to the dining hall for an early dinner. I fought down nervousness as I filled my plate and selected a seat. *You've been in groups before,* I told myself. *Relax.*

It was a futile command. The thick hero sandwich I began to stuff into my mouth suddenly exploded into a shower of ham, lettuce, tomato and onions. As I tried to catch the falling food, my paper plate tumbled to the floor. My feet were awash in debris. As every eye in the room turned to survey the mess, I let out a self-conscious giggle. Immediately the entire room broke out into gales of laughter.

"Looks like you'd better start all over again," cracked a large blonde woman seated next to me. As she turned toward me, I noticed a steel brace supporting her back.

Looking around the room at the now smiling faces, I felt cheered somehow that my blunder had been a welcome icebreaker. Everyone had been as tense as I was.

After dinner the leadership team was introduced, including Terry Kellogg, founder of the Compulsivity Clinics, and we got down to basics. First some important definitions were explained to us.

- **OBSESSION:** recurring, persistent thoughts, images or impulses that occur in your mind. They seem to come from nowhere; they are not voluntary. You do not seem to be able to control or suppress them, though you try.

- **COMPULSION:** an insistent, repetitive, intrusive and

unwanted urge to perform an act that is contrary to one's ordinary wishes or standards. Since it serves as a defensive substitute for even more unacceptable unconscious ideas or wishes, failure to perform the compulsive act leads to anxiety. Performing it relieves anxiety. Yet performing it is also linked with the desire to resist doing it and often a sense of shame. The compulsive link to a particular act, event, experience (like gambling or shopping) or thing (like alcohol) often leads to addiction.

❖ ADDICTION: a pathological link or relationship with a mood-altering act, event, experience or thing that causes major life problems. An addiction is more serious than a compulsion and can be life threatening if it involves substance abuse (alcohol, drugs, or even food and tobacco). It is behavior that continues despite adverse emotional, medical, financial or social consequences.

After the introductory staff comments, the twenty-five of us who had enrolled in the clinic introduced ourselves and spoke briefly about the problems that had brought us there. We were alcoholics, drug addicts, chain-smokers, gamblers and compulsive TV watchers. Many had come with sexual compulsions or severe relationship dependencies. Most of us had one form of eating disorder or another. Some were given to excessive shopping, spending or other types of binge behaviors. It was heartening, somehow, to know that my secrets, my problems, were also the secrets and problems of others. Several faces now brightened with a new sense of hope.

Mic Hunter (who later became the coordinator of the clinic) assured us that what seemed impossible to resist was indeed resistible, that our problems were treatable and curable. He later offered this checklist to help identify compulsive behaviors:

1. Is the behavior ritualized? If interrupted, does the person get upset?

2. Is there time distortion when the person is involved in this behavior? (Does it go on for much longer than he thinks it does or than he expects?)

3. Does the person set rigid rules for himself in this behavior, and then tend to violate them? (For example, he says he'll drink only between the hours of ten and twelve, and then doesn't.)

4. Does the person go to extremes, from overdoing to underdoing, in this behavior?

5. If there are negative consequences, does the person continue the behavior anyway?

6. Is there any "situation stressor" causing this behavior? (A man insulted sexually by a woman who has spurned him, for instance, may launch a succession of promiscuous relationships, but only to prove his masculinity and not as a compulsive behavior. When he understands the reason for what she said, or that it isn't true, he will stop his promiscuity.)

7. Is there preoccupation ("obsessing") about this behavior, in which the person thinks more about it than anything else, so that it interferes with his life?[1]

After the introductory comments, our first group session came in a small room with mahogany-paneled walls and one large window. We all sat on floor pillows. It felt strangely cozy inside these walls, almost womblike. There we met our six group members: two men and four women, including myself.

Our counselor, Maureen, welcomed us: "You are to become a family. You are to eat together, spend time together when we are not in this room and be there for each other. I want you to experience trust and love for one another, something you may never have really known in your own families."

She paused for a moment. "For the rest of the week, please do not contact anyone on the outside. This is especially important for those of you with relationship dependencies. We suggest you don't call out and 'get a fix.' You're here to focus on yourselves, feel your true feelings and confront your fears. I urge you to stay within the framework of our program so as not to become fragmented."

I liked Maureen, a lovely Irish wisp of a woman with a cloud of short auburn hair and a mellow, soothing voice that was competent and reassuring. Maureen described herself as a recovering alcoholic from a strongly dysfunctional family.

"Over 90 percent of American families are dysfunctional to some degree," she added. She defined the dysfunctional family as one in which either father, mother or child has a problem that causes an imbalance in family relationships. A father may be addicted to alcohol; a mother may have a nervous breakdown; a son or daughter may have a serious illness. Whatever the specific issue, the family begins to revolve around the problem, ceasing to function in a healthy, mutually supportive way.

Soon a cover-up of feelings begins. Hurt, angry and confused emotions are stuffed down inside of us, kept concealed even from ourselves. Out of touch with our own deepest truth, we feel driven to do things without knowing why. Compulsive behavior is born.

Fred, a heavyset man in his thirties, sat in the corner frowning. He was a stockbroker in the Gamblers Anonymous program. Wall Street, he confided, was spawning a new breed of gambler, the compulsive investor. Fred spoke slowly, as though physically exhausted.

Maureen bore in on him. "I suspect you are so full of sugar and starch—they act as medication, you know—that your real feelings can't get through. For the rest of your time here, Fred, I want you to abstain totally from all sugar and white flour. You need to cleanse your body of these substances before you can start to *feel* what you need to feel."

The stories that poured out from this group triggered memories and pain of my own:

"I've always had problems with money and men."

"I'm a chain-smoker and addicted to soap operas."

"My wife said if I didn't get some help for my pornography addiction she would divorce me."

"My father raped me when I was eight; then my uncle and my two brothers took advantage of me. I hate them all."

My contribution: "I've had five years of sobriety, but I know I've only struck the tip of the iceberg in working out my compulsive behavior."

Each person spoke with deep emotion, some with anger, some with tears. An ever-present box of tissues was scooted about the room. Complete strangers a few hours earlier, we began to see ourselves by the end of the session as being bound by a common thread of inner pain.

Facing Off

I was too keyed up after this encounter to go to bed, so I took a short walk under the trees. Geese honked on nearby Lake Minnetonka; the smell of burning leaves recalled fall nights in Vermont where I grew up.

I wondered how I had come across. Had I sounded too "put together"? Hollow? Superficial? Defensive? Had I used too many humorous quips to keep people from getting too close because I was too selfish or scared to communicate more meaningfully?

After breakfast the next morning I stopped to talk with the woman in the steel back brace who had sat next to me the night before at dinner. Perched uncomfortably on a straight Naugahyde chair, she was wheezing and struggling for breath.

"Can I help you?" I offered weakly.

She pointed to her pack of cigarettes. "You could take these things and throw them in the lake. But I'd probably be fool enough to dive in after them."

"I used to be hooked on them, too," I said, and then wondered if my "used to" sounded lofty or self-righteous.

The small group session that morning was heavy going. We again sat on pillows in a circle, while Steve, the other male in our group, sobbed uncontrollably and rocked back and forth on his pillow. He told the group about his problem.

"I hate myself!" he kept saying, pounding the oversized pillow beneath him. "I told myself when I came here I wouldn't read that stuff again, but I read it last night before I went to bed. Then I took a fantasy trip and..." He didn't go on.

"Steve, who are you *really* angry at?" Maureen asked.

He was silent for a moment. "I guess it's my parents. It goes way back. As kids, we couldn't be normal. You know, no smoking, no drinking, no dancing, no movies."

"So reading sex magazines was a way to get back at them," ventured Maureen.

Steve nodded. "The only thing my parents ever said to me about sex was, 'Don't do it. It's wrong.' Since they wouldn't answer my questions about masturbation, I felt like a freak." He started to pound his thighs with his fists.

"Steve, stop beating yourself up," Maureen ordered. "I want you to get in touch with how lonely you have been, how isolated you've felt."

13

Steve's realization moments later: "When I started rebelling, voices inside me began saying, 'You're *bad*!' That really scared me. I guess I was scared because I wondered if those voices in my head were from my parents, from God or from the pit of hell."

He talked for half an hour. We all went through his torment with him. Finally spent from this wrenching session, Steve leaned back against the wall. The toes of his stained white tennis shoes were tilted slightly inward, reminding me of a little boy abandoned in his playpen. I had a glimpse then of a little Steve, desperate and lonely, wanting to be picked up and held.

Then the little boy opened his eyes, reached for his horn-rimmed glasses, cleared his throat and was transformed before our compassionate eyes into the Steve of today, the forty-year-old accountant.

Each day there was some kind of breakthrough in a member of our group. Some of the things I heard resembled my own nightmares. Others represented the secrets and fears of other lives.

Peggy, thirtyish, with green eyes and a sprinkle of freckles, was office manager for a small insurance company. Despite her responsible position, she had come to the clinic desperately needy and scared. The oldest girl in a family of four, she had been responsible for the care of her younger brothers and sisters. Her mother, obese and deeply disturbed emotionally, had spent most of her time in bed, getting up only for trips to the bathroom or refrigerator. Her father, a violent and abusive man, had beaten his children unmercifully.

"I became sexually active with boys in my class at age thirteen," Peggy related. "By the time I was seventeen, I'd tried it all, except marriage. That was a disaster. All four of my marriages have been failures. I've lost track of the times I've tried to kill myself...six, eight."

"Why suicide?" asked Maureen.

"Maybe suicide was an attempt to kill that part of me I didn't like. The guiltiest I feel is about my abortion twelve years ago. Since my marriage was breaking up, I thought it would be a mistake to bring a child into the world. I never told my husband."

"Would you like to let go of that guilt, Peggy?" Maureen asked.

Peggy wiped her nose with the back of her hand. "Oh, God, yes! Is there any way I can?"

Maureen moved across the room to where Peggy was sitting and put her arm around her. "We're going to have a memorial service for your child, right here. Would you like to invite the group to be part of it?"

Peggy blinked, her stricken eyes meeting the gaze of each of us seated around the room. "Would you all like to come?" she asked.

Profoundly affected, we nodded.

What Maureen didn't tell us then is that ritual acts often help to break the pattern of guilt that underlies compulsive behavior. That is why cleansing rituals as an expression of real faith—rituals like baptism and communion—play such an important role in many addicts' recovery.

"Does your baby have a name, Peggy?" Maureen asked.

"Yes. Her name is Kim."

"Please invite Kim to come into the room and be with us now."

Peggy moved her lips self-consciously, her eyes filling with tears.

"Would you describe Kim to all of us, Peggy?"

"She is twelve years old. Her hair is blonde, and she has blue eyes. She looks so sad. There are tears in her eyes..."

"Do you know why she looks so sad, Peggy? It's because she doesn't want you to go on mourning for her. She is happy and at peace in heaven. Is there anything you would like to say to Kim?"

Breaking a long pause, Peggy blurted out in a shaking voice, "*Please* forgive me, Kim. I was so confused when I found out I was pregnant with you. I was so frightened and unhappy. I didn't dare to have you. Please forgive me! I love you, Kim. I miss you, and I miss not having you with me now when I could be a mom to you. But I wasn't ready. I hope you can understand that." Peggy broke down, her tears and mascara running together down her cheeks. Most of the women in the group were also weeping.

"Is there anything else you would like to say to her, Peggy?"

"Just I love you...I love you...I know we will be together someday."

"It's time to say good-bye to her and to let her go."

"Good-bye, Kim...good-bye...I love you..."

The six days at the clinic felt like forever, yet when they were over, they seemed to have sped by. We had exercise sessions and lectures on the dysfunctional family, sexual disorders, nutrition and so forth. Information helps us to get a handle on our problems, I learned, because fear plays a major role in compulsive behavior.

The last morning I took an early morning walk alone, past Lake

Minnetonka into the forest. The woods were pungent with the smell of moist earth. I found a sunny spot on a gently sloping hill where leaves protected me from the damp ground. Easing my body to the ground, I looked skyward in self-examination. I felt strangely vulnerable, so I began a deep breathing exercise we had been taught in one of our sessions. In…out…in…out. We had been taught that getting proper oxygen to the brain is often enough to help reduce or eliminate the fear response. Agoraphobics and other people afflicted with fear are often able to reduce their anxiety simply by improved breathing. Hyperventilation occurs frequently during anxiety attacks and makes you feel dizzy and that you are losing control.

The breathing exercise helps compulsives as well. We used it in combination with focusing mentally on our grief, pain or sadness. After a while, a surge of emotion welled up from deep inside me. I sobbed wrenching sobs, thinking of my new friends. The intimate details of our lives we had shared and the mutual support we had given one another had brought us close together.

The Compulsivity Clinic had provided insights into the nature of the problem millions of women face but left me with unanswered questions: How can compulsive people change? Were we wounded ones permanently damaged, or was there a clearly marked path to wholeness? How far along was I? Were there any positive elements in compulsive behavior?

The root cause of all compulsions, we had been told, was fear and shame. I needed to ponder that deeply, to look for the origins of shame in my own background.

The search would take me not only into my own history, but also into the experiences of many others. It would take me to hospitals and clinics, halfway houses and self-help groups, into libraries and research centers. It would set me interviewing health professionals and people struggling with current addictions.

I offer my own story as an illustration of the genesis and growth of compulsive behavior. It is typical of the inhibiting and self-defeating patterns many women live and suffer under. It also illustrates the processes by which you and I can be released from the bondage in which compulsions keep us.

MORE THAN OTHER EMOTIONS, shame involves a quality of
the unexpected; if in any way we feel it coming we are
powerless to avert it. This is in part because of the difficulty we have in admitting to ourselves either shame
or the circumstances that give rise to shame. Whatever
part voluntary action many have in the experience of
shame is swallowed up in the sense of something that
overwhelms us from without and 'takes us' unawares.
We are taken by surprise, caught off guard, or off base,
caught unawares, made a fool of. It is as if we were
suddenly invaded from the rear where we cannot see,
are unprotected, and can be overpowered.

—HELEN MERREL LYND
On Shame and the Search for Identity

THE VIOLATED CHILDHOOD

I learned something about myself from every person at the clinic. Some of their experiences helped me open long-closed doors in my past. Peggy's story was much sadder and more traumatic than mine, but, with her green eyes clouded, she pried open a door I had sealed shut in my childhood. Peggy traced her low self-worth to unremitting abusive treatment by her father and the unsupporting, passive behavior of her obese mother, who became a negative role model for her.

Because her mother was so disturbed, Peggy had to fill the role of mother to the other children. Before she reached puberty, Peggy found a way to prevent her father from beating his children: sex. If she gave in to her father's demands, he would not abuse the younger children.

"My father wanted to have sex with me all the time. I just didn't have the strength to resist, so I let him," Peggy had told us dispassionately. "I felt it was my fault somehow that my mother acted so strangely."

My heart had ached for her. Basically a talented, responsible person— she had held her office job for seven years—Peggy's emotional life was a mess. A compulsive eater and drinker, obsessed by fears, she had been looking desperately for help. The memorial service for her aborted child, Kim, had been a good start. A lot more healing had to take place inside of Peggy before she could acquire positive feelings about herself.

What was the connection, I wondered, between sexual abuse in childhood and compulsive behavior problems in adulthood?

Reading *Silent Scream* by Martha Janssen on her incestuous relation-ship with her father helped me understand Peggy's agony of spirit. Martha Janssen's book is written in blank verse:

> *Daughters love to sit*
> * on daddies' laps.*
> *Me too.*
> *I would scramble up*
> * at the end of the day.*
> *We'd talk until Mother left the room.*
> *Then we'd "play."*
> *Now I know*
> * why I watch so carefully*
> * little girls sitting*
> * on their daddies' laps.*[1]

My mind went back to a clinic lecture. If children are sexually molested, then the "boundaries" of their bodies have been violated. It's as though their right to say no has been stolen from them. Thus they grow up confused, with certain protective limits erased, prone to erratic and compulsive behavior. Such people have a lifelong struggle with shame.

Shame, I learned, has to do with how we feel about ourselves, whereas guilt has to do with our behavior. We incur guilt when we violate some value we hold, but it has a constructive purpose in that it motivates us to make amends. Shame has no such constructive purpose; it turns us away from others and strikes a blow at our very worth as persons. Shame iso-lates and alienates. It makes us feel that we're no good, that we're unwor-thy of respect.

Because shame is almost impossible to communicate, and because a person suffering from shame tends not to talk about his problem—or even perhaps be aware of it—he looks for temporary relief through some outlet like food, drugs, alcohol or any "mood-alterer" to ease his pain.

Estimating rates of sexual violence against women is a difficult task. Many factors stop women from reporting these crimes to police and to interviewers who are collecting statistics on the rate of crime in our country. Women may not want to report that they were assaulted because it is such a personal experience, because they blame themselves, because they are afraid of how others may react or because they do not think it is useful to make such a report. However, there are statistics that demonstrate the magnitude of this problem in this country:

> The Department of Justice has recently released an important new study: "The Sexual Victimization of College Women." Its chief finding is about 2.8 percent of women in college experienced a completed or attempted forcible rape in the previous approximately seven months, only about 5 percent of which are reported to police.
>
> Extrapolating from these figures, the authors suggest 4.9 percent of college women suffer such an assault in any given calendar year, and perhaps 20 to 25 percent over the course of a typical undergraduate career.[2]

Between 1995 and 1996 more than 670,000 women were victims of rape, attempted rape or sexual assault.[3] The study mentioned earlier from the February 1987 issue of *Ms.* magazine compiled striking anecdotal evidence that "women who have been victims of incest or rape are vastly overrepresented among the addicted population."

Only in recent years have women been able to acknowledge their rejected memories and describe their experience. The emotional progression of a victim goes something like this:[4]

1. There is a deep inner hurt and dismay over the sexual violation, a feeling of being damaged goods.

2. There is a fearful resolve not to tell anyone.

3. There is an attempt to bury the episode(s) in one's subconscious, where the memory festers and creates an inner disorder.

4. Adult relationships with men are severely damaged.

5. Trust and intimacy problems with both sexes develop.

6. Suicide can seem the answer—as it had to Peggy.

The road back to health for the victim takes this course:

1. She faces up to the fact of abuse, dredging it up from the subconscious.

2. In a therapeutic setting, she admits to others that it

happened, as Peggy did in our small group. Once this exposure gets the abuse into the light, much of the destructive power goes out of it.

3. She sees it as the abuser's problem and fault, not hers.

4. She forgives him/her for it at the appropriate time.

Peggy's experience, outwardly so different from my own, nevertheless had triggered childhood memories. The change from the emotionally charged atmosphere of the six-day Compulsivity Clinic to the more relaxed pace in my small rural community was what I needed to begin to sort those memories out. I developed a whole new perspective on this period of my life, including one traumatic episode that had burst out of my subconscious. One day with notepad and pen I began to dig into my early years.

At first glance my childhood seemed utterly normal. An only child, I was reared in the small community of St. Johnsbury Center, Vermont. My father, Richard Simpson, was a handsome and gregarious man. He was a salesman, first for an appliance store, later for an automobile dealer. His wife, Elizabeth, my mother, was a fragile, pretty woman who centered her life on homemaking with few outside interests.

For me going to the old Congregational village church was a high point. On Sunday mornings I'd arrive starched and curled, eager for the Sunday school lesson to begin. The smells linger to this day: men's minty aftershave, the musky, damp odor of the church bell rope (how I longed to give it a hearty tug), coffee, cinnamon and ham from the church kitchen.

I can still see the ladies dressed in dotted Swiss and print voile dresses, their "finger-waved" hair-dos as precise as metal washboards. The men in their three-piece suits seemed oddly stiff, as though their legs wouldn't bend in pants with such razor-sharp creases. Their hair slicked down with Brilliantine, noses and cheeks aglow from vigorous scrubbing, their hearty "how-do-you-do" rang through the building.

My classroom was a clutter of small oak chairs presided over by our teacher, my Aunt Ethel. Next to the large blackboard was an oak-framed picture of Jesus. I recall His strong, sensitive face, long, beautiful, flowing hair—and His warm, loving eyes. Jesus was holding the lost sheep in one arm, a staff in the other hand, with a red cape over His long white garment.

"Jesus loves you," Aunt Ethel would intone. "He wants you to come to Him with whatever is bothering you." What was bothering me in those early years was the fact that my father and mother didn't seem to love each other as other daddies and mommies did, but I couldn't even tell Jesus this.

Then my aunt would teach us from the Bible. A verse she often chose was, "He was wounded for our transgressions, He was bruised from our iniquities…and by His stripes we are healed."[5] I couldn't understand these words at all. Aunt Ethel explained that the stripes were the wounds of Christ, but the only wounds I saw in the picture were in His hands and feet. They looked more like holes in His flesh than stripes. Yet the verse was strangely comforting.

The hour of Bible stories always passed too quickly for me. Soon it was time to join the grown-ups in the auditorium, where the organist extracted loud and wondrous sounds from the quaking mahogany organ with her favorite selection: "Yes, Jesus loves me…"

How I loved these Sunday afternoons when we would motor around the Vermont countryside in our slate-gray 1938 Plymouth! Occasionally we'd take the hour's journey to where my Uncle Ralph and Aunt Agnes lived. Aunt Agnes always had freshly fried doughnuts and orange Kool-Aid for us, and her house smelled of lavender and polished wood.

One of these visits, however, was not so pleasant. For many years what happened that Sunday at Uncle Ralph's had been buried deep inside me. Peggy helped me recall it. The rest I discovered in a therapy session. As I began to put the episode down on paper, I trembled so violently I had to get out of my chair and walk around the room.

It happened when I was five. On this particular Sunday we had driven there in time for lunch. Afterward we gathered around the old player piano in the living room for a songfest. Uncle Ralph let me select the music roll from the glass-front cabinet where the player rolls were stored, and then he let me sit beside him on the piano bench.

Mother and Aunt Agnes didn't sing; they just sat nearby smiling encouragingly as Dad, Uncle Ralph and I warbled away. Dad sang tenor to Uncle Ralph's bass, with my squeaky child's voice feebly carrying the melody.

Every time a polka was played, I would slip off the bench and skip about the house. I would skip through the dark hall with its ticking clocks, past Uncle Ralph's gun case with the stuffed animals on top, then out through the kitchen past the black wrought-iron stove with its gleaming chrome trim, on into the dining room. Breathless, I would jump back onto the piano bench, bumping affectionately into Uncle

Ralph as he manipulated the brass levers beside the keyboard.

When the music ended, Aunt Agnes, a gardener of great skill, invited us to help pick vegetables for diner. Usually when she suggested this I'd be the first one out the door, but on this occasion I decided to stay behind while Uncle Ralph rolled his handmade cigarettes, a ritual I found fascinating. All the ingredients were in place to start production when Uncle Ralph sank down into his oak rocking chair. I noticed that his face was flushed and his breathing wheezy.

"Is something wrong, Uncle Ralph?" I asked.

"No, dear, not really, but I would feel better if you'd come over here and sit on my lap."

Eager to please, I approached the seated figure, turning my back to him expecting to be lifted into his lap. Instead his strong hands pressed my small body next to him. He gripped so tightly I could hardly breathe; then one hand groped for my pubic area. I heard his rasping, measured breath, felt the brass fittings on his suspenders digging into my shoulders.

What was going on? Why was he breathing so fast? Now he was pressing and poking and hurting me through my cotton dress.

Terror filled me. Shame…horror. What if Dad, Mom and Aunt Agnes were to walk in now? I could hear their voices chatting nonchalantly outside. "Let's dig some more beets," I heard my father say.

What is this man whom I love and trust doing to me? Uncle Ralph wouldn't touch me *there*…but he is, and he's acting crazy and frantic and his false teeth are clicking in my ears. Oh, somebody help me!

After little short gasps and moans, his hands dropped limply beside me. He slumped back in the squeaking rocker like an exhausted rag doll, his eyes shut, the spittle running down the corners of his mouth. The only sound now was the *tick-tock* of the hall clocks.

Breaking loose from his locked legs, I streaked upstairs to the bathroom, past the stuffed animals. My heart was pounding, my stomach heaving, and my eyes burning with tears of guilt and fright. There was the beautiful ceramic jar with the blue forget-me-nots where Aunt Agnes saved the long strands of her jet-black hair. This saintly and pristine lady, what would she think of me? I let Uncle Ralph touch those private parts that Mother told me no one was to see or touch. Mother and Dad would be furious if they knew! They must never find out. Deep within me something was dying—a joyfulness and a trust. A passage had been made from innocence to something I wasn't quite sure of, something frightening and unclean.

I pressed my body so hard against the washbasin that my chest ached. Gallons of water must have passed through my desperately scrubbing hands. My nightmare was interrupted by a familiar tap at the door. My dad always knocked that way. *Dum-dum-da-dum-dum-da-dum.*

Poking his head around the door, he teased, "Snookie, are you going to use up all the water in the reservoir? We're waiting on you to come help with dinner."

"I'll be right down, Daddy."

Shyly I entered the kitchen, the skipping child of an hour ago now silent, ashamed and wounded by an encounter she neither understood nor could share. Irrevocably I gave myself an order: *I will never, ever tell anyone what happened today.*

The beets stained my small fingers as I scrubbed off the dirt in the old stainless steel sink. My hands were almost raw. Would I ever feel clean again?

Years later at the Compulsivity Clinic, I asked Mic Hunter if this single instance of sexual abuse could be one of the underlying causes of my compulsive behavior.

Compulsivity, he admitted, usually has a complicated genesis. The shame/guilt reaction of the victim in cases of abuse can be a major contributing factor. The key is the way in which the family responds to the person who has been victimized. In my case, he said, there was no one I felt I could talk to. Nor did anyone notice my trauma symptoms. The implication to me as a child was, *Your pain doesn't matter.* So I forced the pain inward and blamed myself.

It was significant, I think, that I tried ritual, obsessive hand washing to cleanse myself.

According to the psychologists Pamela Vredevelt and Kathryn Rodriguez in their book *Surviving the Secret,* there are five common identity and interpersonal problems suffered by sexual abuse victims:[6]

1. Minimizing their own abilities and maximizing others' strengths

2. Tending to take responsibility for others' behavior

3. Having difficulty achieving intimacy with others

4. Tending to think if they please others they will be considered "perfect"

5. Worrying obsessively about problems and sabotaging their own efforts to change

In retrospect, I can see that my experience of being abused shattered not only the trust I had in myself, but also in others close to me—and even of the boundaries of the world as I knew it.

PASSIVE DEPENDENT PEOPLE are so busy seeking to be loved that they have no energy left to love. They are like starving people, scrounging wherever they can for food, and with no food of their own to give to others. It is as if within them they have an inner emptiness, a bottomless pit crying out to be filled but which can never be completely filled.

—M. Scott Peck, M.D.
The Road Less Traveled

3

The Dysfunctional Home

Though I was fortunate that neither of my parents drank—I became an alcoholic in spite of this—it was apparent to me at an early age that my father and mother did not enjoy being with one another. Dad's absence for three years during World War II didn't help. Our home, off-balance because of the problem relationship between my two parents, was dysfunctional.

As the alienation between my mother and father grew, a spirit of sadness took over our home. A dome of silence seemed to settle over us. Yet for years, probably because of me, their only child, my parents struggled to hold their marriage together.

I remember a recurring dream in which I was a lifeguard trying to pull my parents to the ocean's shore. I'd swim frantically to rescue one as the other went under. I could never get them both to safety; one or the other would drown before I could reach him. Choices! Which one to save? Why couldn't I save them both? I'd awaken tangled in my bedclothes, heart pounding, my nightgown soaked in perspiration.

Tensely I'd lie awake until Dad's short, dry cough from the adjoining bedroom and the sound of Mother's steady breathing assured me that all was well.

But all was not well. They were playing a charade called marriage. Sometimes my mind would form a strange fantasy. I imagined that our rambling three-story house was actually made of cardboard. If you cut on the dotted line, you could fold it up and return it to the carton it had come in. One day I'd return home from school and there would be nothing there—just a grassy plot with a few lilac bushes standing sentinel over an empty hole.

Often my heart would race with fear as I hurried up the broken asphalt sidewalk of Elm Street after school. Maybe today was the day the house had vanished. All the other neat clapboard homes were in place, their prim, Priscilla-curtained windows following my anxious odyssey toward home. Eagerly my eyes would sweep up the street to our house on the hill. It was still there!

My steps would quicken. I hoped there would be a simmering pot of chowder on the stove. First I stamped my muddy feat on the square raffia mat, then burst into the kitchen. I was always trying to bring light and sunshine into the house, into my parents' cold marriage.

There was Mother, neatly groomed in her modest cotton house dress, her sad hazel eyes lighting up as her only child came through the door. She seemed so fragile, so vulnerable. I felt responsible for her. How I wanted to throw my arms around her and tell her not to worry, that I would protect her.

After chowder and cookies I would slip out the kitchen door and head for my very own sanctuary. There it was! The golden glow of the afternoon burst through the pink and white blossoms of my apple tree, warming my long braids and sprinkling me with diamonds. My skin was dusted with golden flecks of light. The red clover and buttercups in my hand were celestial blooms.

Vermont disappeared in a misty vapor, our house and garage spinning away into space. Here I was away from sad, unhappy people. My apple tree was a magic place. There was no pain here, no confusion. No one spoke cross or accusing words.

My tree always welcomed me. It never said, "Come back later; I have branches to straighten now." Just, "Come rest in my arms. You're safe here."

My tree had a heartbeat. I could feel the rhythm pulsating as I sat into the branches. I didn't mind sharing my tree with the robins and the fat honeybees.

My earliest "addiction" was for love and approval. There were happy times with my father. He taught me while I was still small to use carpentry tools and do other boyish things. I was only four when I started "helping" him work on our gray Plymouth. He'd take the motor apart, placing nuts, bolts and gaskets in murky baths of lubricating oil. I'd swirl them around with my hands and squeal in delight as the oil ran down my arms. How much I depended on Daddy's approval!

Knowing deep down that my parents' marriage was failing, I tried harder to please. It was at this point that I slipped into what I now know as the "codependent role." I so wanted our family life to be happy that I was ready to play any part that could bring this about. Very early, perhaps as a contrast to the joylessness in our home, I determined to be a "fun person." I was always playing jokes on others, mimicking my teachers and friends. I laughed a lot and developed a reputation as a class clown. I was not yet a true compulsive, but already my gaiety had something excessive about it, as though I were telling myself, "I *will* be happy!" Hurting inside, my defense was a perpetual smile.

Years later I was to read my own youthful situation reflected in the words of social philosopher Helen Lynd:

> The discovery that our parents are not all-wise and all-good and that we must face the uncertainties of our own judgment…is a lonely experience. It becomes still more lonely and poignant, and in a real sense shameful, when it is followed by a realization that, instead of our elders being our interpreters of the world, our protectors, we must, instead, protect them from their own fallibilities and shortcomings, and from the shameful knowledge that we are aware of them.[1]

I was also to learn that an addiction-prone personality like mine typically manifests an exaggerated degree of compliance and is overly concerned with pleasing people and winning approval.

But not even my desperately cheerful facade, as it turned out, could stop the breakup of our home. I was fifteen when Mother and Dad separated and filed for divorce. I retreated to my apple tree on the hill. By now my teenage legs were too long for the "stirrup" limbs, and it seemed pretty dumb to sit in a tree at my age. So I'd lean up against the warm bark, feeling the heartbeat of the moving sap. Was my parents' separation something I had caused? Was there something I could still do?

All year my heart throbbed like a toothache. Typical of young people in dysfunctional families, I felt increasingly responsible to take care of my mother—to fix everything in her life, to "make it all better," the phrase she often used when she kissed a bump or a scratch.

My tree had no answers. So I retreated behind an air of bravado, masking my hurt with a casual veneer. Life was a charade…smile…pretend. I practiced my act before my dressing table mirror—"so-what" expressions, "I-couldn't-care-less" gestures. Cultivate the quick, merry laugh, Sandra Jean. Crinkle your eyes in merriment.

After the divorce, both my parents entered second marriages that proved to be solid and lasting. Not aware of the happiness ahead of them, however, I remained the confused child in-between. Feeling disconnected with family life, I sought love like candy, intensely trying to be more acceptable to my friends.

One of these friends was Linette. She was a sunny blonde with a dazzling smile and a Bo Derek figure that drove the guys at Spaulding High School wild. We were sophomores when Linette invited me to spend the weekend with her while her parents were away in Montreal.

She set out popcorn and potato chips, then poured Cokes from a frosty twelve-ounce bottle. "Should we put some bourbon in these?" she asked.

"That would be fine with me!" I replied in my best Rita Hayworth imitation. I had never seen a bottle of bourbon.

Linette went to a dining room cabinet and flung open the double doors. Before us stood a dazzling array of liquor—vodka, gin, Scotch, bourbon, brandy, wine, creme de menthe, rum, champagne. What an education!

How worldly I suddenly felt as she measured a crystal shot glass of bourbon into each glass of Coke. After stirring the swirling mixture with a pink flamingo swizzle stick, she triumphantly handed me my glass.

"Here's to Spaulding High!" she toasted.

The mossy smell of the liquor sifted through the sweet Coke aroma. Now I was in the big leagues—a rite of passage—a woman at last!

Yuk. The first rush of bubbly liquid hit my tongue. "This tastes awful, Linette."

"It gets better as you go along," she assured me.

Sure enough, the second and third swallows were less pungent. A warm, tingly feeling was taking hold. "I see what you mean. This is OK!"

I burbled, gulping the contents of the glass.

"Hey, take it easy," Linette warned. "You shouldn't drink it so fast!"

Before long my body felt as though it were floating in warm butterscotch sauce. I felt cozy and cared for...and cared about.

"Do you suppose I could have another?" I don't remember how may times I asked this question that evening.

Sometime later Linette telephoned our boyfriends. When it came my turn to talk, I gushed something wonderfully witty into the phone.

"You all right, Sandy?" the boy on the line asked. "You sound funny."

That's the last thing I remember.

I awakened fully clothed, flat on my back on the bed in Linette's guestroom. By flinging my leg over the side, I stopped the room from spinning. Then waves of nausea came, and I rushed for the bathroom. Kneeling on the tile floor I gripped the toilet in a death lock.

I didn't feel at all like Rita Hayworth now.

It would be two years before I had another drink—but I had the exact same chemistry to become an alcoholic. I see myself in this statement:

> The dulling of sensibility, the soothing feeling that all is well, is a powerful experience for some people...Those who depend totally on such an experience do so because it gives their lives a structure and secures them, at least subjectively, against the press of what is novel and demanding. This is what they are addicted to.[2]

After graduating from high school, I enrolled at the Rhode Island School of Design in Providence. On weekends several of us would go to nearby Brown University for fraternity house weekend parties. Feeling like a small-town bumpkin in my homemade clothes and unsure of myself in the company of sophisticated Ivy League girls, I began to depend on alcohol for my security.

During exam week in May 1956, at the end of my second year in Rhode Island, I got a telephone call from my father who was now living in Barre, Vermont, with his new wife, Nora. "The Chamber of Commerce wants Barre to have a contestant in the Miss Vermont Pageant this year," he told me, "so I volunteered you. Your picture ran in last night's paper."

I was too stunned to speak. Dad had always been a practical joker, but this time he had gone too far.

"The pageant is next weekend at the Burlington High School

Auditorium," he continued. "You'll need to be there on Friday with a talent presentation."

Panic set in even before I hung up. What would I wear? What in the world could I do for a talent presentation? Could I lose twenty pounds before next weekend? Fretful hazel eyes stared back at me from the bathroom mirror. Dark circles. Jowls. Why did I stuff myself with all those sugar doughnuts at the Bluebird Cafe?

Somehow I completed my exams, got some clothes together and made the trip to Burlington, Vermont—all in three day's time. The pageant weekend activities were a blur of teas, lunches, interviews and rehearsals. The night of the finals was brutally hot; the makeshift fans that wheezed asthmatically from the gymnasium balcony raised barely a tickle of breeze. As I went onstage to do my talent, I was sure I would faint.

I had decided to repeat a skit I'd done at the School of Design, a pantomime about the precocious little six-year-old Eloise who lived in New York's Plaza Hotel. To my amazement the audience in Vermont seemed to like it, filling the auditorium with riotous laughter and applause.

Still, as the contestants circled the stifling auditorium in formal gowns for the final time, I knew I had no chance of winning in the face of the far more beautiful and talented competition. I was already undressing in the basement as the announcer began to call up to the stage the runners-up for the title of Miss Vermont.

I had just gotten out of my soggy copper-colored velvet gown and was struggling with a jammed hook and eye on my voluminous crinoline hoopskirt when the final announcement came: *"And now, Miss Vermont of 1956, Sandra Jean Simpson of Barre!"*

I couldn't be hearing right.

Struggling back into my clothes, I stumbled up the stairs and burst onto the brilliantly lit stage. Blinking in disbelief, I heard applause pouring from the packed auditorium. People were standing on their chairs. Even the judges were giving me a standing ovation. I was in shock.

A crown of daisies, roses and ferns was placed ceremoniously on my head. It was too big and slipped down over my ears. A brass trophy was thrust into my hands, while a white satin banner affirmed that I was indeed being named Miss Vermont of 1956.

My eyes scanned the audience for my parents' faces. Mother was weeping copiously on the left side of the auditorium. Dad and Nora were clapping wildly on the right. For one addicted to pleasing others, it was a heady experience.

Suddenly I felt somehow terribly alone and vulnerable. The thorns in a mountainous bouquet of red roses pricked painfully at my arm. In all that noisy, spotlight-lit room, only the pain seemed real.

Though I didn't know it, the pain had just begun.

SUPPOSE A BOTTLE SHOULD MATERIALIZE before him full and unopened. Once assured of its reality, how calmly then, all excitement gone, he would open it and pour, almost not needing it in the security the sight of it gave him. But he would drink it, of course. He wouldn't care how bad it tasted—un-iced, without water or soda, lukewarm, stinking, throttling. He would drink a good half-glass at once—and at once the pricking nerves would die down, the thumping heart quiet, the fatigue and ease come warmly over him at last. That's what liquor and only liquor could do for him...

—CHARLES JACKSON
The Lost Weekend

Into the Fast Lane

The morning after the Vermont pageant I awoke in my father's home to the scent of roses. I rolled over in bed and touched the gleaming trophy on the nightstand. So it wasn't a dream; it had really happened.

"Here's the morning paper, Miss Vermont," my stepmother chirped, bringing coffee. "Your picture is on the front page."

Indeed it was. There, above an expanse of bare shoulders, a mass of greenery and flowers obscured my eyes. Only the tip of my nose protruded out from under the foliage like a shiny cautious mouse. "Oh, no," I groaned. "I look like a tossed salad."

Weeks later the same horrid picture glared at me from the slick pages of *Confidential* magazine. The magazine staff had amassed the most unflattering photos of state pageant winners they could dig up and concocted what they felt was a real pageant exposé. The caption under my picture read: *Is This Vermont's Best?*

Shortly thereafter each contestant received an unsettling flood of letters from members of a fundamentalist group as we prepared to go to Atlantic City for the Miss America Pageant. We were informed through elaborate maps and diagrams that we had chosen the road to death and destruction.

My oversized crown was not the only unflattering aspect of the newspaper picture. At 146 pounds I was twenty pounds overweight. A stint as tennis instructor at a summer camp turned out to be a good way to prepare for the Miss America Pageant looming ahead in September in Atlantic City. The campers monitored every mouthful of food I ate, and by late August the twenty pounds were gone.

Meanwhile, filling the duties of Miss Vermont had its perilous aspects. Who, for example, would have anticipated horse shows? At these appearances it was my duty to tromp to the center of the field, present trophies to the victorious riders and pin the ribbons to the bridles of their snorting, grasping mounts. Since horses have terrified me since early childhood, these ribbon ceremonies represented pure torture.

The Stowe Horse Show was almost canceled by heavy rains. But "the show must go on." At the judge's nod I picked my way gingerly through mucky clods of earth toward the biggest, blackest stallion ever born.

As I approached, this black monster reared up on his hind legs. When his right front hoof came down, it pummeled my left foot into the slime, driving my periwinkle pump several inches into the mud. Only my stocking foot emerged, undamaged—but how does one walk off the field with one shoe? My fear of the beast turning to indignation, I began to dig furiously for the submerged pump. Some unseen force was pulling it in the opposite direction. By now my white gloves were two clunky paws. At last I struggled upright, clutching the oozing shoe, while a nervous judge helped me off the field past the tittering onlookers.

Unaware that my insecurity had turned me into an all-out-people-pleaser—especially with men to whom I automatically looked for approval—I accepted blindly all suggestions put forward by the Vermont Development Commission, the Chamber of Commerce and the Vermont Ski Association. In spite of the fact that September was breaking all heat records, I agreed to travel to Atlantic City dressed in ski garb. The outfit they chose made me look like a raspberry-colored walrus. (Raspberry was the newest and most daring shade in skiwear in 1956.) But I lived to please.

Departure day at Burlington's airport was the initial test. Approaching the plane I had my first tussle with my cumbersome skis and poles. Even though laced together, they clearly had a mind of their own and poked out of my frantic grasp in all directions. Trying to be terribly nonchalant, despite the trickles of perspiration running down my face in the 80-degree heat, I stumbled up the narrow stairs of the DC-7, my ski boots massive lead weights. Somehow the stewardess and my traveling companion, a charming woman named Barbara who was director of the Vermont Pageant, got me sandwiched into the narrow seat.

Getting off the aircraft at LaGuardia Airport for a change of planes was difficult, but a breeze compared to my encounter with the revolving doors inside the terminal. Barbara sensed impending disaster. "Clasp your skis and poles close to your body," she urged. "Take teensie steps until you get around, then step out slowly."

Holding my breath, I clattered into the swirling cubicle. What happened next I can hardly describe. Skis, poles and I flew from the spinning contraption like an exploding pinwheel. Barbara darted to safety as a pole zipped by her head. Stunned onlookers peered in disbelief at the tangled mass of steel and bamboo that lay sprawled on the marble airport floor.

We did eventually arrive at the Atlantic City airport where we were whisked into a pageant limousine. When we emerged at the Claridge Hotel, Barbara collared the photographer who had been assigned to record my arrival. Where was that promised brisk breeze from the ocean? I was about to faint from the heat.

"Let's set up the shot on the beach," the photographer suggested, leading us across the boardwalk and onto the scalding sand. There I strapped the skis to my boots and crouched in my best downhill position while he took shot after shot. The blowing sand caked my perspiring face and stuck in my teeth. My knees felt as though they'd never unbend.

Afterward I clomped off dutifully to Registration. Assembled contestants floated about the palatial ballroom perfectly coiffed and groomed—immaculately pressed, buttoned and zippered. Over in the corner, by contrast, was propped a wretched raspberry robot, fumbling with skis and poles.

The net result of the ski publicity attempt:

1. No picture in any paper—local or otherwise

2. Two huge blisters on both heels

Pageant week continued to provide one glitch after another. I spilled food and broke my zipper at a crucial moment. At the end of my talent presentation, I forgot the presence of stagehands and bustled about cleaning up my equipment, causing, to my mortification, a burst of laughter from the audience.

Yet this very laughter served as my escape. As I had learned, first as a child, then as a teenager, I covered my confusion with pranks and prat-falls. It won me acceptance from the other contestants, who voted me Miss Congeniality.

Once again the press handling did little for my ego. One reporter noted that my listed weight of 146 pounds (recorded before I had dropped the twenty pounds) was the highest of any contestant and wrote this caption under my picture: *Fattest at Pageant Is Friendliest.*

Nevertheless, my future seemed full of promise. The day after the Miss America Pageant (beautiful Marian McKnight of South Carolina won that year), I was flown to New York and introduced to the Broadway columnist Walter Winchell. Winchell delighted in discovering young talent and creating opportunities for them. Thus began an unusual friendship. Probably because my naivete intrigued him, he took a fatherly interest in my career.

One night I was escorted by Winchell and Joe DiMaggio to a party for Judy Garland at the Plaza Hotel. The small-town girl from Vermont gazed around the room awestruck at the celebrities from sports and show business. In the glow of the flickering candles and flowing champagne, the world seemed a warm and wonderful place. I became hooked on the celebrity lifestyle. Hoping to launch me in an entertainment career, Winchell got me breaks on television variety shows. But even his clout could not compensate for that fact that I was a lousy actress.

By now I was going to classes at the Parsons School of Design in New York City and working part-time at the Vermont Development Commission office in the Radio City Music Hall building. There I met the Operations Manager of Disneyland, who offered me a job as an artist doing caricature sketches of tourists. Soon I moved into a Newport Beach, California, beach house with three other girls.

After a two-week apprenticeship under a Disneyland instructor, I was assigned a location at Sleeping Beauty's castle. My first assignment might have served as a warning of trouble to come. A young mother with three sons signed up to have each child sketched. The first two likenesses flew easily from my pad. Not so the third. The little boy wiggled, slid down from his chair, made faces and stuck out his tongue. The first three tries were disastrous, the fourth barely acceptable.

I was close to tears. What was wrong? Why was my hand shaking?

Into the Fast Lane

Could it have been because of the beach party that had gone on until two that morning? My roommates seemed to feel fine after these late nights. Why couldn't I stop after one or two drinks the way they did?

In any case, the Disneyland job lasted only for a season. Pepsi Cola, one of the Miss America Pageant sponsors, offered me a position in their public relations department with a good salary and an expense account. I moved back to New York City.

One of my first assignments was to go to Providence, Rhode Island, to help with a fashion show promotion put on by the local Pepsi bottler. While strolling down the familiar streets—it was hard to believe three years had passed since my father's phone call ended my stint at the Rhode Island School of Design—an episode occurred that, once again, should have alerted me to the excessive side of my personality.

Ahead I saw a familiar storefront logo: *Kays of Newport*. As a student, I'd drooled over their gorgeous shoe windows, but I could never afford a single pair, even on sale. Today the store windows were swathed in wide paper banners: *Relocation Sale! 50–75% off!!*

Seated inside the store on a plush velvet chair, I smiled nervously at the salesman. "I was thinking of a little evening sandal in silver," I said, trying to sound sophisticated.

Soon he returned balancing six shoeboxes.

"Ooooh," I squealed amid a flurry of fuschia tissue paper, as he slipped a gleaming sandal with rhinestone trim onto my foot.

"I'll take them!" I gasped enthusiastically, not wanting to appear gauche and ask the price.

"Would you care for something similar in gold?" he asked.

More boxes, more mountains of tissue. "These lucite sling pumps with rhinestone heels are very new…"

If they were very new, I wanted them. After all, I was expected to be a trendsetter, wasn't I?

Back and forth from the treasure trove behind blue velvet curtains he bounced, arms laden with boxes—black patent pumps, red espadrilles, blue and white candy-striped "slings," purple iridescent slippers, navy suede sandals, charcoal gray dinner shoes, yellow flats with flower trim.

"Yes…yes…yes," I kept saying.

By now the tower of boxes around my chair was obscuring me from the rest of the store. The sales staff were clearly impressed. So were other customers. Who was this extravagant mystery woman? I loved the attention.

An hour later my shopping binge was complete: twenty-two pairs of shoes, five matching handbags. One entire month's salary gone. The purchases would be delivered to my hotel that afternoon.

How was I going to pay my rent? Somehow that didn't matter. I floated back to the hotel in a euphoric trance. From then on, shopping would give me what almost amounted to a chemical high.

Dr. David J. Juroe, writing in his book *Money*, comments on just this kind of reaction:

> For those inclined toward buying, compulsive spending sprees keep them on excitable highs, away from being bored or listless about life. What really happens is that the compulsive striving, in this case spending, sustains the constant activity that is needed to distract them from the real inner disturbances.[1]

I was to become very much like the woman described below in "Compulsive Shopping":

> It is 7:00 P.M. and twenty-eight-year-old Liza Moran [not her real name] is in tears because her boyfriend has just called to cancel their dinner date. This has happened four times in the past month; Liza is afraid the relationship is falling apart. She looks at the clock, realizes the stores are open until 9:00 tonight, and heads out the door.
>
> Several hours later, Liza returns home with a $200 cashmere sweater and a $150 pair of suede boots. She would have bought even more but she had already used up most of her available credit on an earlier $1000 shopping binge that began after her boyfriend canceled a weekend in the country.[2]

The article went on to describe Liza as a compulsive shopper. When anything goes wrong in her life, she spends money. Liza even uses the language of drug addicts to describe her shopping sprees and their guilty aftermath. "I get high when I catch the first whiff of perfume from the cosmetics counters," she says. "I'm flying the whole time I'm in the stores. The crash comes the next day, when I look at the pricetags on everything I've bought. I tell myself I'll never do it again, but I know I will. The high is worth the letdown."

Into the Fast Lane

The pace of my own life speeded up. Early morning plane departures. Cabs, terminals, hotel hobbies. Hands to shake, speeches to make, an endless blur of faces and places. Lonely room service dinners. A drink to blunt the loneliness. Better still, two drinks...

The glamour soon began to wear off as I battled the pinchers and strokers who grabbed at me. At times I felt like a plastic wind-up Barbie doll; at other times I felt like a trained seal: "Throw me a fish, and I'll balance a ball on my nose!"

"How many other gals are raking in the dough you're making, doll?" one Pepsi bottler asked me.

True. I would be silly to quit such a rewarding job. Yet if people only know how grim it was to live out of a matched set of turquoise Samsonite luggage. Finally I placed a call to my boss in New York: "Mitch, I can't go another mile. I've been on the road now for five weeks straight. May I take a rest?"

"Sure. Why don't you take a few days in Palm Springs and soak up the sun?"

Sitting by the pool of a fancy resort hotel, I let the warm California sun melt away my battle fatigue. I knew I was drinking too much. Often I had made promises to myself...one more drink and I'd toddle off to bed. Too often there'd been a rising sun on those words. Time only for a shower, a change of clothes, then it was back to the cola wars.

Reaching for the suntan oil I realized hours had passed. The pool waiter was certainly efficient. I wondered if he had counted all the drinks he had served me. It didn't matter if he had. I was an important public relations woman. I was in the big leagues now.

Weaving slightly toward the thatched snack hut, my toe caught in a chaise lounge leg, and down I went onto the pool tarmac. Four waiters in safari uniforms leaped to my rescue. Gently they seated me at a glass table under a tilting purple canvas umbrella. "May I bring you something to eat, miss?" one asked.

My skinned knees burned. "Yes, bring me one of those pineapple things with shrimp...and perhaps a vodka martini on the rocks."

After all, it was lunchtime, and the guys back in New York would be at the Cub Room starting on their Bloody Marys. I missed the camaraderie and the comfort of that coterie of bodies pressed together at our end of the bar, the Bloody Marys and the inevitable London broil accompanied by soggy sliced tomatoes and mushy green beans. Nirvana!

Another martini arrived. The whiff of juniper pricked my nostrils as the first bracing jolt of the velvety liquid exploded my taste buds.

Wow, Simpson, you're a fireworks gal! You glitter. You flash, You dance in the sky.

Although for me...at least at first...alcohol acted as a stimulant, it is known to depress the activity of the central nervous system.

In their book *Self-Watching: Addictions, Habits, Compulsions,* Drs. Ray Hodgson and Peter Miller describe the effects of alcohol as follows:

> In small doses [it] results in a lessening of tension and a feeling of relaxation and lack of inhibition. Increased dosage, however, leads to a progressive loss of control over judgement, skills and emotions, often accompanied by violence and aggression. In large doses alcohol poisons the whole system and may result in coma followed by death. Alcohol also has a long history of inducing a dependence which is notoriously difficult to break.[3]

Traveling with the current Miss America became one of my greatest challenges at Pepsi. (I was now the coordinator of the Miss America/Pepsi Cola Scholarship Foundation.) It was my responsibility to see that her public appearance schedule was kept within limits, which was not an easy task when the host bottler was paying a thousand dollars a day and wanted her to visit his favorite Aunt Minnie for "just a couple of minutes."

Then there were those harrowing evenings when the new queen was to appear at the same function where Mrs. Alfred Steele (Joan Crawford, wife of the Pepsi Board Chairman) was also attending. As Walter Winchell warned, "Don't invite Miss America (any Miss America) and La Belle Crawford to the same party." When it happened, as it had to, we staffers went into maneuvers not unlike a beachhead invasion, complete with walkie-talkies, to make sure those two stellar females didn't cross paths. Mrs. Steele didn't like to share the spotlight with beautiful younger women.

I used to have the cold sweats hearing in Mrs. Steele's icy voice the words I most feared: "Miss Simmmmmmmmsunnnnn!" Joan Steele was a diminutive dynamo in matching couture creations. Her hat, gloves, handbag and dress were frequently stitched from the same bolt of fabric; those high-heeled sandals with clear plastic ankle straps were her trademark. The famous crystal-blue eyes, flashing under the black slashes of her eyeliner, and the stony set of her crimson, butterfly-shaped lips could transform me into a pillar of salt.

I developed an especially close relationship with Marilyn Van Derbur, Miss America of 1958. One evening after a long, stressful afternoon of appearances, Marilyn, her official pageant traveling companion and I decided to have dinner sent up to her suite in an Atlanta hotel. We ordered filet mignon, which arrived on a pink linen-skirted room-service table, along with a bouquet of pink sweetheart roses.

"Thank God this day is over!" I gasped as we kicked off our shoes and collapsed into chairs about the table.

"Why don't you do just that?" Marilyn urged.

"Just what?" I asked, trying to blink away the rum punches I had gulped down in the hotel bar before coming up.

"Thank God. Why don't you say grace, Sandy, so we can start on this gorgeous dinner?"

I was nonplused. I didn't know a grace to say. I couldn't even remember the last time I had heard one.

Then she rescued me. "That's OK, Sandy. I'll say it. You've had a rough day."

Softly Marilyn thanked God for His goodness, for His protection and for her responsibilities and privileges as Miss America. I suddenly wished I could talk to God as she just had. How may years had it been since I had gone to Sunday school or church? Five? More like ten.

What I couldn't understand was why I wasn't enjoying my life more. I was meeting glamorous and important people; I had a solid income (although never quite enough to cover my shopping flings) and all the travel and excitement I had ever dreamed of. Yet I was empty and frustrated and needy and scared. Nothing was filling that void in my chest regardless of what I tried to stuff inside me. It was a hole so empty that the wind seemed to blow through it.

I was twenty-two and alone too much. I was drinking by myself more and more. On lonely evenings my mind would travel wistfully the "white-cottage-and-rose-trellis" route. Maybe it was time for me to get out of the fast lane and settle down somewhere.

Colette Dowling writes:

> [The Cinderella complex] used to hit girls of sixteen or seventeen, preventing them, often, from going to college, hastening them into

early marriages. Now it tends to hit women after college…after they've been out in the world awhile. When the first thrill of freedom subsides and anxiety rises to take its place, they begin to be tugged by that old yearning for safety: the wish to be saved…the Cinderella complex.[4]

But where is Prince Charming when you really want to find him?

For me he turned up in a most unlikely place: Billings, Montana. The Pepsi bottler there had arranged for a blind date for me.

"Oh, no," I groaned, recalling the disastrous evenings set up for me in other cities.

"But he's Billings' most eligible bachelor!"

"Maybe the most eligible bachelor in the whole Northwest," the Pepsi supplier chimed in.

"And to top it all off, he's a *doctor!*"

Bells went off in my brain. Wedding bells. A doctor. That rose-covered cottage. Security. Prestige. A man to depend on. A man to love me. I had myself walking down the aisle in yards of white Chantilly before I had even met him. And when I did, he was ruggedly handsome—a tanned, angular face, sandy blond hair, tall, athletic frame.

The evening flew by…a blur of cocktails at his apartment, dinner in a dimly lit Chinese restaurant, dancing at the Skyline Club atop the rimrocks that formed the northeast border of the city. My heart was dancing as fast as my feet.

Parked outside my hotel in the wee hours of the morning, Werner leaned an arm on the wheel of his Thunderbird convertible and looked me straight in the eye. "Young lady, I think I want to marry you." Nine weeks later we were en route to Europe on our honeymoon.

Who is this stranger I married? I thought, waking in a Paris hotel to see a tousled head on the pillow beside me. We knew so little of each other. A flurry of phone calls, flowers, *I love you* letters. So little time together… maybe two weeks total, if that.

I was suddenly frightened. Marriage was such a big step, and I was so ill prepared. Maybe this isn't really happening. Maybe I'll be getting on a plane in a little while, on my way to some Pepsi promotion. But no, I was replacing one treadmill with another.

The honeymoon was a string of riotous days and nights. Afterward Werner stayed on for a radiology conference scheduled months before, while I went on ahead of him to New York. A week later I met him at the International Arrivals Building at Kennedy Airport with some unexpected news. I felt sure I was pregnant. His face dropped. So did the ever-present pipe in his mouth.

"All those people in Billings will think we had to get married," I wailed as we headed for home.

"That's OK, honey," Werner assured me. "Let them talk. You and I have got the world by the tail."

Wrong. I had a tiger by the tail, and its name was alcohol.

The invitations started as soon as we got back to Billings. Who was the beauty queen from the East who had snatched the town's most sought-after unattached male? Many seemed dying to know. Dinner parties, luncheons, summer barbecues…an endless flow of social engagements.

Usually parties were my forte. Not when I was pregnant, I soon learned. Would I ever be able to stop carrying my little bag of soda crackers?

Sitting on the lawn of our lovely new brick home on Rimrock Road during Werner's long days at the hospital, I would look out at the college campus across the street, wrestling with the feeling of unreality that still swept over me. The collie dog at my side looked up at me with adoring moist brown eyes. Was this really me? The doctor's wife in Billings, Montana?

Nine months after our marriage our son was born. We named him Bradford, after Brad Frapart, the business manager of the Miss America Pageant who had become a good friend. Our Brad was adorable, a cuddly bundle. It was almost like playing dolls, only this doll cried and shrieked.

I had never been around a baby before. Werner assured me that motherhood would come naturally. In his eyes, apparently, mothers were all capable. Twenty minutes after his son and I came home from the hospital, he headed out the door to go bowling.

Brad was four months old when my doctor told me I was pregnant again.

To help me adjust to this news, Werner took me to Mexico. We left Brad in Billings with Werner's parents—strict, Old World German Swiss who still spoke with heavy accents. I was intimidated by my mother-in-law. She towered over me in every sense. She was a devout Christian always talking about "the good Lord." I couldn't remember what was so good about Him.

"Bring me another Margarita," I said now to the hovering beach waiter.

Brent burst into the world feet first the following April and never stopped running. An active, cheerful, precocious baby, he kept me running, too. I was lifting him from his bath one morning when I caught sight of Brad grinding the contents of a can of coffee into the gold carpeting of the dining room with his little saddle shoe.

"I'm not cut out for this," I moaned as I raced to retrieve the can from Brad's chubby fist. "I need a drink. I deserve a drink."

Brent was four months old when the doctor again had staggering news.

"I'm pregnant again, Polly," I told the woman who was living with us now to help care for the two little boys.

"That's wonderful!" she exclaimed. "Wouldn't you like to lie down and rest?"

Lie down? I wanted to flee—somewhere, anywhere. There was a Junior League meeting that afternoon. Or was it the Medical Auxiliary? An addict to volunteering, I belonged to every organization in town that could keep my mind off the growing silence between Werner and me.

Nancy Friday's best-selling *My Mother/My Self* described the kind of anxiety-ridden, angry, compulsive woman I had become:

> The compulsive housekeeper, the lioness of the Anti-Porn Society, the nonstop charity-worker, the overprotective and critical mother who does it all for someone else's good—who can fault these people out loud?...Very often, these women are obsessive/compulsives—suffering from forms of behavior that seem to have nothing to do with anger. Unlike depressed people who turn their anger within, against themselves, the obsessive/compulsives express theirs outwardly—but in such an indirect way they never need face their furies at all.[5]

My third pregnancy was the hardest of all. In my sixth month, regularly as clockwork at one in the afternoon, the premature labor pains would begin. Hospitalization was the only way to prevent the baby from being born too early. For six weeks I lay in a room on the maternity ward. And every afternoon at one the familiar pains would begin.

Into the Fast Lane

Lisa was a beautiful little girl with dark curls. Six weeks premature, her head was barely larger than a tennis ball. So fragile. So helpless. So in need of dedicated mothering.

With Lisa's birth I'd had three children in less than three years. Lying in bed in the hospital through the weeks of waiting had provided a time for reflection. How little of this there had been in my twenty-five years! I seemed to have careened through life with my motor racing. I couldn't seem to turn it off. *I want...I want...I want* had fueled it. "Anything worth doing is worth overdoing" seemed to be my motto.

But surely now, as a mother with three children, I could stop scrambling for whatever it was that kept eluding me. Now I would slow down, savor, devote myself to raising my family.

I returned home with my daughter in my arms and high resolve in my heart—and was soon driven as frenetically as ever. I didn't yet apply the word *compulsive* to my behavior.

Nor had I ever considered an observation like that of Stanton Peele, a social psychologist and probably the foremost expert on addictive behavior: "A person will be predisposed to addiction to the extent that he cannot establish a meaningful relationship to his environment as a whole, and thus cannot develop a fully elaborated life. In this case, he will be susceptible to a mindless absorption in something external to himself...his susceptibility growing with each new exposure to the addictive object [or experience]."

In fact, there were a succession of habits I seemed powerless to stop. The more I hated myself for them, the more I did them. The chain-smoking that had begun in lonely hotel rooms now launched the day: I couldn't get out of bed until I had a lit cigarette in my hand. The four-letter words I'd acquired as "one of the boys" popped out increasingly when I least intended them.

What to do about my bulging waistline? I hated the flab and knew I needed to do something about it. Exercise! Jogging! I bought black tights and a leotard for workouts, a warm-up suit and a pair of running shoes for jogging. At a women's program at the Y, I groaned and moaned through my first session. Agony! Next I donned my running gear and jogged around the wooden running track until cramps forced me to stop.

Day after day it was the same routine: exercise, jogging, then I pummeled my fat on the wooden rollers and my hips with the canvas vibrating machine. My body began to revolt. Cramping, nausea, clouded vision. I simply didn't know when to stop.

"Jogging…can become addictive in its own right," writes psychotherapist Howard M. Halpern in *How to Break Your Addiction to a Person*. "I have seen people so obsessed with running and so uncomfortable and anxious about missing a planned run that the activity begins to interfere with other important areas of life."[6] (See section on Compulsive Exercising on page 233.)

Far from cutting down outside activities, however, I continued to volunteer for every civic cause that came along. I'd open my mouth to say *no* and out would come, "Of course! I'd be glad to."

Where was my backbone? But Polly was so competent with the children, so patient and steady…so unlike me. The only part of married life in which I felt confident was entertaining—and a doctor's wife did lots of that.

So the years slipped into a pattern: part-time mothering, full-time socializing. The drinks required to get me into a party mood grew in number. So did the awkward moments, the blackouts and the incidents I simply could not remember.

Like the turkey episode one Thanksgiving. Our guest list had grown to twelve. Preparation the day before had involved marketing, fixing dishes ahead of time, fussing over the table setting and arranging fresh flowers. Before dashing out the door for a luncheon date, I decided to stop at the super market and pick up a larger bird on my way home.

Four o'clock already! How I hated to pry myself away from those after-lunch coffee-and-brandies at the Golden Belle to face the teeming hordes at the grocery store.

The turkey department was a free-for-all. People were pushing and elbowing one another to extricate the frosty birds from their refrigerated nests. A twenty-five-pound frozen turkey isn't the easiest object to maneuver. As I lowered mine into my cart, waves of dizziness and nausea swept through me. Why did I drink so much? I didn't seem to be able to stop anymore. *I'll start cutting down tomorrow,* I promised myself.

Back at home I faced a new problem: *Where was I going to thaw the turkey? The clothes dryer! The perfect place!*

Thanksgiving morning I crawled shakily out of bed to get the turkey into the oven. A bird that size would take many hours. Now where was it? Not in the refrigerator, I quickly discovered. With increasing frenzy I searched the car trunk, bathtub, downstairs shower, outside barbecue, the roof of the tool shed...

How many drinks had I had yesterday?

An attic-to-cellar search aided by all three children failed to unearth the elusive bird. Twelve guests were arriving at three o'clock! I was in a panic. While making a last-ditch sweep through the laundry room, I saw hanging limply from the open dryer door a golden tag: *Swift's Butterball*.

A scarier episode occurred many months later after a party at the Yellowstone Country Club. I didn't remember driving home. Around 3:00 A.M. I awakened to see lights glaring into the bedroom window.

Struggling to my feet and pushing back the drapes, I observed a peculiar scene in our front yard. There on the lawn sat the white Jeep Wagoneer I had driven alone to the party. (My husband had had to attend a special meeting and had gone in his own car.) The Jeep's high-beam headlights were blazing into my aching eyes. Both doors were wide open, and an inside ceiling light illuminated the car's interior.

At first glance it looked like an errant UFO. I stumbled out the front door and through the thick grass to the lighted vehicle. Cautiously I backed the Jeep across the lawn, over the short curb into the street, and then into our driveway.

Back in bed I noted gracefully that my husband had not awakened. *You lucked out this time, kiddo. When are you ever going to learn?*

The next morning I dragged myself out of bed, started the coffeepot, and then headed out the front door to fetch the morning paper. As I passed by the Jeep, my glance turned into a stare of horror. Red stains covered the splash panels behind the front wheels. Long, ugly reddish streaks were splattered on the white door. The touch of a trembling finger confirmed my worst fears. It was blood.

What had I done? Had I run over someone last night? Had I killed someone?

Dashing to the mailbox, I yanked the Sunday paper from the metal box with such intensity I skinned my knuckles. Tearing the rubber band from the paper, I searched the front page for a hit-and-run story, forgetting, of course, that there had not enough time to make today's news.

Nothing there. Frantically I spread the paper on the ground, tearing and flailing at the pages to find the item I didn't want to see. Still nothing.

Gathering up the mangled newspaper, I headed back for the kitchen, my heart pounding. My head was splitting from front to back. What had I done?

"Lord God, I will never, ever drink again! Just tell me I haven't killed anyone, and I'll go on the wagon for the rest of my life!"

My husband entered the kitchen and eyed the jumbled newspaper. "Did this thing get hit by a bus?" he asked, reaching for the sports section.

I was standing pressed up against the sink, taking short breaths so as not to faint from fear.

"Did you hear that dogfight this morning?" he went on. "I had to go outside and turn the hose on them. The setter across the street got bitten badly; his blood is all over the Jeep."

The relief that flooded through me made my knees buckle. "Gosh, no, I didn't hear a thing."

My vow never to drink again lasted exactly ninety minutes. As I fixed my children's breakfast I decided to treat myself to a Bloody Mary. I had something to celebrate!

These 1999 statistics from the National Council on Alcoholism and Drug Dependence are certainly nothing to celebrate: More than half of all adults in America have a family history of alcoholism or problem drinking.[7] Nearly four million American women ages eighteen and older can be classified as alcoholic or problem drinkers, one-third the number of men; of these women, 58 percent are between the ages of eighteen to twenty-nine.[8]

New research indicates that women apparently metabolize alcohol differently from men—due, perhaps, to hormonal levels, the menstrual cycle, birth control pills or even women's lower percentage of water content and higher percentage of body fat.

Whatever the cause, observed *Ms.* magazine (February 1987), it adds up to the fact that "alcoholism and all its health consequences tend to 'telescope'—proceed at a much faster pace within a female body." Researchers for the *Ms.* survey, moreover, found that as drinking increases, so does other addictive behavior.

According to psychoanalyst Theodore Rubin, alcohol, drugs, tobacco and food "are often used as sedative and anesthetic devices in an attempt to relieve self-hate. [Such people] put themselves into a temporary haze in order to escape their feelings…This device is also unfortunately and nearly always unconsciously used as a form of slow suicide."[9]

Below is a questionnaire developed by John Hopkins Hospital in Baltimore, Maryland to assist people is seeing whether they have a problem with alcohol.

Are You an Alcoholic?

To answer this question, ask yourself the following questions, and answer them as honestly as you can.

1. Do you lose time from work due to drinking?

2. Is drinking making your home life unhappy?

3. Do you drink because you are shy with other people?

4. Is drinking affecting your reputation?

5. Have you ever felt remorse after drinking?

6. Have you ever gotten into financial difficulties as a result of drinking?

7. Do you turn to lower companions and an inferior environment when drinking?

8. Does your drinking make you careless of your family's welfare?

9. Has your ambition decreased since drinking?

10. Do you crave a drink at a definite time?

11. Do you want a drink the next morning?

12. Does drinking cause you to have difficulty in sleeping?

13. Has your efficiency decreased since drinking?

14. Is drinking jeopardizing your job or business?

15. Do you drink to escape your worries or troubles?

16. Do you drink alone?

17. Have you ever had a complete loss of memory as a result of drinking?

18. Has your physician ever treated you for drinking?

19. Do you drink to build up your self-confidence?

20. Have you ever been to a hospital or institution on account of drinking?

If you answered *yes* to any one of the questions, there is a definite warning that you may have a problem with alcohol.

If you say *yes* to any two, chances are you have a problem.

If you answer *yes* to three or more, you definitely have a problem with alcohol.

REAL LIFE IS HARSH. It is constantly injuring our sensibilities. The temptation to escape from it by flight is the stronger the more sensitive we are: We run away in order to protect our sensitivity, to escape the conflict which wounds it. The land of dreams is close at hand, so that one an escape into it at any moment, far from these painful realities…It is a secret treasure into which he pours the best of himself. It is his way of turning the tables on harsh reality.

—PAUL TOURNIER, M.D.
The Healing of Persons

5

The Cultist

I didn't want to face my furies. I wanted someone else to do it for me. Compulsive people are particularly vulnerable to the quick fix of mind-bending fads and cults. We are dependency-prone. We want to please. And from childhood I'd been attracted by the invisible world.

"Have you noticed what a vivid imagination Sandra has?" relatives would say of me. Being an only child in a household of adults created companionship problems. So I created imaginary playmates. The characters in my fairy tale books became real people to me. Draped in lace curtains and tottering in Mother's high heels, I was Cinderella swirling in the arms of Prince Charming at the ball.

On warm, sunny days I'd scamper through the tall grass of our neighbor's pasture to my magic hideaway in the woods. It was a small mossy shelf to the right of the path, which I pretended was my majestic medieval bed. My headboard was an enormous Vermont maple with low-hanging branches, my footboard a bush of wild roses.

Sometimes I'd bring along Ted, my lambskin teddy bear. Ted and I were great friends. I'd prop him up on my chest facing the rosebush so he could see what I could see. His black silk eyes were far more perceptive than mine, and he could spot an elf or a fairy at a hundred yards.

Once as we were sitting there, a yellow butterfly landed delicately on my chest. I hardly dared to breathe for fear I'd frighten this glorious visitor. As the butterfly remained balanced there, I felt our souls touching at some mystical level. So real were these fantasies that it was often hard for me to return to everyday life.

Beautiful and innocent childhood fun, surely. Where and how does it begin to turn into something not so pure and good?

We often had a chicken wishbone at our house drying on the windowsill over the kitchen sink. Dad and I would wait till it was completely dry for the ritual of breaking. Whoever got the longer piece would have his wish granted.

Superstition was part and parcel of New England life:

- Never walk under a ladder.
- If you spill the salt, throw some over your left shoulder.
- Never put your hat on the bed.
- Never let a black cat cross your path.
- Never open an umbrella in the house.
- If you leave the house and have to go back for something, sit down and count to ten before proceeding on your way.

There were rabbit's foot keychains and horseshoes nailed over doorways. (Make sure to mount them properly, or the luck will slip through.)

Then came the Ouija board craze. Great mysteries were revealed by this means, I was assured by one neighbor. She had special clairvoyant insights and could tell you where you had lost things. The police used to go to her to ask about missing persons. My mind whirled at such powers. In my early teens I made frequent visits to her house seeking answers to all kinds of problems.

Once as a seventh-grader I attended a magic show at the Barre Municipal Auditorium. My friend Betty Lou and I arrived early to get front-row seats. The magician, the Great Garlock, was a character right out of my fairy tales. Tall and handsome (who wouldn't look that way in a tuxedo—the first I'd ever seen), he wore a magnificent floor-length black satin cape.

He needed twelve people to be hypnotized. Were there any volunteers? Betty Lou and I streaked to the stage. Perched on wooden folding chairs, we stared obediently into his intense blue eyes. "Count backwards with me," he told us. "One hundred…ninety-nine…ninety-eight…" Somewhere in the eighties I lost consciousness. When I awakened, it was to gales of laughter. Later friends told us that after being given hypnotic suggestions, we had scratched frantically as if covered by fleas and shivered violently from icy cold blasts.

Afterward the volunteers stumbled down the steep stairs from the stage. I crumpled uneasily into my seat. Something was wrong. My mind wouldn't focus. I felt confused, disjointed.

The Great Garlock spoke. "If any of you who were just hypnotized have any problems bringing your mind back to focus, I'll be here tomorrow morning in the director's office to help you readjust."

Next morning I made the mile walk back to the auditorium. The building smelled of varnish and perspiration. At my knock the door to the director's office was flung open, and there stood the towering black figure from the night before. He was wearing the long satin cape, yet somehow it looked tawdry in the morning light.

"I'm one of the people you hypnotized last night," I told him. "I've felt strange ever since you woke us up. My mind seems fuzzy. Everything is all mixed up."

"You must be one of the very sensitive ones," the Great Garlock replied. "Really, what I did last night was routine. Perhaps you went into a higher plane of consciousness than the others."

The man in the black cape fixed his eyes on mine and started the countdown from one hundred. I was aware of the onions on his breath.

Suddenly I had the strangest sensation—as though something unknown, something dark and disagreeable, were trying to climb right inside me. My heart started pounding. "I don't want to do that again," I wailed.

"But you must if I am going to help you."

"Can't you do it any other way?" I pleaded.

"Well…perhaps."

He pulled a chair beside mine and explained that he would call upon a higher power to help me. I didn't understand the words he used after that. *Magicians must have their own language,* I thought.

Ten minutes or more passed. His voice trailed off into a chant. I was feeling very uncomfortable.

"You should have no further problems now, miss," he said at last.

I thanked him weakly and backed out of the room. Did I feel any better? I wasn't sure. A part of me felt violated that had felt safe and secure before last night.

Psychic phenomena, however, continued to fascinate me. It wasn't long after the Miss America pageant that I visited a woman who told fortunes with a deck of cards.

"Your parents are divorced," she revealed. "They live in close proximity."

Quite true.

"You have just won a national honor," she went on. "It will carry you into new horizons of job opportunities and influential relationships."

This woman is wonderful, I thought.

The shoe-buying orgy in Providence was my first look at my own tendency toward excessive behavior. Alarmed by this lack of control within, I started looking for control outside myself. Soon I was searching regularly for the "Today's Horoscope" column in newspapers. If my horoscope said to beware of short trips, I'd hesitate to cross the street for a cup of coffee.

When marriage to Werner failed to supply the needed external control, I sought out a psychic in Billings. She called herself Madame X—a pot-roast of a woman, solid, round, with watery brown eyes and hair pulled into a tight bun at the back of her neck. I began to depend on her for most of my decisions.

At one visit (fifteen dollars per session) she announced that we had been joined by her "spirit guide," who also happened to be her dead mother. Together they went into the previous lifetimes they said I'd had, including one as the wife of a cruel Chinese warlord who sold me as a prostitute. I was anxious to believe these revelations, my imagination captivated by the intrigue of my supposed past.

To expand my psychic awareness Madame X encouraged me to attend the weekly class she taught. At these group sessions, held in the basement of her modest home, she'd speak of members who were absent, telling us what they were doing at the precise moment we were meeting.

One mind exercise she taught was billet reading. We would write things on pieces of paper, fold them up and pass them around in a basket. Picking one at random, we were to feel the vibrations of the message and "read" it without opening it up. I got to be pretty good at it.

One of my friends tried to warn me against all this. Influenced no doubt by her Roman Catholic faith, Lois Ann, a stately brunette with compelling blue eyes, called such practices "occult." They were, she informed me, "an abomination to God." She even brought a Bible to my house one day and read me a passage out of Deuteronomy:

> Let no one be found among you…who practices divination or sor-
> cery, interprets omens, engages in witchcraft, or casts spells, or who
> is a medium or spiritist who consults the dead. Anyone who does
> these things is detestable to the LORD…
>
> —DEUTERONOMY 18:10–12, NIV

It struck me as a little far out, but I didn't say anything.

The person who brought the most stability into my life at this time was our cleaning woman, Hilda Best, an outgoing, energetic woman with copper red hair. (Polly had gone to be with her grandchildren.) Hilda was more than an employee. She was a surrogate grandmother who had great strength, endurance, love and tenderness. I often turned my responsibilities to my children over to Hilda so that I could focus on civic projects and my social engagements.

Sometimes I would catch her looking at me sadly: "Sandy, you have to spend more time with these kids. They need you. You don't have to volunteer for every committee in town. The years will slip away, the kids will grow up, and you'll have missed the most important time in their lives."

I knew she was right. And I loved my children dearly. But, compulsively driven as I was, I could only overwhelm them with gifts and affection in sporadic efforts to make up for lost time. What little I was able to pass along to them issued right out of my own compulsive traits.

Take, for example, my perfectionism where clothes were concerned. I used my design training to see that the family's wearing apparel was color-coordinated. And then one day I discovered that Lisa, age four, was changing her clothes several times a day. If her socks didn't match her dress or sweater, she went into a frenzy, tearing through her dresser drawers for just the right combination. The thought that my daughter was growing up like me was scary.

What I *didn't* give our children was time. My husband and I came home late from a country club party to find Brad, Brent and Lisa asleep in the hall instead of their bedrooms. For solace—or for companionship?—they had wrapped themselves in their nylon comforters like three little quilted cocoons. Remorse tore at my heart. Why didn't I stay home more? What was I doing to these tender little lives?

Werner too was seldom available to them. Every daylight hour he spent at the hospital or tennis court. In addition, his practice took him to other towns in Montana. When I went to Madame X with a litany of complaints against my workaholic doctor husband and his absenteeism, she consulted her spirit guide and reported that we were not right for each other. I already knew that: At the ten-year point of our marriage I was rationalizing my heavy drinking as a result of our deteriorating relationship. Werner and I were two utterly unconnected people wandering in our own worlds. Strangers when we married, the passage of years had not brought us much closer.

What advice did Madame X have for improving my marriage? The psychic shook her head. "You and your husband are working out your karma from other lifetimes. Perhaps the next time around will be better for both of you."

Since I had suffered the trauma of my parents' breakup, divorce was the last thing I wanted for myself and our children. Nevertheless, it took place—legal separation in 1970, divorce the following year. I moved to our weekend home in Red Lodge, sixty-five miles from Billings, and entered the three children in school there.

It was a miserable time for us all. The children missed their father and their friends back in Billings. One fall morning my older son Brad, then ten, announced he was running away. He put on his corduroy jacket over his jeans and shirt, packed a pair of socks, a flashlight, two cans of tomato soup, a knife and a fork in a brown paper bag. Then he headed up the street, kicking the brown and yellow aspen leaves as he went.

I watched him from the living room widow, set to jump into the car and follow him the moment he was out of sight. Where the road turned, however, he stopped. For a long while he stood there, head bowed. Then slowly he retraced his steps. Inside the house he emptied the contents of the paper bag onto the foyer floor. "I'm back," he said. I hugged him fiercely, his cowlick tickling my nose.

Brad's unhappiness with the current arrangement remained, however, and a few weeks after this episode he went to live with his father. Several years later Brent would join him.

Meanwhile, I married again. The answer to all my problems, I decided, was another husband. Perhaps this man could fix what was wrong with me and fill that empty place. The need for someone who could show me what to do, who could bring control and order into my life, was compelling.

The Cultist

"Too often," writes Dr. Sonya Friedman in *Men Are Just Desserts,* "women marry to escape their true selves, believing that marriage will make life work for them. Operating under the assumption that they are incomplete, unformed, lacking the capacity to take care of themselves financially or emotionally, they seek out a man who will be caretaker, benefactor, love, and hero—'everything' to them."[1]

Similarly, psychoanalyst Karen Horney, in her classic *Feminine Psychology,* referred to "neurotic women who feel unhappy, insecure, and depressed as long as they do not have someone devoted to them, who loves them or somehow cares for them."[2]

My new husband Randall was a sharp Billings trial lawyer, a man of striking good looks. The children and I were glad to be back in Billings again, where we could see Brad more often, where Brent and Lisa could visit their father and where I could resume my hectic social schedule. In my obsessive busyness it didn't occur to me that no amount of outside activity, only a transformation inside, could satisfy. In my neediness I continued to cry out for answers from anyone and everyone.

One day I saw an advertisement in the newspaper that read something like this:

Who Are You? Why Are You Here?

Looking for Answers?

Is inner contentment eluding you?

Come Wednesday night to a lecture of

The International Serenity Society*

and revitalize your life.

8 P.M. Comanche Room, Warbonnet Inn.

I have a date with destiny tonight, I told myself as I pulled my car into the overflow parking lot of the hotel. I was disregarding the advice of Lois Ann who had warned, "Sandy, stay away from all that hocus-pocus! You're playing with fire."

I tuned out her words as I hurried up the concrete sidewalk and into the sprawling dark-brown stucco building. Inside I found a registration table strewn with alluring color pamphlets of the Serenity Society. I

---

* Not the real name

grabbed a handful and headed for the crowded lecture room. The evening's speaker was a stocky, handsome woman named Velda. She had short salt-and-pepper gray hair curled tightly about a strong square face and bright dark eyes that snapped knowingly behind thick glasses.

"The International Serenity Society has totally revolutionized my life," she began. "For years I suffered from depression, asthma and painful arthritis, but this simple program has given me the tools to overcome these problems. Any one of you can change your lives this way, too."

The lecture lasted an hour and included facts, graphs, humor and even Scripture. Velda had a mixed bag of technical data and psychic techniques. I was captivated by her presentation and wanted to know more, so I made a date with her for a special counseling session the following morning.

At 10:45 A.M. I swung into the driveway of the address she had given me, a crisp twenty-dollar bill in my pocket. Velda greeted me at the screen door and invited me back to a book-lined study. A tall grandfather clock ticked in the shadows, reminding me suddenly of Uncle Ralph. Feelings of helplessness, of the desire for some kind of external control, flooded me.

When I was seated, Velda explained how she would help me contact my "spiritual guides" through her own guides, a process that involved much eyes-closed concentration. Apparently sensing uneasiness on my part, Velda assured me, "You have nothing to be afraid of. These guides are spirits who have been with you ever since you were born—and even before that. They are committed to helping you as long as you are on this side."

Further revelation: I had nine guides, which supposedly meant I had a very important earthly mission. Most people have but four or five.

"You are a very old soul," Vera told me, "a master who has returned from many lifetimes. You didn't have to come back this time, but *you chose to.*"

My head was spinning, the ticking clock setting the pace of my heartbeat. "What are you trying to tell me?" I asked.

"That you are a prophet," she answered, "with strong visionary capabilities—gifted in intuition, but confused in the feeling part of your psyche." Before dismissing me, she urged me to attend the summer camp of the International Serenity Society, which would be held in Idaho at a place called Spirit Lake.

Should I go? How I wished I had Madame X to advise me. She'd died recently of gallbladder trouble—a terribly grubby, earthly ailment, I thought, for such an ethereal spirit.

In Madame X's classroom I'd heard about people who received answers via "automatic writing." Back at home I sat down at the kitchen table with pencil and legal pad borrowed from my new husband's desk. With pencil poised, I waited self-consciously for some message from the spirit world. "Should I go to this camp?" I wrote at the top of the page.

Now what? Would some unseen force seize my fingers and spell out the answer? Would the pencil write by itself? How did these discarnate spirits communicate?

For a long time nothing happened. Frustrated, I cried out, "OK, if there are nine of you guides out there, or in here, or wherever you are, somebody please tell me something."

I felt my arm begin to shake with small tremors. Placing the pencil on the writing pad, my hand scribbled, "YES. GO."

Thrilled with this outward sign of affirmation, I sent in my application.

I was a cauldron of conflicting thoughts and emotions when I returned from Spirit Lake. Part of my conscious mind was telling me it was all nonsense—maybe even dangerous nonsense, as Lois Ann had warned. Another part was telling me how fascinating this new knowledge was. Why, it even contained Scripture. Well, what sounded like Scripture.

What I didn't realize was that the compulsive woman unrecognized inside me was finding a "high" in these experiences. Psychic phenomena—offering experiences like altered states of consciousness, trances, perceptions of auras surrounding objects, even the exaltation of becoming divine—attract people seeking a mood change, and they can deliver just as effectively (and addictively) as alcohol or drugs.

In fact, new research suggests chemical explanations for so-called transcendental states of consciousness.[3] Arnold Mandell, brain chemist and professor of psychiatry at the University of California, San Diego, theorizes that meditation inhibits the action of the neurotransmitter serotonin, ordinarily a brain-quieting hormone. The result: increased electrical discharges. In Dr. Mandell's words, "Affectual and cognitive processes characteristic of religious ecstasy."

Eugene d'Aquili, a psychiatrist and neuroscientist at the University of Pennsylvania, postulates that electrical stimulation of the parietal lobe of the brain corresponds with advancing states of transcendence, all the way to "ultimate mystic experience."

I knew nothing of such chemical explanations, of course, but was drawn by the intrigue and spiritual euphoria promised by the International Serenity Society. Since I had agreed to be the Montana representative, our home soon became the destination of a steady stream of visiting ISS "counselors," each one stranger than the last. My new husband Randall had welcomed these visitors good-naturedly at first, but his attitude soon changed to frustration, then outrage at the constant intrusions, the endless long-distance phone calls. He was totally turned off by my new psychic vocabulary: chakras, auras, reincarnation, karma.

Desperate for help with my out-of-control drinking and the eating binges with which it alternated, I began calling these counselors for advice. To each I described my inability to concentrate; the mocking, haunting voices in my head; the ugly faces that zoomed in and out of my mind whenever I closed my eyes.

"You've picked up some angry souls from a past life who are out to get you, now that they have your attention," one told me.

"There is an astro-soul counselor in the Denver area," another said. "He could regress you through your former lives to find out just exactly who is harassing you." But the process, it seemed, would take months and be very expensive.

A third adviser suggested I try cold showers. "These dark spirits cannot stand the cold. Cold baths work well, too. You might want to throw in a couple of trays of ice cubes." Later this same counselor called back long-distance (charges, of course, were always reversed). "We're having a conference here in Los Angeles this weekend. Friday night at ten o'clock sharp we will all send you our energy. Be standing under a cold shower so you can receive it."

At ten o'clock that Friday night (eleven o'clock my time) I was shivering in the shower stall. Was I receiving the promised energy? The only observable result was a miserable cold.

Days, weeks, months passed while the sinister voices and the hideous faces became more insistent. Nothing could shut them out—not alcohol, not the cakes and other sweets I'd slip into the kitchen to gorge on in the middle of the night.

My weight was now crowding two hundred pounds; coloring and setting my hair, taking time over my clothes, everything had become too much trouble. Once as I was standing in the checkout line at the grocery store, I overheard a woman behind me whisper to someone else, "She was in the Miss America Pageant? She couldn't win a livestock show the way she looks now!"

One day in desperation I remembered that my daughter possessed a two-inch silver crucifix on a black silk cord; I found it in her top bureau drawer and clutched it for comfort, the sharp edges embedded in my frantic palms. But nothing seemed to help.

Nor did any person. My husband was bewildered by the change in my appearance and my enslavement to the bizarre practices of the International Serenity Society. Brent and Lisa would come home from school and greet me with troubled faces. One day when I was out, the two of them rifled through my desk drawers and threw out what they could find of my International Serenity Society literature, explaining when I discovered the loss that it made me "act funny." I ached to be a real mother to them. Yet I had nothing to give. I was totally consumed with self—self-hatred and self-pity—and spent endless hours in bed with the covers pulled up over my head and the drapes closed to shut out any prying rays of the sun.

I had everything to live for, yet something inside me was pushing me straight into a dark pit.

Today, "channeling"—men and women giving up temporary use of their bodies in order to channel the messages of spirits, ostensibly wise old "ascended masters"—has become a multimillion-dollar business. Fifteen years ago, according to the May 10, 1987 issue of the *New York Times,* consumers could consult a reincarnated "spirit" for as little as $10 per hour or as much as $1,500 an hour. The best-known channels (formerly called mediums) charged admission fees of $200 to $400 at weekend seminars that attract hundreds of people. Just imagine what the fees are today!

The same *Times* article quoted Marcello Truzzi, professor of sociology at Eastern Michigan University who specializes in paranormal research:

"What we have is a tremendous democratization of religion, allowing many people to be the pathway to the almighty. Everybody has a pipeline, be your own guru; everybody is their own priest. It assuages guilt, tells people that what they are doing is all right…"

Psychiatrist Scott Peck, on the other hand, writes tellingly of the attempt to escape the anxiety and pain of being responsible for one's self. It is this anxiety that drives the compulsive person to self-destructive acts and perilous dependencies:

> The difficulty we have in accepting responsibility for our behavior lies in the desire to avoid the pain of the consequences of that behavior…Whenever we seek to avoid the responsibility for our own behavior, we do so by attempting to give that responsibility to some other individual or organization or entity. By this means we then give away our power to that entity…In attempting to avoid the pain of responsibility, millions and even billions daily attempt to escape from freedom.[4]

CULTS

When the compulsive woman seeks help through involvement with a cult, her behavior will often get more and more out of control.

Occult practices

Those who are finding healing through Scripture and the Lordship of Jesus Christ need to be aware that occult practices can get them off track, as they did me. God warned the Israelites as follows: "Let no one be found among you…who practices divination or sorcery, interprets omens, engages in witchcraft, or casts spells, or who consults the dead. Anyone who does these things is detestable to the Lord" (Deut. 18:10–12, NIV).

The New Paganism: A new world religion

The cover story of the August 2002 issue of *Whistleblower* magazine is "The New Paganism," subtitled "How America's Christian churches are being invaded by radical environmentalism, goddess worship and global government."

> For years, Christians have stood by helplessly as their once-dominant religion has been increasingly scoffed at, marginalized and demonized. They have watched a dizzying succession of outrageous court

decisions—outlawing the Ten Commandments in schools and court-rooms, forbidding acknowledgment of God in practical ceremonies such as graduation speeches, and most recently, declaring public recitation of the Pledge of Allegiance unconstitutional...

This "new" religious worldview is sugarcoated with high-minded and universal ideals of environmental protection and species preservation, but the ultimate agenda behind the movement is much darker.

The ultimate purpose of "green religion" is to convince the people of the world to embrace world governance—which for a free nation like America represents a massive loss of national sovereignty and personal freedom—for the supposed sake of Mother Earth ("gaia") and the environment. After all, it is a lot easier to administer world government if all the people believe it represents their salvation, rather than tyranny...

"The vanguard of this movement," explains Henry Lamb in "The rise of global green religion," "people like James Parks Morton, James Lovelock, Robert Muller...Timothy Wirth and many others, have been 'enlightened' through their biocentric belief in gaia"—the belief that the earth itself is a conscious, living organism—"and therefore they know what is best for the planet. They also know that the only way to protect the sacred gaia is to control the people who are degrading her. The only way to control the people is through an omnipotent government that is, at this moment, consolidating its power into an evergrowing bureaucracy,now stretching around the globe, extending its tentacles into every corner of human life, creating de facto global governance."[5]

Superficially, it appears like a freak show, ranging from the seeemingly harmless "Entertainment Paganism" ("Dungeons and Dragons," "white witchcraft," "Buffy the Vampire Slayer," "Witchblade") to "Teen Cult Paganism" (teens in Gothic drag, freaky hair colors, tattoos, body piercing, "body art," black garb, studs and chains) to "Ecology Theology" (free-form sexual morality, "gaia" worship, native spirituality rituals) to the wide-ranging "New Age Movement" (believes humankind is on the cusp of a new dawn, beginning new phase in evolutionary history) to "Dark Paganism" (believes there's no such thing as "evil," and that destruction and death are forms of beauty) to "Wicca" (witchcraft is reportedly the fastest growing religion in Australia) and "Satanism" (consciously acknowledges Satan as master, and seeks power to corrupt all things, especially Christianity).[6]

MIND-MANIPULATING GROUPS: ARE YOU OR A FAMILY MEMBER A VICTIM?

The following statements, compiled by Dr. Michael Langone, editor of *Cultic Studies Journal,* often characterize manipulative groups. Comparing these statements to the group with which you or a family member is involved may help you to determine if this involvement is cause for concern. Keep in mind that this checklist is meant to stimulate thought, not "diagnose" groups. We suggest that you check all characteristics that apply to you or your loved one's group.

- The group is preoccupied on a living leader to whom members seem to display excessively zealous, unquestioning commitment.

- The group is preoccupied with bringing in new members.

- The group is preoccupied with money.

- Questioning, doubt and dissent are discouraged or even punished.

- Mind-numbing techniques (such as meditation, chanting, denunciation sessions and debilitating work routines) are used to suppress doubts about the group and its leader(s).

- Permission is required from leaders to date, change jobs, get married and so forth; leaders may prescribe what types of clothes to wear, where to live, how to discipline children, and so forth.

- The group is elitist, claiming a special, exalted status for itself, its leader(s) and members. (For example: The leader is considered the Messiah or an avatar; the group and/or the leader has a special mission to save humanity.)

- The group has a polarized us-vs.-them mentality, which causes conflict with wider society.

- The group's leader is not accountable to any authorities (as are, for example, military commanders and ministers, priests, monks and rabbis of mainstream denominations).

- The leadership induces guilt feelings in members in order to control them.

- Members' subservience to the group causes them to cut ties with family and friends and to give up personal goals and activities that were of interest before joining the group.

- Members are expected to devote inordinate amounts of time to the group.

- Members are encouraged or required to live and/or socialize only with other group members.[7]

Below are some other occult practices that should be avoided:

- Acupuncture
- Anthroposophy ceremonial practices
- Astral projection/travel
- Astrological Life Charts
- Astrology
- Automatic writing
- Bahai
- Biofeedback
- Black/white magic
- Blood pacts
- Black Mass
- Buddhism
- Cabbage Patch Dolls
- Celebrating Halloween, the satanic equivalent of Christmas
- Channeling
- Christadelphians
- Nintendo
- Nostradamus predictions
- Ninja Turtles
- Numerology
- Omens
- Oriental astrology
- Ouija boards
- Paganism
- Palm reading
- Parakinesis
- Parapsychology
- Phrenology
- Pokemon
- Powder Puff Girls
- Psychic healing
- Psychic hotlines
- Psychic reading
- Pyramid power
- Rebellion

- Christian Science
- Clairvoyance
- Confucianism
- Divine Light Mission
- Divine Science
- Dream Catchers
- Dragons
- Druid worship
- Edgar Cayce
- ESP
- Fantasy games
- Father Divine
- Fortune telling/
  crystal balls
- Freemasonry
- Guided imagery
  (spiritual guides)
- Gurus
- Hare Krishna
- Harry Potter (makes
  witchcraft/magic
  appear to be miracles)
- Hinduism
- Horoscopes
- Humanism
- Hypnosis/self-hypnosis
  (trance inducement)
- Inner Peace Movement
- Iridology
- Islam/Black Islam
- Jehovah's Witnesses
- Kabbala
- Karate
- Karma
- Ku Klux Klan
- Levitation
- Mantra chanting
- Mardi Gras
- Martial arts (those that
  invoke supernatural,

- Reflexology
- Reincarnation
- Religious Science
- Rosicrucianism
- Satanic rock music/
  heavy metal
- Satanism
- Scientology
- Seances
- Seers
- Silva Mind Control
- Shintoism
- Skinheads
- Sorcerers
- Spiritism
- Spiritual Frontiers
  Fellowship
- Star Gazing/Zodiac
- Supremacist/Separatist
  groups (of any kind)
- Table Lifting
- Tae Kwon Do
- Tai-Chi
- Tarot cards
- Tea Leaf Reading
- Telekinesis
- Telepathy
- TV magician
  extravaganzas
- Theosophy
- The Way
- Transcendental
  Meditation
- Trolls
- Unicorns
- Unification Thought
  and Theology (Moonies)
- Unitarian Universalist
- Unity
- Voodoo

spiritual power)
- Mediums
- Metaphysical healing
- Mind control
- Mind expansion
- Mind science
- Mormonism
- Nature worship
- New Age Movement
- Water-witching/ Divination
- Wicca
- Witch Doctors
- Witches and warlocks
- Wizards
- Worldwide Church of God
- Yoga
- Zen Buddhism

The list seems endless. Also be aware of how the occult may operate through physical objects: Ankhs (a cross with a ring at the top), amulets, Egyptian "cartouche" pendants, any jewelry with skulls/bones/other death signs, birthstones, charms (e.g. for wart removal, etc.), crystals used for healing, hallucinogenic drugs, "heavy metal" rock, hex signs, "lucky" symbols, pagan fetishes or religious artifacts, planchettes, talismans, zodiac charms.

Particularly dangerous are religions that misrepresent the Person, the nature or the redemptive work of Jesus Christ. The New Testament, for example, presents Jesus Christ as "God manifest in the flesh," but Jehovah's Witnesses teach that He was a created being. Again, Islam rejects the claim of Jesus to be the Son of God, and denies that He ever actually died on the cross. Yet the atoning death of Jesus is the only basis on which man can claim forgiveness of sins.[8]

For more information on Satanism and other cults write:

Spiritual Counterfeits Project (SCP)
P. O. Box 4308
Berkeley, CA 94704
510-540-0300; 510-540-1107 (fax)
www.scp-inc.org
access@scp-inc.org

International Cult Education Program (ICEP)
American Family Foundation
P. O. Box 413005, Suite 313
Naples, FL 34101-3081
239-514-3081; 732-352-6818 (fax)
www.csj.org

I DO NOT BELIEVE a real urgency to die produces the suicidal act, so much as the feeling of not knowing what else to do to ease the Pain. The person is all out of struggles.

—ARTHUR JANOV, PH.D.
The Primal Scream

6

WHY LIVE?

I t was not until I attended the Compulsivity Clinic, years later, that I gained true insight into my suicide attempt. Just as Peggy, in our small group there, had started me thinking systematically about my early years, so another group member helped me look into the depths of the pit I had finally reached.

Ginny was a small, thin brunette with a soft voice, eyes full of hurt and an apologetic manner. At the Compulsivity Clinic she had listened to the lectures and small-group revelations with no sign of emotion. Confronted by our group leader, Maureen, for her passiveness, Ginny had opened up enough to say she loathed herself and had tried four times to commit suicide.

"You're full of anger, Ginny," Maureen informed her. "That is what's behind your suicide attempts. Suicide, you know, is the ultimate angry gesture."

The mousy little woman shook her head in shocked denial.

"Yes, you are angry, Ginny. You're angry with your father for abusing your mother. You're angry with your mother for putting up with it. And you're angry with them both for neglecting you. You've stuffed these feelings down for years. When they wouldn't stay down, you turned this rage on yourself."

Ginny again denied harboring such emotions.

"Everyone in this room is full of anger at someone, or they wouldn't be here," Maureen persisted. "We're going to do something about yours right now."

With that she opened the closet in our small conference room and brought out a hollow plastic bat. Then she instructed the rest of us to make a pile the cushions on which we were sitting in the center of the room.

"Now, Ginny, your father is here, sitting there in the corner watching you. Go ahead and whack these pillows as you talk to him. Let it all pour out. You need to get rid of your rage if you're ever going to be healthy."

Protesting that it was silly, Ginny did it halfheartedly at first. Then something seemed to explode in her. Soon the room was reverberating with her fury. Quiet little Ginny had suddenly become the mouse that roared.

"I hate you, Dad!"

Whack! Splat!

"...for your filthy, rotten mouth!"

Whack! Blap!

"...for getting drunk all the time!"

Whack! Thump!

"...for beating Mom all those times when she couldn't fight back!"

Thunk! Whap!

"...for leaving us without money for food—and spending it on your creepy friends!"

Whack! Crack!

"...for cheating on my mother!"

Whap! Klap!

"I hate you...I hate you..."

Whack! Whack! Whack!

Ginny was so into it now that she began kicking the pillows right through the open door into the hall, all the while screaming, "I hate you, you rotten, miserable s-o-b!"

We were drained just watching her. Ginny returned to the conference room red-eyed but peaceful, spent by her outburst of pent-up emotion.

"That sure felt good," she exclaimed. "Now I need some hugs." Soon she was in my arms holding onto me as if she would never let go, our tears running together.

I could identify with Ginny completely, for I was remembering the time several years before when I too had tried to end my life and the tremendous store of repressed anger I myself had found. Therapy had helped me discover a lifetime of bottled-up rage—which was, Maureen insisted, the major factor in most suicides. I did not have the kind of traumatic memories Ginny acted out. But I had grown up in an environment that blocked the free expression of negative emotion, an environment that encouraged peace at any price.

There might be another reason for my anger, too. The echoes roused in me at the sight of Ginny's distorted face made me wonder suddenly: Did all of us share an inheritance of fear and rage, roots deep in the human past that I could have unwittingly tapped into when I opened myself to the visitations of "spirit guides"? By the time I arrived at the Compulsivity Clinic I no longer believed the International Serenity Society's far-out theories about previous existences. But those rage-twisted faces, those shrieks and curses hounding me asleep and awake, had been real enough. Could I have invited anger itself into my unconscious?

By the time of my second marriage I had also started seeing a psychiatrist, but we did little but spar with words. Several times I was a patient for a period of weeks on the psych ward of Billings' Deaconess Hospital. These served as brief drying-out times only. Back home each time I resumed my drinking to blot out the voices, the faces, the reality of my failure as a human being. One advantage of alcohol as an escape is that it occupies your mind even when you're sober. All my creativity went into subterfuges to disguise the amount I was consuming.

One example was the Tuesday morning trash collection ritual. The moment I heard the familiar grinding of the garbage truck down the street, I would speed out to the garage where sat our two green plastic trashcans. Stealthily I would lift a white dress box from under a dusty stack of discarded magazines nearby and place it into one of the containers.

A gentle shake of the box satisfied me. The bottles didn't rattle: I had wrapped each one in tissue paper and Scotch tape. Inside the box six empty Smirnoff bottles lay like silent soldiers, shrouded for burial.

Quickly I would open the garage doors, push the cart containing the bottles out to the street, and then run back into the garage and fumble for the button to close the garage door. Whew! One more time I had gotten the bottles out of the house before Randall found them.

Getting rid of the empties had become an increasingly challenging ritual. They were always wrapped carefully so that the garbage men wouldn't see them. Heaven forbid these four faceless men (I never had the nerve to look out the window to see what they actually looked like) should know how much I drank!

An all-out commitment to soap operas was another way I drowned out the painful situation around me. The soaps had become my reality since it was too difficult to face my failure as a mother and wife.

At 11:00 A.M. sharp I'd be seated in the den waiting for *All My Children* to begin. I would surround myself with a nest of pillows on the black Naugahyde couch, make sure I had a fresh pack of cigarettes and sometimes a six-pack of Pepsi with an ice bucket and vodka bottle. The phone came off the hook. I didn't want any interruptions.

As time went by, my repertoire of soaps expanded: *The Young and the Restless, The Days of Our Lives, Search for Tomorrow, The Edge of Night, Another World.*

The characters in the dramas became good friends. I talked about them as though they lived next door. Each tragedy I eagerly identified with, each triumph accepted reluctantly—for my own life was still in shambles.

Even my grocery list was a problem. Why burden my mind with more decisions than I could cope with? List in hand, I'd drive to the small neighborhood grocery store, wrapping the paper around the steering wheel so as not to lose it. Once things got into my purse, they could be lost forever, and I couldn't risk losing anything as important as this. I had to get dinner. That was one function I still performed. Yet it was becoming increasingly hard to stir and sauté and chop and fry.

Grocery shopping would have been impossible without the woman at the checkout counter. Somehow Shelly seemed to look past my rumpled clothes, the dried vomit in my hair, my confused manner. If she suspected that the boxes of candy and cookies were not for "those hungry kids" but for myself, she said nothing. Sometimes she'd leave her checkout line and help me assemble each item on my list. *She cares about me,* I thought on more than one occasion. *I wonder why.*

One morning as I laced my steaming cup of black coffee with a healthy slug of vodka, I remembered suddenly that Lisa's sixteenth birthday was the following day. By now Brent had joined Brad at his father's, but Lisa still lived with Randall and me.

Why Live?

Visions of a glorious birthday celebration suddenly danced in my head. Lisa, radiant and smiling, her bright-eyed young girlfriends seated about a candlelit table. Great baskets of field flowers everywhere. A spectacular concoction of marzipan, whipped cream and candied violets ablaze with sixteen candles illuminating the contours of her beautiful face. "Make a wish and blow out your candles," I would urge her gaily. "*All of them,* or your wish won't come true!"

But it was only a vision. There wasn't time to invite guests. And anyway, Lisa's mother was too sick to do it. None of Lisa's wishes were coming true. The smiling sixteen-year-old of my daydream was in reality a fretful, stressed young fawn, blinking shyly as she surveyed her disenchanted forest. Life in her stepfather's home was increasingly tense; my remarriage was already floundering under the strain of my progressing addictions.

Well, if it was too late to ask friends, at least we could have her brothers over—make it a warm and wonderful family celebration! At the grocery store Shelly greeted me courteously and helped me find the things I needed for the birthday dinner. Back in my kitchen, I would have just one beer before starting. Three beers and two hours later, I plodded through the motions of unpacking the groceries.

I must make tomorrow special for Lisa! After all, a sixteenth birthday is very important. I recalled how often as a tiny girl she had stood by my bed with a bottle of Vicks syrup and a spoon in her little hands when she heard me coughing in the night.

Closing my mind to such memories, I tried to focus on the job at hand. The cake. The birthday cake. The cake for my child. The child who is taking care of me. Do something special for her, for God's sake!

I picked up the box of chocolate cake mix. *Add two eggs and one cup water.*

I put the box back on the counter, sat down in the middle of the kitchen floor and wept. I couldn't cope with cake mix. It was too hard.

A call to the bakery produced an angel food cake with pink icing. The next day I muddled through a family birthday dinner that was strained and sad.

But that dinner was not as sad as the following Mother's Day. On my breakfast plate was a card—*To the Most Wonderful Mother in the World*—with a verse that brought wrenching sobs to my gut. Late that afternoon my husband and I went to visit friends. There were many drinks.

At 11:30 P.M. we returned home. The dining-room table had been set lovingly with our best dishes and gold-filled flatware. In the center of the table was a bouquet of handpicked flowers from our yard arranged in my favorite crystal vase. Loving touches from the loving hands of a girl wanting to please her mother, to honor her mother on her special day.

I lurched woozily past the pan of dried-up barbecue ribs Lisa had tried valiantly to keep warm for the Mother's Day dinner. I lifted the lids from the pots on the cold stove. Rice…broccoli…carrots. I sampled each pot's wilted contents, wiped my mouth with the back of my hand and headed for Lisa's bedroom.

She was still awake. She had been crying.

Weakly I tried to apologize. "Lisa, I'm so sorry…" The excuse was threadbare by now.

"Where were you, Mom?" she asked, her voice anguished. "I've been so worried…"

"Please forgive me, honey. It will never happen again." As I bent down to kiss her she turned her face into the pillow.

As the number of alcoholics has increased over the years, a new category of damaged people has emerged. According to statistics, there are now from 28 to 34 million children of alcoholics in the United States, of whom seven million are under the age of eighteen.[1] One out of every eight Americans is the child of an alcoholic. Here are further facts:[2]

- Alcoholism runs in families.

- Sons of alcoholic fathers are four times more likely to become alcoholics.

- Daughters of alcoholic mothers are three times more likely to become alcoholics.

- Children of alcoholics are often grandchildren of alcoholics.

- Daughters of alcoholics are more likely to marry alcoholics.

Many of us who have contributed to these statistics are trying to rectify the damage done to our children, to rebuild their sense of self-worth, to help them find fulfillment in life. It can happen, but not easily or quickly. Because of their upbringing, adult children of alcoholics (ACOAs) develop the following tendencies:[3] The same would apply to adult children raised in compulsive/addictive homes.

1. Adult children of alcoholics guess at what normal behavior is.

2. They have difficulty following a project from beginning to end.

3. They lie when it would be just as easy to tell the truth.

4. They judge themselves without mercy.

5. They have difficulty having fun.

6. They take themselves very seriously.

7. They have difficulty with intimate relationships.

8. They overreact to changes over which they have no control.

9. They constantly seek approval and affirmation.

10. Usually feel they are different from other people.

11. They are superresponsible or superirresponsible.

12. They are extremely loyal even in the face of evidence that the loyalty is undeserved.

13. They are impulsive. They tend to lock themselves into a course of action without giving serious consideration to alternative behaviors or possible consequences. This impulsivity leads to confusion, self-loathing and loss of control over their environment. In addition, they spend an excessive amount of energy on cleaning up the mess.

I was forcing my children, especially Lisa, into this life of misery. I despised myself. The taunting voices in my head were growing insistent: *Give everyone a break…kill yourself. Go ahead! Do it! Get out of this life!*

No question about it—everyone would be better off without me. The angry little men who inhabited my inner world had been pointing this out for some time. Sometimes I'd fondle the handle of Randall's hunting rifle. No, I couldn't possibly shoot myself. Or use a razor.

At the very back of the top shelf of the bedroom closet was my exit visa from the world: a cache of sleeping pills that I'd ferreted away in a fat orange plastic cylinder.

Clutching it in a shaking hand one late April afternoon in 1978, I headed for the cherry cabinet where stood a tall, clear bottle of vodka, almost full.

"You'll soon be where you can't do any more damage," I promised myself as I poured the liquor into a water glass at the kitchen sink. Opening the plastic container, I dumped the pills onto the black Formica counter where they rolled about in a riot of color.

The yellow wall phone caught my eye. From far away something said, *Don't do this. Think of your children, your husband, your parents. For God's sake, don't do this. Call someone. Get help.*

No. Death would be a welcome relief. I was dead in so many ways already.

Scooping up the skittering capsules, I stuffed them into my mouth and washed them down with an enormous gulp of the bitter vodka. More pills…more vodka…until the capsules were gone. Then more vodka to kill the taste of the gelatin coating. Two cups of strong black coffee—half coffee, half vodka. I reasoned that the hot coffee would melt the capsules in my stomach faster and speed the whole process.

Outside, the gray Montana sky increased the sense of doom. Anyone glancing up at the brick ranch-style house with the white shutters would see a manicured lawn, majestic blue spruces and a glorious willow tree sweeping the ground. No one would suspect that the figure standing at the kitchen window in a red bathrobe was waiting for death.

My lips started forming words. In a quivering voice I began to sing, "Jesus loves me, this I know, for the Bible tells me so…" How peculiar that I would think of that song at such a time! The happy Sunday school tune of years ago marched persistently through my mind. I could think of nothing else.

I placed my hand on the kitchen counter as if it were a ballet barre and practiced ridiculous leg positions, all the while singing "Jesus Loves Me."

Did everyone revert to childhood at a time like this?

Drowsiness was stealing over me. I had to get into bed before I collapsed. I didn't want Lisa or Randall to find me on the floor. Locking the bedroom door, I turned back the bed covers, lowered myself onto the cool sheets, and pulled up the blankets.

I plumped the pillow around my head, the way Mother used to tuck me into bed at night. My eyes scanned the familiar walls of our bedroom for one final time. On the dresser the chocolate-brown digital clock stared back at me, its green fluorescent numbers blipping away the final moments of my life.

My eyes rested on a framed watercolor of a red barn. A Vermont barn. Then inky blackness. A howling wind. Nothingness.

Where was I?

I smelled adhesive tape and ether. A blinding light was shining from somewhere above. Then the sound of my husband's voice: "Sandra, are you awake?" Randall's anxious face looked down at me.

I struggled to comprehend. The pills, the darkness…but I wasn't dead.

"Who found me?" I managed to mumble.

"Lisa," my husband answered. "She crawled through the bedroom window."

Self-loathing filled me. Lisa had found me. I had planned all this carefully so that she would be spared needless horror. What kind of monster was I?

"You've been in Intensive Care for twenty-four hours," Randall was saying. "It took three medical teams to bring you around. They'd given you up, but then someone felt a faint heartbeat. You were lucky…"

I didn't feel lucky. I felt sick. Despairing. I couldn't even succeed at killing myself. I rubbed my nose, and my fingers came away stained with dark-gray crystals. Charcoal. They had used it to save my life. Why had they bothered?

I had reached the bottom of the pit.

Thirty percent of all suicides, according to the Department of Psychiatry at Cornell University, are committed by people suffering from severe depression mixed with alcoholism and drug abuse. Recent statistics on suicide, available through the National Center for Health Statistics, indicate that in 2000 there were 28,332 successful attempts at suicide.[4] Many more people than that attempt to kill themselves every year for a variety of reasons.

"It seems incongruous," writes Arthur Janov in *The Primal Scream*, "to say that the aim of killing oneself is to live, but my experience with the attempted suicides makes it difficult to reach any other conclusion…As a rule, the attempt at death is one more neurotic plea to be loved. In this sense, the attempt at death is a cry for life."[5]

AT THE TIME ANY PERSON comes for psychiatric help he is lacking the most critical factor for fulfilling his needs, a person whom he genuinely cares about and who he feels genuinely cares about him.

—WILLIAM GLASSER, M.D.
Reality Therapy

7

Breaking the Cycle

It was at the bottom of the pit that change for me began. I have since come to learn that this is typical of compulsive personalities. As long as we can keep up the slightest pretense of normality, we deny the seriousness of our problem. And until a crisis comes, those around us do not confront us with our unacceptable behavior.

With my near-suicide all this changed. At the insistence of my psychiatrist and my husband, I entered Montana's hospital for mental disorders at Warm Springs, two hundred fifty miles from home and one of very few facilities in the state then available to treat people with addictions.

I arrived at the hospital dazed and lethargic. There were perhaps eighteen men and women on the ward where I was placed; at that time addicts were mixed in with the mentally ill. The best way the staff knew to keep their charges functioning and manageable was through medication.

The turning point for me occurred in this hospital, but it did not come through chemicals; it happened in another, totally unexpected way.

As one hopeless day slid into another, I sat staring through the greasy, nicotine-streaked windows at the dazzling blue Montana sky outside. How had I gotten myself into such a miserable state, locked up like a criminal? I really didn't want to answer that question. For whom could I blame but myself? Two husbands, my children, my parents, my friends had all tried to help me. Lord knows how hard they had tried.

Family visits were infrequent because of the distance. Friends sent me helpful books. One, *Beyond Our Selves* by Catherine Marshall, I carried about for days, but never got beyond the dedication page: "To Len," whoever he was. I seemed to have a block about reading anything religious. At the worlds *God* or *Jesus* my eyes would simply refuse to focus.

One afternoon my roommate, "Jackie," a wispy, angular waif with sad, dark eyes, and I were sitting on our beds waiting for the dinner bell to ring—a signal for us to line up by the front door to be counted before being picked up by the asthmatic old bus that took us all to the central dining hall. Just then a nurse brought a new patient to the room adjoining ours. The young woman collapsed on her newly assigned bed, sobbing and plucking at the bed covers.

Jackie and I looked at each other uneasily. This show of raw emotion was not uncommon at the hospital, but the moans of this poor girl were unnerving. "Oh, Jesus! Jesus! Jesus!" she intoned over and over.

"Karen, try to pull yourself together," the harried nurse implored. "It's almost dinnertime!"

"I don't want to eat; I want to *die*," came the muffled sobs.

Catching sight of Jackie and me, the nurse came to our doorway. "Karen is very upset. She was to be married next week, and her fiancé has been killed in a car wreck. Perhaps you two can speak with her and persuade her to come to dinner with the rest of the unit."

Jackie got up swiftly from her bed and stepped into Karen's room. I shuffled self-consciously behind her, alarmed at this new patient's wailing and writhing. Karen was not to be consoled. "Jesus, help me!" she kept crying out. "*Please,* Jesus—help me!"

I was to hear these words hundreds of times in the days that followed.

When Jackie and I returned to our room after dinner, we were startled to discover Karen up and walking regally about the hall. The change in her appearance was startling. Before she had been a crumpled, sobbing body in rumpled sweater and jeans. Now her short auburn hair was neatly combed, framing a gracefully beautiful oval face. Huge luminous brown eyes shone beneath thick lashes. She had changed into a long white bathrobe and white slippers, giving her an angelic appearance as she glided down the hospital corridor.

Breaking the Cycle

I was struck by her loveliness—such a powerful contrast to the other disheveled, vacant-faced patients. She fascinated me and frightened me at the same time. I wanted to reach out to her, but her constant calling on Jesus grated on my nerves.

As a little girl I had loved to hear Aunt Ethel tell us Bible stories and to stare at the picture on the Sunday school wall of Christ holding the lost sheep. Somewhere along the way I had lost that connection to Him. So I felt a grain of envy for Karen's faith. Even through the personal torment I sensed within her a quality of grace.

Later that first week after Karen arrived, I was alone in the room when I looked up to see her in the doorway. "May I come in and talk to you?" she asked shyly. "I'm scared of this place...of some of the men..."

This was the first of endless visits to our room. Karen seemed to appear in a puff of smoke—suddenly she'd just be there. It soon became apparent that Karen had appointed me her special friend and protector. I never had to guess who was behind me in the food line, her beautiful brown eyes searching for assurance that it was OK for her to be around. She would be waiting in the corridor when I got out of the shower room, by the door at the close of my therapy session.

Before long we became close friends. She shared her love for Jim, her deceased fiancé, and the dreams and plans they had made for their lives together.

One sultry July night, tossing restlessly in the heat of the stuffy hospital room, I was aware of Jackie's deep, regular breathing in the bed next to me. How could she sleep in this oven?

Then I sensed another presence in the room. Half-sitting up in my bed, I saw a familiar white-robed figure. There was Karen standing in the doorway, her long robe startlingly bright in the moonlight. As she approached my bed I could hear her crying. "Oh, Sandy, does Jesus love me? Does Jesus *really* love me?"

The pleading in her voice sounded as though this was the only thing in life that mattered to her.

What to do? What to say? Some instinct in me longed to comfort this weeping child. I got up gingerly, not sure how to console this quivering soul—how to reassure anybody of anything. Taking Karen in my arms, I patted her damp hair. It had been a long time since I'd held anyone to offer comfort. I had always been the one demanding comfort.

Clearing my throat awkwardly, I said, 'Yes, Karen, Jesus loves you."
Her sobbing stopped in an instant.

My heart was beating furiously. I felt cold and warm at the same time.

Karen detached herself from my embrace, wiped her eyes with the back of her hand, thanked me in a voice of childlike gratitude and slipped back to the adjoining room.

I lay back down, puzzled at a strange lightness, almost giddiness, that was pulsing through me. The full moon dipped lower in the west. The room seemed filled with a fragrant coolness. I slept peacefully until dawn.

As I write these words years later, I am filled with awe at how a fragile little event like this can change the direction of a life. We compulsives travel down one road after another, willfully driven on toward growing darkness and a dead end. In fact, road signs along the way warn that we proceed at our own risk. But pride and stubbornness compel us on.

Then something happens. Perhaps an encounter with another traveler, the breakthrough of a new idea. A change takes place—perhaps only a slight change, as in my case through Karen, but a change nevertheless. The traveler changes direction, hesitantly at first. And the way becomes lighter.

The turning point for me was no more than a flicker in my spirit. Shortly after her nighttime visit Karen was discharged, her leaving as sudden as her arrival. Lying on my bed one early morning a few days later, my eyes drifted to the room next door, resting on the rumpled bed that had been Karen's. Priscilla, a burned-out rock singer, was now camped there. Her bed was a shambles of posters and *Rock Star* magazines. A hand-tooled leather belt with thunderbolts etched around the word rock hung limply to the floor like a fleeing snake.

A chill rushed over me. I recoiled at the thought of this violation to Karen's special place. She'd brought such light to those dreary surroundings.

Shifting to a sitting position on the side of my bed, I stared out the window into the small grassy courtyard. The morning sun had appeared over the building annex, exposing the drabness of our rooms. The windowpane was covered with dusty rivulets from last night's thunderstorm. How I longed to polish the window to crystal clarity. The dirty windows everywhere represented more walls—transparent walls, but still walls further reinforcing my feeling of confinement.

Glancing down at my lap, I was astonished to see my hands in a prayer position. Across my skirt and onto the floor marched a shadow pattern from the slotted roof overhang—a pattern of *stripes*.

"By His stripes we are healed."

Where had those words come from? Of course! I'd heard them as a child in Vermont from Aunt Ethel. I didn't have any more idea what they meant now than I had then, except that they were somehow good words. Strong words.

My eyes went back to Priscilla's snake belt on what to me was Karen's bed. What if there really were two worlds at war, good and evil?

The breakfast bell jarred me back to the reality of hunger pangs. I really felt hungry! I hadn't felt anything for so long.

"Good morning, Gus," I chirped to our pudgy Scottish bus driver.

"Well, gud mawrnin' to you, Miss Sandy. An' if you aren't a bright-lookin' lass!"

After breakfast, another change. Somehow this morning the thought of gulping down my nine o'clock medication was repellent. The inevitable line was forming, patients clutching yellow Dixie cups to receive their juice and pills.

I inched forward at the end of the "meds" line, my eyes sweeping the dingy lounge strewn with old magazines and pots of pathetic scrawny plants, finally resting on the blaring TV set suspended from the ceiling (a precaution to keep the inmates from wrecking it). I saw NBC announcer John Chancellor appear:

> We interrupt this program to bring you a special news bulletin. The Pope has died in Rome."

I felt a rise of tears burn my eyes. Why should I react? I wasn't even Catholic. I remembered with a pang the off-colored stories I'd told about the Pope. Being funny had given me power. All at once I was repulsed by my "gutter humor," which, like foul language, slipped so readily from my tongue.

I had almost reached the cart where two nurses were mechanically filling the cups and dispensing the medications. I didn't want to swallow these pills anymore. What would happen if I didn't take them?

As the person in front of me moved away, I approached the nurses station with newfound resolve. "Here are your meds, Sandy." One nurse filled my Dixie cup while the other proffered gray capsules in a small pleated cup.

Her tired blue eyes stared at me as I popped the pills into my mouth and swished them quickly under my tongue, at the same time swallowing the canned orange juice "chaser."

As they pushed their squeaky cart back to the nursing station, I slipped into the women's bathroom. My heart was pounding as I entered the wooden stall. Flushing the toilet, I spit the bitter pills into the swirling water.

No more pills. The words seemed to come from outside of myself. Suddenly it mattered what I took into my body.

"Going against medical advice can be dangerous," my first husband had said many times from hard-won experience as a doctor. True, if arbitrarily you discontinued medication for something like diabetes. But these pills were chiefly to pacify and control.

Leaning against the rough plaster wall, I felt a tremulous stirring of well-being in that squalid little stall.

Like many women alcoholics, I had become addicted to prescription drugs, creating a dependency I was hardly aware of. The addiction continued when I was institutionalized during the 1970s, because the use of drugs was a standard procedure in the treatment of patients during this period. Today most treatment centers have patients go through a detoxification procedure before entering their program; drugs then administered are done only after careful evaluation of the patient's medical history.

Many of these treatment programs, moreover, see a good rate success. Kitty Dukakis, for example, wife of former Massachusetts governor and presidential candidate Michael Dukakis, announced in July 1987 that she had been treated successfully for a secret twenty-six-year addiction to amphetamines—diet pills. "I am now drug-free and I have been for five years," she was told an audience. "I'm very proud of that...I am telling my story because I want to help others."

It was a sign of the times that her confession elicited not criticism but respect, and even sympathetic identification.

As knowledge has increased about cross-addiction (for example, a patient is freed from an addiction to alcohol only to become addicted to sweets), patients are treated for their basic compulsive-addiction personality disorder. Cross-addiction, for me, also meant that at one time I was addicted to several substances (alcohol, tobacco, sweets and so forth).

At the well-publicized Betty Ford Center in Rancho Mirage, California, only 10 to 15 percent require prior hospitalized detoxification, but it takes at least a week for the different drugs to leave a patient's system. Whether the problem being treated is alcoholism (their number one problem), cocaine or prescription drug abuse, or often a combined addiction, that first week represents the hell of withdrawal—shakes, headaches, nausea and exhaustion.

Even withdrawal, however, is only the first step. The person trying to break any addictive pattern is subject to an extraordinary degree of internal conflict. She wants to break the pattern, and she doesn't want to. Symptomatic of this conflict is *dissociation,* a sense of separation from oneself, which sometimes results in a woman's feeling like a helpless spectator to her own self-indulgence.

"Dissociated feelings," write Drs. Hodgson and Miller in *Self-Watching,* "are linked with anxious and depressed states of mind in which willpower, planning, and reasoning are difficult to sustain. In helping people to overcome habits, then, it is not enough to identify why habits arise and how they are triggered. The individual must be equipped with the necessary skills to survive episodes of conflict, when morale and motivation are likely to be at their lowest ebb."[1]

TO ACKNOWLEDGE [OUR NECESSARY LOSSES] and neverthe-less find our freedom, make our choices, recognize what we are and what we might be, is what a responsi-ble adult is all about. Bowing to necessity, we must choose. This freedom to choose is the burden and the gift that we receive when we leave childhood, the bur-den and the gift that we take with us when we come to childhood's end.

—JUDITH VIORST
Necessary Losses

8

Do It Now

What was this change inside me after Karen?

At first it was simply in my attitude. Less despair. A glimmer of hope. And the resolve to take no more of the daily medication.

When there was heavy traffic in the john, I would slip the pills into an empty cigarette pack and hide them temporarily in my suitcase. I was careful about this because I'd seen what happened to patients who refused to take their medication. Off to the "Quiet Room" to be strapped to a table and given their medication by injection.

I couldn't risk discovery. My progress was slow—imperceptible some days—but I rejoiced at the new freedom I felt. Freedom from the inner fuzziness produced by the Quaaludes and the effect of the Thorazine, which seemed to fling my nerves against my body walls while I drifted in and out of reality. How could I ever get well in a psychedelic haze?

I knew that for some patients—the more violent ones—chemical stabilizers were the welcome alternative to physical restraint. Yet I sensed that in my case true recovery could not begin until I was free of artificial aids.

A second resolve was to regain my sense of personal dignity. My clothes had been confiscated for "special laundering" when I was admitted. There had been a forced shower and shampoo ordered by the impersonal admitting physician who inspected me like a side of beef, charting my scars, birthmarks and tooth fillings. Even my wedding ring was taken from me, the last vestige of my "belonging" to somebody.

I felt like a faceless number among murderers, rapists and manic-depressives. Every conceivable type of mental illness was baking in an asphalt pressure-cooker. Helplessness and despair had all but swallowed me whole.

To restore my sense of dignity, I began spending more time on personal grooming, taking more interest in my crafts class, even standing straighter. I stuck all my greeting cards on the wall over my bed as a cheery reminder that I was loved.

As I lay on my bed during rest time one afternoon, my spirit felt lighter. I fell asleep contemplating a return home to my family. Then a nurse was shaking my shoulder. "Wake up, Sandy. The staff wants to see you at once."

I followed her apprehensively down the corridor. What could the staff want to see me about?

As I entered the conference room I saw nurses and doctors assembling in a circle of chairs ready for "report." They were sipping coffee and shuffling papers and patients' charts. My eyes fell on Harry, the hospital administrator, the ever-present unlit cigar jammed into the corner of his mouth. Today he looked particularly disgruntled. My heart sank. I was in trouble, but I wasn't sure why.

At a nod from the nurse I threaded my way past the outstretched feet and lowered myself into an orange plastic chair.

"It has been brought to our attention that you have not been taking your medications," Harry began. "Unswallowed capsules were discovered in your suitcase this morning. Not taking your prescribed medicine is a serious violation of hospital rules. Do you have anything to say for yourself?"

Panic gripped me. Visions of being strapped down in the Quiet Room almost paralyzed my voice. Then something happened. My voice acquired strength. Purpose. I requested formally to be taken off all medication. To my surprise I had moved suddenly from defense to offense.

"I also need a week at home with my family to see if I can adjust to the outside world. Please," I concluded, "just give me a chance."

Surprised looks. Clearly they had been caught off guard.

"Reactions?" Harry queried his staff.

At first there was mild dissent. I pressed my point, stressing the progress I had made in recent weeks.

Do It Now

"I'll need to clear it with your doctor," Harry said uncertainly. "If she says you may go, I guess there's no reason a week at home wouldn't be all right. OK, staff?"

There were reluctant nods of agreement around the circle. When queried, my doctor, a warm-hearted Filipino woman, was favorable. The only stipulation: stay on my medication. Before week's end I was on a bus to Billings.

My husband was waiting at the bus station. On the drive home our conversation was strained. Later I stood in my own kitchen for the first time in four months and looked about in childlike wonder. Was this really my home? Somehow everything looked strange. Different.

I was suddenly aware of the depth of my emotional and physical exhaustion. As tired as I was, however, I dreaded going to bed with this stranger I was married to. Randall must have felt it, too. A silent wall separated us that night. He, so vibrant, bright and productive; I, so frightened and uncertain, a failure at everything.

The temptation to stay in bed the next morning was nearly overwhelming. A late August breeze was puffing the green shantung drapes in languid little bursts. Why not just roll over and go back to sleep? It would be so easy to do that. I really wanted to.

Yet deep within a kind of inner knowing gnawed at my soul. If I didn't get started right this morning, my life might never get straightened out Today was the first day of the rest of my life. With this realization came the practical message I most needed to hear: *Get up! Get moving! Do something to help yourself! Do it now.*

There had been countless mornings when I'd had this choice and had chosen to avoid the world, to hide in my bed with blankets pulled over my head. When I finally would get up, I would go from doctor to doctor, psychic to psychic, friend to friend, desperately hoping one of them could "fix" me, somehow transform me magically into a whole person, sound of body and mind. The answer over the years had become agonizingly obvious: No one else could do it for me. The effort to change, to get well, was going to have to start with me.

In describing this freedom to choose, Dr. Theodore Rubin wrote in *The Winner's Notebook:*

> The decision I arrive at is uniquely my own and born of my freedom
> to struggle through my feelings to either act or not act...This kind of

freedom to feel and to decide and if necessary, to experience conflict and to struggle through conflict to an answer produces values. This kind of tapping of one's own feelings and arriving at one's own individual values produces a sense of self-responsibility and identity.[1]

Now, from my bed, I gave myself a set of commands: "Get up, take a shower and get dressed!" My body obeyed reluctantly. These seemingly normal routines had been almost impossible during my periods of depression.

Wiping the steam from the bathroom mirror with the sleeve of my pink cotton robe, I peered at the anxious face that stared back at me. My appraisal:

- *Eyes*: Apprehensive. Needed the usual help from a mascara wand and eyeliner. I hadn't bothered with eye makeup for months.

- *Eyebrows:* A jungle growth. Get out the tweezers fast!

- *Skin:* Ghastly! So dry. Like an alligator suitcase. Alcohol and cigarettes do a job on skin. I looked at broken spiderweb veins around my nose. Quick, where's the face cream and liquid foundation?

- *Hair:* A disaster area. Stubborn wisps of gray hair were spiraling through the tangled auburn mop like errant bits of barbed wire. It had been months since I'd cared about coloring my hair.

To signal the change that I hoped was taking place inside, I would start today to make over the outside. I dressed carefully, then went across the hall to the den where I had a small desk. There I made a list of the things I wanted to accomplish that day—simple things: Make a date at the hairdresser. Take my soiled dress and slacks to the cleaners. Buy nail polish. I came up with nine items.

As I searched for the hairdresser's number, the old temptations flooded back. *What's the hurry? You've been four months in a grubby hospital. Sit down and have a cigarette. Bet there's a cold beer in the refrigerator. You deserve a break. What are you trying to do—win a medal?*

For a moment it was an all-out battle. My new resolve vs. the old pattern. Oh, how I was tempted.

Do It Now

Do it now!

Those three words snapped me out of it. I found the number and reached for the telephone.

That nagging little voice pursued me all day. *Are you some kind of slave driver? Take it easy.*

Then from inside came the rebuttal: *You've had enough rest. Get on with your life. Do it now.* At the end of the day, to my astonishment, I'd completed all nine items on my list. I'd also made a decision not to take the tranquilizers given me by the hospital.

The high point came when I went to get my hair done. What is there about the sounds and smells of a beauty shop that rejuvenate even before the work begins? As Rod, my favorite hairdresser, snipped and whirled me about in the dance that hairdressers do, visions of a new me spun through my brain. For some reason my mind flashed back twenty-two years to the summer of 1956 before the Miss America Pageant. I had felt the same sense of adventure, of a life-changing journey. The clinging coat of depression was dropping away from me like hunks of hair from Rod's scissors.

Wow, what a difference! I thought when Rod had finished. I couldn't believe my eyes. The "before" and "after" were staggering.

My husband did a double-take when he walked through the door that evening. "Can this be the same woman I said good-bye to this morning?" he asked with an astonished smile.

Settling for the week into a household routine after months of hospitalization, however, wasn't as simple as I'd thought. The second morning I wondered, *Should I dust? Should I iron? Should I bake something?* Such mini-decisions seemed overwhelming.

I wandered from room to room trying to reacquaint myself with my surroundings. Gingerly I examined each object in the living room as though reintroducing myself to old friends. Why did everything look so strange? A sudden fear began to strip away the fragile self-confidence built up by the first day's small achievements. Would I be able to stick out the week?

Our house was full of old ghosts—dreadful, painful memories. The chair where I did my heaviest drinking and planned my suicide seemed to menace me each time I passed it. Maybe it should be stored in the basement where I couldn't see it. No, that would be ridiculous All the furnishings held memories of some sort.

Taking a deep breath, I entered Lisa's now-vacant room. She had moved to her father's house to live with him and her brothers during my hospitalization. I was grateful that the children had pulled together while their mother was falling apart. I wondered if they knew how much I loved them, how guilty I felt.

As my sickness had worsened, it had become increasingly difficult to hug them, to show them warmth. My heart had become an icy lump sprouting from stainless steel ribs, my body home to miles of nerves that twisted and tangled around wooden bones. I had felt no life, just desperation.

Lisa's room still had her fragrance about it. The Love cosmetics popular with teenagers sat in a pristine row on a mirrored tray. Her dressing table was immaculate, each item in meticulous order. The stuffed animals she had left behind stared up at me from her red plaid bedspread. Clutching an armful of them, I sobbed into their soft plush bodies. Lisa had often held them for comfort. *Oh, Lisa, what have I done to you? To all of us?*

In the hallway outside her room, the white stucco walls seemed to close in on me. Then they expanded like rubber bands stretching to some far-off horizon. Back and forth. Back and forth.

Perhaps I belonged back in the hospital. Apparently I wasn't as strong as I'd thought. It had seemed so easy in my daydreams at the institution. Was I becoming a robot like so many of the patients there? Had I developed an institutional mentality? Was I unable to make any decisions or do anything for myself?

An insistent inner voice shouted, *No! Get busy. Do something. Do it now!*

This was going to be the toughest battle of my life.

One night that week my husband took me out to dinner. He seemed so proud of the "new me" and scrambled to open the car door and help me with my chair at our favorite table at the Rex Hotel. For the first time in months, I felt special.

As I took dainty sips from my chilled glass of white Chablis, I forgot the panic in the hallway. My husband was newly attentive, my self-confidence straining to break through the years of self-loathing. The rather attractive woman reflected in the bar mirror was really me. I tried not to stare at her.

From our table in the back room next to the wall, Randall liked to watch the stream of diners drift in and out. He had the lawyer's observing mind—every detail, every nuance. I admired him so. Yet our marriage had stretched on the brink of disaster for five years. It would take a miracle to breathe new life into it after so much damage.

I tried not to think back to only two years before when we'd sat at the same table on my fortieth birthday. I was on medication and had sat in this same chair in a fuzzy haze. My size eighteen dress did not cover the bulges from my binge eating. I'd felt like an overstuffed chair—a black-and-white print chair. The dress was hideous, but it was the only one I could still get into.

Now, while Randall ordered dinner, I took another sip of Chablis to wipe out the memory. A little wine never hurt anyone. After all the heart-break, I had still not faced up to my drinking problem…

On the six-hour bus ride back to the hospital, I thought back over the ups and downs of the week just ended. The visits with my children had been too short and tense to be satisfying. They had stared at this "new" mother, doubtless wondering whether they dared trust the changes they saw.

What had been accomplished by these seven days? A start…and the latching hold of a three-word principle: *Do it now.*

When I arrived back at the Warm Springs Hospital, it was afternoon. Since the entrance door was always locked, I rang the buzzer for admittance. A nurse named Gretchen peered through glass at me. "May I help you?"

"Gretchen, it's me! Sandy. Don't you recognize me?"

"Good heavens, no! You look so…good. In fact, you look terrific! Come on in."

Patients and staff alike gathered in the smoky lounge foyer to survey the returning patient. Incredulous stares greeted me, as though I were an alien from outer space.

Harry almost bit through his cigar as he rounded the corner of the nurses' station. "Looks like Billings agreed with you, Sandy. We're about to staff. We'll want a report on your week."

My doctor's round face was wreathed in smiles as she spotted me. "You look wonderful," she declared in her thick Filipino accent. And to the rest of the staff: "We can all see the positive results of home visits!"

Harry was staring at me with questioning, "show-me" eyes. "Give us a report, Sandy."

The pressure was on, every eye in the room riveted on me.

"I-I got along fine," I began. "The hardest part was to walk back into a house that held so many memories of pain and failure—and to know my time there was an experiment only. Could I change old habits? Could I start over? In many ways I was like a baby who had to learn to crawl before she could walk.

"I knew I had to set a schedule for myself that I could follow. I've always put unrealistic goals on myself. I've been such a perfectionist. If I couldn't do something perfectly, I wouldn't try at all. That's been a real trap for me all my life.

"I decided to choose a few simple tasks and do them. Not to expect perfection, but to make progress—any progress—on functioning normally. I wasn't sure that I could, but I did do what I set out to do. I was able to relate to my husband and my children as an adult instead of a sick-o. They were all surprised about that. I got up each morning, showered and dressed and accomplished my housework.

"The first morning I decided to do something about the way I looked on the *outside* to show that things were changing on the *inside*. I made an appointment to have my hair cut and colored. After coming out of a mental hospital, it took courage to walk back into that shop and face all those beauty operators I'd known so well. I was amazed at the warm way they all welcomed me! Since I'd let fear paralyze me for so long, it felt good to take a risk and have it work out. It's given me confidence to face the next hurdle."

Harry's bulldog face was set in rapt attention. The cigar was teetering in the corner of his mouth.

Gretchen seemed puzzled. "You make it sound so easy, Sandy. It's hard for me to believe you could adjust so quickly. You didn't show that kind of initiative here…"

My heart sank. Did the rest of the staff feel this way, too?

"Let's let Sandy continue," urged my doctor. "I'm sure she has a lot more to tell us."

Now what? What could I add? Frantically my mind raced ahead, trying to second-guess what would impress these staffers. I had never been in a situation like it—except the judges' interview at the Miss America Pageant. The thought of that experience in this setting was so ludicrous I almost laughed. It was the comic relief I needed.

"I don't know what else to say," I told them. "Obviously Gretchen finds my new resolve hard to believe. But I've had a lot of time to think while I've been a patient here. What do I want to do with the rest of my life? I want to get well. I want to have a good marriage and be a good mother. I want to be the best I can. Thus far I've been pretty much of a goof-off. I want to get on with the rest of my life."

"All good intentions," Harry interjected. "How do you plan to accomplish all this, Sandy?"

My heart was beating like a thrashing machine. My eyes were stinging. What to say?

"I've made some progress. My husband is supportive, and my children are anxious to have their mother back. That's a good start. I have a solid base to go home to. I'd like to find a job. I feel optimistic about my life in Billings…about my chances to get well there. Frankly, I don't believe I belong in this hospital or in any hospital."

My doctor was smiling at me. Patting my clammy hand, she spoke softly. "Staff, I'm going to ask Sandy to leave the room while we process this. Just have a seat in the lounge, if you will, Sandy."

I struggled to my feet and all but fled.

"Somebody give me a cigarette," I commanded in the lounge area. My roommate, Jackie, offered me an unfiltered one. The bitter jolt of raw nicotine almost spun me around.

"How can you smoke these things?" I gasped.

"I've always said if you're going to smoke, smoke a real cigarette," Jackie retorted. If she only knew how many nights I'd been awakened by her racking cough. Suddenly I felt very tender toward her.

It seemed like hours, but it was probably only twenty minutes before I was readmitted to the conference room. Taking the vacant orange chair, I awaited the verdict with lowered eyes

"It is the consensus of the staff," my doctor announced, "that you are capable of being released from this institution as soon as we can process your papers. We feel you have shown favorable initiative and sufficient resolve to adhere to a solid program of recovery. You've been a cooperative patient. I especially will miss you, and I wish you much good luck in your life outside this hospital."

Tears welled up in my eyes and slid down my cheeks as the staff applauded.

IT IS INDEED POSSIBLE for us to mature out of a belief in God. What I would now like to suggest is that it is also possible to mature into a belief in God. A skeptical atheism or agnosticism is not necessarily the highest state of understanding at which human beings can arrive. To the contrary, there is reason to believe that behind spurious notions and false concepts of God there lies a reality that is God.

—M. Scott Peck, M.D.
The Road Less Traveled

The Pain in Change

My hospitalization and recovery period introduced me to a new word in the treatment of compulsive behavior: *enabler*. An enabler is the addict's spouse, parent and/or child who, because of embarrassment or a sense of guilt, attempts a cover-up to protect the family, *enabling* the addict to continue his destructive behavior.

An enabling wife is one who calls her husband's office on Monday morning and tells his boss that her hung-over spouse has the flu. A whole pattern of deceptive practices, involving all members of the family, is under way. The addict's sickness is all too obvious; the rest of the family's "sickness" is not so recognizable, yet it is just as real and needs to be treated.

"No matter what personality type you live with," writes Mary Ellen Pinkham in *How to Stop the One You Love from Drinking*, "*all* members of the family will react to the alcoholism, and as the alcoholic becomes more involved with his drinking, *you* become more involved with *him*. You will eventually experience identifiable and pathological behavior that is as predictable as the pattern of the alcoholism itself."[1]

If, as the National Council on Alcoholism and Drug Dependence estimated in 2000, each of the 18 million alcoholics in the U.S. directly affects four other people, then there are at least 72 million people intimately involved with alcoholism.

Family members, through embarrassment and guilt, will try to cover up the destructive behavior of the addict. Husband and children will adjust their daily routines and even go through psychological change in their efforts to protect the addictive wife and mother. In doing this, they become enablers. They not only do not help the addict; they become sick, too. (See page 281 to check your own codependence.)

The addict's sickness is usually obvious to family and close friends; the rest of the family's "sickness" is not so recognizable, yet it exists and needs to be treated.

An enabling husband will often assume the role of peacemaker in the family when his wife is an addict. A family friend in his forties, for example, was married to an alcoholic for twelve years. When she died, he took his two young children quickly into a second marriage with a widowed woman and her teenage daughter. The result: tension and conflict in the home.

"When I tried to resolve these squabbles, they dubbed me 'peacemaker,'" the friend revealed. "The term was often used contemptuously. It took an Al-Anon meeting to make me see that in my first marriage my role as enabler had, in a sense, made me sick, too. My ability to act openly and forthrightly was impaired. I did seek peace at any price, and my second family was calling me on it."

My own past is most painful to reflect on when I see the effect of my compulsive behavior on my family. All tried valiantly to help me: my parents, two husbands, my children, my parents-in-law. All became enablers in one way or another in their efforts to protect me, damaging themselves in the process.

My husband Randall, for example, used to watch the liquor cabinet to see how much I consumed. I knew this, so one winter morning I conspired to outwit him. After he left for work I plucked a full bottle of vodka from the cabinet, plotting to use just one shot in my morning coffee. I planned to add a touch of water to fill it up, then restick the seal with glue. He would never know. Besides, Randall never drank vodka in the winter anyway—just Scotch.

At 11:30 I was on my second pot of coffee, and the bottle was half-gone. *I'll run out later this afternoon and get another bottle,* I promised myself. By four o'clock it was snowing, and I was in no condition to drive anywhere. I had to sober up and fix dinner. When Randall arrived home at 6:30 the vodka bottle, filled with water, was back in the liquor cabinet, paper seal in place.

The Pain in Change

Randall sat down in his favorite chair and started to peruse the evening paper. "How about fixing me a vodka and tonic tonight?" he asked.

My heart pounded. I was caught. "There's no vodka," I murmured.

"What do you mean no vodka? There's a full bottle in there."

"I'm afraid it's full of water."

There was no confrontation. He had resigned himself to the hopelessness of the situation. I wondered how he could go through this little drama without blinking an eye. *No wonder he's such a good trial lawyer,* I thought to myself.

Like millions of other husbands with alcoholic wives, there were times when he did get angry at my heavy drinking and rail at the family upsets that resulted. But over the years he drifted into the role of enabler, protecting me as best he could from myself.

When I returned home from the Warm Springs hospital in the fall of 1978, I had made only the tiniest start on the road to recovery. At my departure my doctor had given me a list of medications to take, most of which I had already decided against using. As the months passed, I had no idea what further steps to take.

There had been some kind of spiritual change inside me, but I didn't know what to do about that either. I even sensed God had spared me— but why? I was still tormented at times by angry inner voices.

My deepest desire was to rebuild my home situation, become a good wife and develop closer relationships with my children. But how was I to do that? Probably by working to conquer my destructive behavior patterns. Three areas especially concerned me: smoking, overeating (especially sweets) and drinking. (I was not ready to admit I could not drink at all.) How should I attack these problems? Will power, I concluded.

A flutter of resolve stirred within me. I wanted to change. I knew I had to change. But how does change happen?

I decided to begin with nicotine, which had already been demonstrated scientifically to engender genuine drug addiction, not just an addiction to the activity of smoking.[2]

I'd first tried to quit eight years earlier, when a doctor warned me that smoking was damaging my lungs. I had agreed. It was time to stop. Besides, I hated the spidery lines that were forming around my lips from my constant puffing.

I had done it back then on sheer will power. My first act of a morning had been to *not* light up as soon as my eyes opened, but to reach for a LifeSaver. If I had forgotten to leave these "savior" packs by the bed, I'd fly into a frenzy. What to stick into my mouth? Ballpoint pens, frayed toothpicks, paper clips, anything I could lay my hands on. Every pair of eyeglasses I owned soon had their bows chewed so badly that they scratched my temples.

What had happened then should have alerted me to the fact that it was not tobacco I was battling—or alcohol, or overspending, or any of my other excesses—but a compulsive personality beneath all the specific cravings. Eliminating cigarettes eight years before had simply brought about a switch in compulsions. Chocolate had then become my slave master—in any form, at any time. I'd stir from my bed at ungodly hours and bake a pan of brownies or struggle through the ritual of a devil's food cake mix. "Aptly named," I'd sigh as I stumbled around my kitchen in the darkness.

My clothes had gotten tighter and tighter as the fibers strained to cover my ever-increasing thighs and derriere. My nocturnal baking sessions baffled my children at first, but soon they looked forward to fresh-baked "surprises" for breakfast. Brownies and cereal. Brownies and eggs. Brownies and pancakes.

After two years off tobacco, one day for no reason I had picked up a pack of cigarettes. "I merit a Merit!" I joked weakly to my drinking companions. The first puff slammed against my throat in a burst of welcome relief. Every dormant nicotine sensor screamed to first-alert: *Welcome back! We knew you'd give in someday.*

I had begun to smoke more than ever. Two packs a day. Three packs if I got up early and stayed out late. I would have smoked in the shower if I could have figured out a way to keep the thing lit.

I had hated myself for caving in. What had happened to all the resolve? I had resigned myself to the fact that it was better to smoke than to be fat—just the opposite of what I'd told myself before as I'd waited those endless hours for my cakes to bake. I had thought will power was the answer—if only I were *strong* enough. I know now why that is a typical, erroneous thought of a compulsive person: "Will power as a pure act," writes Dr. Theodore Rubin, "invariably comes from compulsive drives and contracts and further contributes to compulsion. There is no real self involved in an attempt to overwhelm a disastrous situation by an act of 'strength' alone. It just doesn't work. Insight, on the other hand, involves real knowing of self and real self-involvement on the deepest level."[3]

I had no such insight into the driving force of my own inner compulsions.

Today the hard evidence against smoking is overwhelming, connecting smoking with cancer and diseases of the heart, lungs and circulatory system. Smoking is dangerous to one's own health, to nonsmokers in the vicinity of the smoker, and even to persons not yet born. Smoking is a problem on the job. Each year smokers are absent from work 50 percent more often than the nonsmoker. Counting smoking damage, health insurance and other factors, the smoker costs his or her company thousands of dollar per year.[4]

Despite the almost irrefutable evidence, however, about 48 million Americans are still smoking, including 22.6 million adult women.[5]

Dr. Virginia Ernster, associate professor of epidemiology at the University of California at San Francisco School of Medicine, observes that cigarette companies worldwide perceive "the working woman, under stress, as the ideal candidate for their product."

Nicotine is extremely addictive; its addictive characteristics are now being compared to heroin and cocaine. What's more, although individuals involved with other addictions such as alcohol or hard drugs sometimes take a break from their usage—from a few days to weeks and sometimes even a few months—smokers never take a break. They smoke every day, through all their waking hours. Some even have difficulty making it through the night without smoking.

Dr. Ellen Gritz, director of the Division of Cancer Control at UCLA's Jonsson Comprehensive Cancer Center, points out that "cigarettes are often used to control negative moods and stressful feelings. When a woman quits, she may start expressing these negative feelings, and people around her get upset. I've had lots of women tell me that their families begged them to go back to smoking."

Even if a woman can escape this pressure and survive the pain and discomfort of cold-turkey withdrawal, she is met with a psychological attachment that is extremely difficult to break. Some of the following suggested ways to curb the urge to smoke might prove helpful:[6]

- If craving a cigarette, delay lighting up, five minutes at a time. Distract yourself with some other activity.

- If cigarettes give you an energy boost, try modest exercise, a brisk walk, deep breathing exercises and a balanced diet, avoiding foods high in sugar.

- Go places where you can't smoke.

- Keep a glass of water nearby, and instead of smoking, take sips through a straw. Do this with other beverages as well.

- Don't linger at the table after a meal.

- If you do slip and smoke a cigarette or two, decide why you succumbed to temptation; set a new goal of not smoking—and not slipping up again. Nicotine happens to be the most addictive substance known to man— despite what the cigarette manufacturers would have us believe. It's easier to kick a heroin addiction than nicotine.

Remember, the urge to light up lasts only five to ten minutes. You *can* do it!

One day I was visiting with a friend going through a painful separation. We were commiserating with each other about the messes we had made of our lives. I took out a pack of cigarettes, my third of the day, and struggled with the stubborn cellophane wrapping.

"I'll quit if you will," she challenged me suddenly. "Let's put money on it. The first one who smokes owes the other…fifty dollars?"

Realizing it wouldn't be possible to extract that much in secret from my household budget, I declined the contract. "We can do it without any bets. I know we can."

Enthusiastically we pumped each other's hands. We could kick this thing. Later, to reinforce my resolve, I rolled down the window of my car as I drove home.

"Farewell, evil weeds!" I intoned, tossing the fresh pack out the window. Suddenly it was as though Karen were sitting in the car beside me. I heard her voice as I'd heard it so many times in the hospital at Warm Springs: *Please, Jesus—help me!*

The Pain in Change

"If You really exist," I whispered, "and if You really do help people…
will You help me quit smoking? *Please.*"

When I awakened the next morning, my eyes greeted the sunny
morning with a strange new clarity and an unaccustomed sense of peace.
The frayed edges of my ragged nerves were somehow knitted together.
The craving for tobacco was simply and amazingly gone. I stared won-
deringly through the bedroom window at the dazzling blue Big Sky of
Montana.

As before, however, doing without cigarettes seemed to activate my
taste buds. My urge for chocolate returned stronger than ever. I tried to
resist, but defeat followed defeat in my kitchen. The inner voice seemed
to gloat, *Weak, hopeless, failure.*

At the time I didn't understand that if checked in one area, the compulsive nature will break out in another, that the sickness was not this
addiction or that, but deep inside me. I was upset when I went to yard
sales and came home with items I didn't need—or even want. Clothing
sales drew me like a moth to a flame. When closets bulged with "bar-
gains," I hid the overflow in bags under the bed.

Harvard psychiatrist George Vaillant has observed just this kind of
cross-addictive behavior, reporting that former alcoholics often shift to
new dependencies—candy, compulsive work, hobbies, gambling and so
forth. Indeed, in the groundbreaking *Ms.* survey, women confessed
addictions to a large variety of behaviors, including shopping, walking,
running, yoga, exercise, cleaning, sleeping, work, daily routines, credit
cards, nail-biting, even using the phone.

For me there was always a monster lying in wait, ready to take charge
again: my craving for alcohol. I still sipped wine at the dinner table and
drank at parties—but no longer could I count on the numbing relief, the
rush of exhilaration that had always accompanied the flow of alcohol
into my system. More and more often now there was only a fearful gray
fog whenever I took a drink. I longed to stop altogether, but lacked the
will power—or, as Dr. Rubin points out, the self-knowledge.

The answer came unexpectedly. It was Valentine's Day, 1980. That
night I was hostess for a dinner party in my home.

The day began with feelings of nervous anticipation, a desire that the
party be a dazzling success. I had made a special quilted tablecloth, spent
hours planning the food—even to colors that harmonized—and

arranged elaborate floral decorations.

It would be a night of striving to win the approval and acceptance of my husband's friends and law associates. I'd be under the microscope. Being scrutinized wasn't new, but an ex-mental patient always seems to have more to prove. Could I pull the evening off?

As the guests arrived, I fluttered in the kitchen, hovering over gurgling pans and checking the oven obsessively. Somehow the meal materialized on my flower- and candle-bedecked table. There were so many decorations there was barely room for the food. Profuse compliments flowed as fast as the dinner wine. Then Randall tapped his wineglass to signal "toast time."

I grasped the stem of my goblet. As I did, the dark burgundy sloshed about, creating swirling purple rings in the crystal. And in those rings I saw, as clearly as if they had been etched in the glass, three words:

- *Poison*
- *Death*
- *Insanity*

I wanted to scream. I stared incredulously at the telltale words. The others were raising their glasses, laughing and talking. Couldn't they see the message inscribed in wavering purple letters?

I don't want to drink this. I don't want to drink anything alcoholic ever again.

A feeling of warmth coursed through my body from head to toe, a renewed sense of being protected. Was it Karen's God revealing His love to me on Valentine's Day, the day for lovers?

Days passed. As with cigarettes, the craving for alcohol was startlingly and totally gone.

For other women, of course, the battle is more drawn out, especially when they are faced with social situations in which they are urged to have "just one" drink. The following suggestions from *Self-Watching* help to develop skills for coping with those social situations likely to arise:[7]

1. Stay for a half hour, and then leave if I feel uncomfortable.

2. Get over my anxiety by just listening to people. Forget about trying to impress.

3. Try drinking a nonalcoholic beverage with lemon or lime. Others will be less likely to pressure me into drinking.

4. If I feel a craving coming on, then I will pick up the phone and call my AA sponsor or someone who is aware of my resolve for recovery.

5. I must remember how good I felt at the office party two months ago when I successfully resisted the pressure to drink.

6. Be assertive. Simply say, "I am not drinking, so please do not offer me one."

Despite the fact that I had suddenly, completely lost the desire for alcohol, I had *not* lost the desire for chocolate. Or the sudden yearnings to go shopping. And the pain was still in place.

In an effort to understand my compulsive tendencies, I started reading everything I could lay my hands on. One report, "The Nature of Craving," showed that monkeys and rats, even when hungry chose cocaine over food.[8] When given free access to cocaine, the animals "went into a frenzy of drug-taking activity."

The study suggested that some machinery for addiction is built into our brains. To combat this innate tendency, the author called for a joining of biological, psychological and sociological forces. No mention was made of spiritual forces having any part to play.

As I read this report, I had a picture of all the antiseptic hospital halls I'd walked down, of intellectually determined and well-meaning medical men talking in scientific jargon about my problems, of pills prescribed and then more pills, and of a kind of emotional and spiritless sterility that surrounded it all.

Scott Peck refers to this sterility of spirit in *The Road Less Traveled:* "It is indeed tempting for psychiatrists to view themselves as knights of modern science locked in noble combat with the destructive forces of ancient religious superstition and irrational but authoritarian dogma."[9]

Meanwhile I struggled with the volcano of compulsion inside me. Why did eating binges and shopping splurges so quickly follow my victories over tobacco and alcohol?

I asked this question of a neighbor. Kathy was about my age, mid-forties, with a pert nose and a short, chestnut pageboy haircut. She responded by inviting me to a prayer meeting. Because I was hungry for answers, I agreed to go. So one bright June morning I walked into a living room filled with smiling women who welcomed we warmly. Nervously I perched on the edge of a green sofa. The pastor of the Methodist church was there, giving me a sense of assurance that I was not involved with spiritual oddballs.

At the prayer meeting someone suggested that because of my exposure to the occult, I should get rid of everything related to it. I went home and burned all my occult books and horoscope readings. It was amazing the amount of psychic material a scavenger hunt revealed. I even discarded items of my clothing that had signs of the zodiac and jewelry with arcane symbols. Part of me argued that the whole performance was nothing but superstition and fanaticism. Yet with these things out of the house I felt...lighter, somehow. Purged.

Was it my imagination, or in the days that followed were the angry voices in my head fainter, farther off—often silent for long periods.

But the craving for food, especially chocolate, still drove me. I still slept late too many mornings, had trouble getting myself organized. My needs were visible to everyone.

Kathy, however, was one of those caring people who sees a friend through the long haul. I especially remember the morning she appeared on my doorstep clutching a book. Eyes filled with concern, she thrust the book into my hands as I stood behind the slightly cracked door.

"Here, Sandy, maybe *this* will help..." Then she ran back to her idling car and sped off down the street.

Shutting the door, I thrust the book into my pocket of my rumpled bathrobe. In the walnut-framed hall mirror I caught a look at myself.

Good grief! Who is that?

Backing up in disbelief, the leering image gaped back at me. That couldn't be me! It must be some beached whale wrapped in a chenille robe.

And those haunted eyes ringed with wilted mascara. Raccoon eyes!

A beached whale with raccoon eyes.

Tears flooded my eyes, splashing down my cheeks onto my robe. I was suddenly aware of the deep hollow in my chest. I knew how to fill it. There was afresh half-gallon of chocolate ice cream hidden in the freezer under the Brussels sprouts. I could count on my dark, cool, sweet friend to bring me relief.

The Pain in Change

To the freezer! I'd need a serving spoon. Yes, a *big* spoon, for I intended to eat it all.

The just-delivered gift of love, Kathy's book, now rested forlornly on the dark pine kitchen table, its pristine newness smudged with brown dribbles from my chocolate binge. I'll read it *tomorrow*, I promised myself.

Several weeks later Kathy's voice on the phone sounded bright and enthusiastic as she told me about an upcoming workshop at her Methodist church. I wasn't so sure, except that since I'd stopped drinking I needed something to occupy my mind. There were so many raw emotions coming to the surface that I couldn't deal with: frustration, fears, anger, and—oh, God—the guilt.

"Sandy! Welcome!" Entering the church for the workshop I was smothered with hugs of well-wishers, many of whom I'd known socially over the years in Billings. I tried not to be preoccupied with the hug wrinkles on my meticulously ironed blouse and scarf.

The workshop leaders were a couple from Spokane, Washington. As the husband spoke I glanced at the shadows on the far brick wall—a syncopated pattern of stripes. I thought of the stripes I'd seen across my lap in the hospital.

The speaker was opening his Bible. "Turn with me to Isaiah 53, verses 4 and 5," he said. Then he began reading:

> Surely he [Jesus] hath borne our griefs, and carried our sorrows: yet we did esteem him stricken, smitten of God and afflicted. But he was wounded for our transgressions, he was bruised for our iniquities...and with his stripes we are healed.
>
> —KJV

I stared at him open-mouthed, stunned at the timing of the words, and felt a transfusion of hope.

"Are you coming to the healing service Sunday night?" Kathy asked later. "I'll be happy to pick you up."

I shook my head. "I'd better pass it up."

Sunday evening Randall and I ate dinner in silence. I tried not to look at the kitchen clock that indicated twenty-five minutes until the healing service began. While scraping the dishes, I wondered what my priorities should be. On the one hand, my husband's negative attitude toward my churchgoing was clear. Religion almost seemed more of a threat to our marriage than my drinking. On the other hand, something inside was pushing me toward the church. That, obviously, would be a mistake.

I changed into my faded blue jeans and slipped on a baggy gray sweater for an evening of watching TV. When I entered the den, Randall was already settled in his black leather chair, the set tuned to the Sunday night movie. I sank into the couch.

A moment later I was back on my feet. "I have to go to church," I said lamely. "I don't expect you to understand why. I'm not sure I do either."

I raced out the front door with the image of his puzzled stare following me. Was I being driven by yet another compulsion?

Organ music was filling the church with a mighty crescendo when I entered. Such joy flooded the sanctuary that the putty in the stained glass windows must have struggled to keep them from exploding outward.

The memory of my husband's disapproving look was dissolved in the majesty of the music. When the invitation was given to come forward for healing, I rose from my seat and walked down the center aisle. People were streaming toward the front from all over the church. There was just enough room for me to squeeze in at the altar rail.

A large white cross hung from the ceiling over the marble altar. In the brilliance of the ceiling spotlights its whiteness was dazzling. My eyes fell on the enormous open Bible resting on the marble missal stand. Below it in brushed brass letters were the words *This Do in Remembrance of Me.*

At first, as I grasped the thick oak altar rail, my mind was racing. Scenes: the living room at Uncle Ralph's; wearing the flower crown of Miss Vermont; awaiting death at my kitchen window. Places: Atlantic City, Disneyland, Deaconess Hospital here in Billings. Faces: Brad, Brent, Lisa, my mother and father, Shelly at the checkout counter, Karen. Like whirling dancers they sped past. Then calm—a holy silence.

A few minutes later a woman minister joined me at the altar rail and listened to my litany of pain. Then she placed her hands on my shoulders and looked straight into my eyes as the following words flowed with quiet authority from her lips: "If God has forgiven all your sins, how dare you not forgive yourself?"

My eyes smarting, my nose running, I offered up my prayers to God— and felt the deep-down happiness of being accepted for what I was. I was the object of a love greater than any I had ever known.

"To forgive your own self," writes Lewis B. Smedes in *Forgive and*

The Pain in Change

Forget, "is almost the ultimate miracle of healing! To forgive yourself is to act out the mystery of one person who is both forgiver and forgiven. You judge yourself: this is the division within you. You forgive yourself: this is the healing of the split."[10]

Later, as I reflected on what happened at the church, I saw it as major step toward health. Since compulsive behavior, by its very definition, entails acts we experience as involuntary—in which our wills are over-whelmed by a desire that feels as if it comes from outside ourselves—the remedy for such behavior lies in submitting ourselves to a countervail-ing positive force. Alcoholics Anonymous call this force a Higher Power. Many therapists construct other ideals "outside" the patient.

A skeptic might argue that by this procedure the compulsive person merely exchanges addictions. I don't agree. Every sufferer knows the dif-ference between pain and release from pain. As Dr. Stanton Peele writes in *Love and Addiction:*

> The difference between not being addicted and being addicted is the difference between seeing the world as your arena and seeing the world as your prison...If what a person is engaged in enhances his ability to live—if it enables him to work more effectively, to love more beautifully, to appreciate the things around him more, and finally, if it allows him to grow, to change, and expand—then it is not addictive.[11]

Though other compulsive women may find other "Higher Powers" that release them from enslavement to detested but irresistible urges, I can speak authentically about only one. For me, Christian conversion and faith was the necessary outside force to break the grips of the pat-terns that held me in thrall most of my life.

A sociologist might say that compulsive individuals in our culture are predisposed toward a Judeo-Christian solution to their behavior. Whatever reasons may be given, I can only say personally that it worked for me. My compulsive lifestyle was reordered by a power outside myself, which since that night in the church I continue to experience and call Jesus Christ.

FOR SOME REASON, I CAN TELL YOU where each person in that room was sitting; the floor plan is burned into my brain…And they all proceeded to confront me with a second intervention. Only this time, they meant business…All of them hurt me. I collapsed into tears. But I still had enough sense to realize they hadn't come around just to make me cry; they were there because they loved me and wanted to help me.

—BETTY FORD
The Times of My Life

10

INTERVENTION

As I probe back into my recovery, and the recoveries of other compulsive people, and see how the sick and defeated are transformed into healthy and productive people, one central fact comes through: *Recovery seldom comes about through one or two experiences. Recovery is not an event; it is a process.*

Encountering Karen at Warm Springs Hospital was a beginning, the activation of a long-buried desire to respond to the hurt and need of someone else. John Schwarzlose, president and CEO of the Betty Ford Center, explains: "Alcoholics and addicts have isolated themselves for years. We want them to form relationships again."

The discovery of those three little words *Do it now* was also a step to healing, the coming to life of a part of me that wanted to take responsibility. It too was part of the process.

After throwing my cigarettes from the car window and uttering what might have been the first real prayer of my life, I was loosed from bondage to nicotine. When months later I was released from the desire to drink at the Valentine's Day party, I thought I was now free from all addiction. (Far from it. My compulsions to overeat and go on shopping binges were to reemerge stronger than ever.)

And after the beautiful cleansing experience at the Billings Methodist Church, the mental and physical listlessness brought on by years of abusing my body was replaced by a powerful infusion of energy. I felt more alive than I had in twenty years. Yet this healing was also only a step on the long road back to health.

During the recovery process, I encountered attitudes that were troubling. Some new church friends took the position that I would find all the healing I needed through prayer alone. God's work in me might be endangered, they said, if I got involved with any secular scientific treatment. The medical world, on the other hand, expressed indifference and even hostility toward any healing that came about through "religion," saying it came either from mass hysteria or a kind of self-hypnosis. Yet I could see value in what both camps offered.

In any case, there were few effective medical treatment centers for addictive people until the 1970s. Before then alcoholics and drug addicts were often institutionalized, as I had been, right in with the mentally disturbed. Once separate facilities were set up to help addiction sufferers, a new era began. These medical centers usually worked closely with Alcoholics Anonymous (AA), the one approach to alcoholism that had proven effective statistically since it was started in 1935. A significant discovery was that the basic Twelve-Step program of AA worked not only for alcoholics, but for other compulsive behavior problems, too. (See page 180 for how to apply the Twelve-Step program.)

Recovery begins, counselors discovered, when patients face reality— as required by the all-important First Step of the program. But oh, how hard it is for the addict to change years of practiced deception and self-delusion. Our emotions are defensive, self-protective. Facing truth can be like pulling teeth without anesthesia...as I was soon to discover.

For weeks after my healing at the Methodist church, Bible study and prayer groups became the doors to a new life while I tried not to look at the wreckage of two homes.

My three teenage children were living with their father and had their own lives and activities, where I did not fit. Randall and I were growing farther and farther apart. Many months had passed since my last drink. My resolve was intact, but my body was behaving strangely. Sometimes I talked like a machine gun. I raced from the supermarket to a prayer meeting to home again at a frantic pace.

"Are you sure you're OK?" friends would ask. "You seem so revved up. Slow down and catch up with yourself!"

Any sense of peace had lit momentarily like the butterfly that had enchanted me in my childhood hideaway, then flitted off elusively. A restless gnawing often filled my heart. I couldn't seem to focus my mind anymore. Blaming the symptoms on the stress of my personal life, I didn't realize I was heading straight for a "dry drunk" condition when a recovering alcoholic exhibits deceptive, unrealistic or "hyper" behavior without the use of alcohol. (See Checklist of Symptoms on page 185.)

Thinking a change of scene would help, I decided to drive out to a seminar in Seattle. On the way I could spend the weekend with my new friend Cathy and her husband, Dirk.

At their home in Red Lodge, Montana, Cathy and Dirk welcomed me warmly. Feeling exhilarated by our evening of discussion, I lingered in the cozy living room of their log cabin lodge long after Cathy and Dirk went off to bed.

Classical music from an FM station set a dreamy mood. I drifted about the room, rolled back the braided rugs and danced barefoot on the smooth varnished floor.

The sound of a male voice fractured my reverie. It was Dirk. "What in the world are you doing at this ungodly hour?"

Startled, I just stared at him.

"Sit down, Sandy. I want to talk to you," he exclaimed as he tightened the tie of his terrycloth bathrobe. "You may not like what I'm going to say, but I have to say it anyway."

He studied me for a moment in the soft light. "I know how much progress you've made sine Cathy and I first met you and how fragile you are right now, but I have to tell you that your behavior is absolutely bonkers. You are on one heck of an emotional binge, kiddo—a dry drunk. If you don't do something about it, it may turn into a wet drunk, and God knows what would happen to you then.

"You are in absolutely *no* condition to drive to Seattle by yourself. Or anywhere else for that matter. You need to go to a treatment center. And fast. I mean tomorrow. Before the sun goes down.

"Meanwhile, quit prancing around like a princess and get to bed. You need rest. We'll call St. Mary's when the office opens at eight o'clock and see if we can get you in. You've got to go, Sandy. Your life depends on it. You're a lot sicker than you think you are."

I hated him. I was fine...just on a slight roll. I argued, stormed and wept, but deep down I knew he was right. His words pierced through all my denial. I couldn't run any longer. My life was still out of control. It was time to face my sickness head-on. Dirk helped me face the truth—that I needed professional help.

The next day I was on my way to St. Mary's Treatment Center in Minneapolis.

The "dry drunk" is a common experience for recovering addicts if there has been no inner healing of the emotions. The message to me was pointed: "You may have stopped drinking, Sandy, but you are still binge-ing emotionally." My compulsive nature was still in control. Turn off tobacco, turn on sweets; turn off alcohol, turn on a "spiritual" high from music or overtalk.

What Dirk had done for me was a spontaneous form of an increasingly popular treatment approach called *intervention* (see page 123). The purpose: to get the sick person to face up to reality The method: confrontation. "Your behavior is bonkers, Sandy. Your very life is at stake. Get to treatment—fast."

Intervention is "a move initiated out of love and concern by the people who care about the alcoholic," writes Mary Ellen Pinkham. "It involves their getting together to tell the alcoholic the facts about his disease and how it is affecting him. It's the only kind, gentle, and caring way to help a chemically dependent person. It's the only thing that works, the key to stopping someone whose life is in danger."[1]

If too many family members have been "codependents" with the addict for too long a period, they lose their ability to be honest with each other, to share true feelings. An intervention reverses this process of denial and deception by the family and facilitates their facing up to truth—and dealing with their loved one—in a loving, caring way.

Since family and close contacts are too involved emotionally to lead an intervention, a specialist is needed. Such a professional can usually be found through a local drug or alcohol council, Alcoholics Anonymous or a mental health department.

Interventions are structured carefully, with as many as six or more people involved. The ideal combination is the spouse, a parent, one or more children, a doctor, the employer and the family's pastor.

Preparation for an intervention calls for a series of meetings between family members and the intervention professional, usually at a location other than the addict's home. The professional explains the process and rehearses the concerned persons as to how they will present their facts. Very often this is the first time the family has actually sat down together and discussed what is going on in the home. All those involved make a list of events in which the addict's behavior has hurt and embarrassed them. Then they practice their presentation. Intervention works for drug abuse, bulimia, anorexia, gambling and other compulsive behaviors.

Other suggestions include the following:[2]

- Timing is crucial. Most successful interventions take place early in the morning when the addict is most vulnerable. It is not advisable to do an intervention when the addict has had time to fortify herself with alcohol or drugs. This is when her denial and defenses are highest.

- Firmness of resolve. The spouse and family should have a plan for separating themselves from the addict if she refuses to go for treatment. The employer should be ready with an ultimatum: treatment or loss of job. Often the threat of the loss of one's salaried position is the most persuasive factor.

- Who to exclude from an intervention: Anyone who would be too legalistic or moralistic; anyone whose mental balance is questionable; family members too full of hate to perceive the addict as sick and in need of help.

- Have a specific treatment plan ready. If the addict agrees to go for treatment, have a time and place firmly set. If there is too much delay, the addict will change her mind.

- If the intervention fails. Sometimes the addict will storm out of the meting. If possible, try it again. Remember that there is tremendous anxiety inside the addict, who is involved in all-out denial. What doesn't work at one setting will at another. Also the intervention, even if it fails, can start a healing process in the family by bringing members together to face the truth of their situation.

Is there any type of person for whom intervention won't work? None that I know of. When I went to a treatment center, I met doctors, pastors, two lawyers and a judge, all of whom were patients. Addiction grips people in the highest and lowest job classifications—which is why Betty Ford calls alcoholism an "equal-opportunity disease."[3]

There is new hope for all these people in that 97 percent of alcoholics, given the intervention procedure by a specialist, go to treatment within forty-eight hours. The process is so simple that few can believe it works—but it does.

I hated being confronted by Dirk just as much as I had hated being confronted three years before by my friend Lois Ann. For this was the second (not the first) time someone had cared enough to play this uncongenial but necessary role in my life. Three years earlier, at the height of my involvement with the International Serenity Society, when each new "spiritual counselor" sent me spiraling deeper into craziness and depression, Lois Ann had organized her own version of intervention.

One day she had invited me to her house for morning coffee to meet a special friend. The friend turned out to be a vivacious blonde who had just gotten out of an alcohol rehabilitation center in Minneapolis. Her sky-blue eyes danced as she excitedly related her twenty-eight day experience there. "I feel like a new woman," she rhapsodized, "like I have a second chance in life. I can't believe how much better I feel."

I took an instant dislike to this lovely creature. She looked too happy, too put together. I suddenly felt terribly tacky in the tired black polyester pantsuit I'd had on for several days. My head itched from need of a shampoo; the runners in my pantyhose looked like the Los Angeles Freeway. *What a slob you are,* I had thought to myself.

Lois Ann cleared her deep voice and began in halting phrases. "I've invited you here today for a very specific reason, Sandy. I don't know much about alcohol, but perhaps this is your problem, too. Perhaps you need treatment. I can't bear to see what you're doing to yourself..." Taking a deep breath as though to muster a new burst of courage, she added painfully, "Have you looked at yourself in a mirror lately?"

Her words burned into my soul. She had hit a raw nerve. But alcohol wasn't my problem! I drank to escape my problems.

"I'll be glad to phone and make arrangements for you," the friend volunteered. "I know a marvelous counselor there who can answer any questions you might have."

Soon I was chatting with a pleasant-voiced older man. "We'll take good care of you here, Sandy," he said. "When you get out, you'll be the woman your husband fell in love with."

That challenge registered. I promised Lois Ann I'd speak with my psychiatrist and my husband. At my doctor's appointment that afternoon, I broached the subject. He thought it was worth a try. The sessions with him were clearly not working.

Randall was more skeptical. The last three years had diminished his faith for my restoration. He saw such devastation and hopelessness in me. He lived with it and in it. Nevertheless, he agreed it was worth trying.

One January morning in 1977 I was on a Northwest jet headed for Minneapolis.

The intervention set up by Lois Ann had succeeded to the extent that it got me into a treatment center. In the majority of cases today, these specialized facilities get the addict turned around. I was one of their failures. The twenty-eight-day treatment, like my short stays on the psychiatric floor of Billings' Deaconess Hospital, removed me temporarily from my destructive lifestyle and started me on new disciplines. But when I returned home and tried to deal with the old problems, the old pitfalls were too many. I chose to ignore the "aftercare" plan that had been set up for me. I'd been confronted with truth, but at that period in my life I had had no resources to undergird me, and I couldn't cope with it. I had opted for the "out" of suicide and had begun squirreling away sleeping pills on a closet shelf.

Perhaps, though, it was that first intervention by Lois Ann in 1977 that prepared me for this second one, in June 1980, which got me into a treatment program that worked.

CONTRITION...IS NOT AN AMERICAN VIRTUE, and, indeed, mere contrition could admit everything, and change nothing. To find culprits is more our style; but culprits, in taking their punishment, take our part of the guilt with them. Liberation can come only from insights into the relevance of past guilt and into the place of ethical choice in the reformation of identity.

—ERIK H. ERIKSON, M.D.
Dimensions of a New Identity

FACING TRUTH

L ooking back, I sometimes think Dirk's intervention, unstructured as it was, saved my life. I had been trying to put up a good front with Randall, my children and my friends; underneath I was confused and frightened. What to do about my marriage? Though Randall had supported me during six bad years, I had sensed his rejection in a number of ways. Now that I'd stopped drinking and was on the road to recovery, he expected me to fit back into his lifestyle. I couldn't do it. It was this social scenario that had kept me in trouble for so long.

"In our society," writes Betty Ford in *The Times of My Life,* "we get to know one another over drinks, we associate feats and celebrations with liquor. We think we have to drink, that it's a social necessity…It's romantic as long as you can handle it—for years I could and did—but it's misery when you become addicted."[1]

Randall didn't understand all this, or why my new religious faith was suddenly important. Since I was no longer the wife he married, and since we were going in different directions, we agreed to separate.

My children were completely bewildered by my decision to go to a treatment center. To them, I was more stable than they could ever remember me. Why did I have to go back to the hospital? I couldn't explain to them how desperately insecure I was, how close to the breaking point.

In mid-June 1980, I entered St. Mary's Rehabilitation Center, a twenty-eight-day treatment facility for alcohol and drug-related addictions in

Minneapolis (a different facility than the one I had gone to three years earlier).

The three-story treatment center contained, in addition to patients' rooms and counselors' offices, a number of small meeting lounges, a large lecture room, a small chapel with stained glass windows, nurses' stations and a large recreation area with pool tables and a piano.

I had a small single room with cream painted walls, a hospital bed and built-in dresser and desk. The daily schedule given us was:

> Breakfast, 8:00 A.M.
> Morning lecture, 9:00 A.M.
> Group therapy, 10:00–11:45 A.M.
> Lunch, 12:00 noon
> Afternoon lecture, 1:00 P.M.
> Group therapy, 2:00–4:30 P.M.
> Free time/relaxation therapy, 4:30–6:00 P.M.
> Dinner, 6:00 P.M.
> Evening lecture, 7:00 P.M.
> Free time/alcohol support group meetings/reading/home-work, 8:30 P.M. on

At intake I was given a physical, a blood test, a psychological testing (Minnesota Multiphasic Personality Inventory—the "MMPI"). I also met with a staff psychiatrist who suggested Lithium therapy for my mood swings. For the first few days my blood pressure was monitored frequently.

For me, group therapy would be the cutting edge of the program. Six of us met together twice a day for close sharing led by a staff counselor. In our group there was Gwen, our counselor, in her late forties; Max, a stockbroker, maybe sixty; Carol, fiftyish, a clothing saleswoman; Larry, a balding middle-aged businessman; Sue, a tense, depressed girl barely twenty; and myself, now forty-four.

We met in Gwen's office, a plain room with a desk pushed into the corner and six plastic chairs placed in a circle. On one wall hung a chart of the Twelve Steps of Alcoholics Anonymous. I got as far as the First Step— we admitted we were "powerless over alcohol, that our lives had become unmanageable"—and stopped reading. *Powerless. Unmanageable.* Tough words.

Facing Truth

Gwen passed out a worksheet to each of us—homework to be done in our rooms that evening. In response to a series of questions we were to write out our drinking history. I did not look forward to that. "You need to get the garbage in your lives out on the floor and sort through it," Gwen explained. "You will need to know if you're in touch with how it really was, because it will hurt. So I wish you a lot of pain, because then something is happening to you."[2]

After two hours of sharing and teaching, Gwen closed the session. Holding hands in a circle, we recited Reinhold Niebuhr's Serenity Prayer (a staple in many treatment programs): "God grant me the serenity to accept the things I cannot change, the courage to change the things I can, and the wisdom to know the difference."

That night I sat down to tackle the homework. *The sooner I get going,* I told myself, *the sooner I'll get it over with.* At the little Formica-topped desk, I began reading the sheet of questions. "Effects on character. List thirty values important to you and give examples of how you have compromised them as a result of your usage."

Suddenly my mind was swirling with indictments—ignoring people's feelings, lying, wasting money, forgetting my children's needs, taking advantage...Now the whirlpool was sucking me down toward unbearable horrors. I flipped the sheet of paper over and slapped my hand down on top of it. "I'll do it later."

I wandered into the big lounge and joined Carol, the fiftyish clothing salesperson, and Sue, the depressed, twenty-year-old. "It's so awful to be a woman and an alcoholic," Carol was saying. "The hiding you have to do, the denying—it really grinds your insides.

Sue nodded bleakly.

"What made me really mad was the unfairness," Carol continued. "It was OK for the men to be at the bar having fun. I was stuck at home. My husband and I had equal status till we got married, and then all of a sudden, *plop!*"

I nodded, remembering my days at Pepsi Cola: "I wanted to drink like a man so I could be with the men."

Our group sessions, while the cutting edge of the program, soon became the most difficult part of treatment for me. There was always a knot in my stomach as I approached the door to our counselor's room. How could I escape Gwen's penetrating green eyes? I admired her, but I feared she could make mincemeat of my carefully cultivated poise if she probed too close. I would sit in the circle with my best Miss America training: knees and ankles together, one foot tucked behind the other, my Miss America smile intact. I'd learned to smile early. "Put on a happy face," my mother would tell me.

When my turn came to give a brief biography, I described my hospital experiences in Billings and Warm Springs, and how I'd since stopped smoking and drinking. I touched lightly on my healing that night at the Methodist church, trying hard not to come across as a religious fanatic. Most of the group looked impressed with my progress. Gwen's eyes were expressionless.

"You paint a positive picture of yourself, Sandy. Just why are you here?" Gwen asked.

"My friends think I'm on a dry drunk."

"Do you agree with them?"

"I guess so."

"But you're not sure?"

"My life is sort of a mess. My marriage is breaking up—that is, my second marriage. My three children are living with their father, my first husband. And…"—to my disgust, tears were filling my eyes—"and I'm… well, not sure of myself at all."

"In short, you could fall off the wagon tomorrow."

"I guess so. I came here to Minneapolis for treatment back in 1977. Stayed sober for two months afterwards, then took that one drink. I know I shouldn't drink."

"Correction. You know you can't drink, but you're not sure you won't."

"I'm pretty sure."

"Sandy, I'll be blunt with you. In some ways you're the sickest person in this room. You spout pious phrases, you hold people off with your sense of humor and your light approach, but you're not in touch with your feelings. I've yet to hear you say how you feel."

"Right now I feel like I've been kicked in the butt."

"Good."

"And I'm miserable underneath all these smiles." The tears were flowing again. "And I'm scared. And I hate myself for what I've done to my family."

"Much better, Sandy. For the first time you come across as real." She turned to others in the group. "What is your feedback to Sandy?"

"Likable, but too pious," ventured Carol. "I felt she was determined to show us she didn't belong here."

"Trying too hard," offered Max. "She was out to win us from the start. A people-pleaser. A lot of froth on top to cover up something underneath she didn't want us to see."

"Hear that, Sandy." Gwen's eyes were boring into me. "Because you've been to treatment before and because you've been dry for a while, you felt you were above the others."

Devastating. Carol handed me some tissues. I felt naked before these people.

Inner healing had begun.

The purpose of these group sessions was to get us to open up, be honest, be vulnerable and express what we felt, not what we thought we ought to feel. At the next session, Gwen zeroed in on my relationship to Randall. "How did he react to your drinking?"

"Frustration at first. Apathy at the end. As a lawyer it bugged him that he couldn't persuade me to stop. He was used to being able to control people and situations."

"So you showed him that he couldn't control you by drinking more than ever."

I shifted uneasily in my chair. "My drinking was a problem before I married him."

"Would you have drunk so much if he had been less controlling?" Max asked suddenly.

Startled, I thought a moment. "Maybe not," I admitted.

Max kept pressing, "Why?"

I jammed my hands under my thighs. "Well, I got so mad…maybe there was some revenge mixed in there."

"I just heard something honest," Gwen said, "and I congratulate you. What was your reward for getting mad?"

My mind swam. My mouth was dry. Leaning forward, I stared at the toes of my shoes. Maybe if I leaned far enough the floor would open and swallow me. "I don't know. Maybe I was getting something out of my system."

"There was a great big reward," Gwen said, "and I'm not sure you want to give it up yet."

I could feel the circle of eyes watching me. Finally I said tentatively, "Maybe part of the reward was an inner permission to drink more."

"Part?" asked Gwen, cocking an eyebrow.

"A lot," I said.

"Do you see," Gwen said, "that your anger has been one of the dynamics of your alcoholism?"

There was another long pause. I felt a fear I could not explain. "But sometimes I drank because I was happy."

Max asked, "What would make you so happy you'd take a drink?"

I laughed. "Not taking a drink."

Gwen was not smiling. "I don't know whether you do that in all your relationships, but humor is a way of getting off the hook and stopping communication. As I see it, Max was trying to help, and you made a joke. Then he's down and you're up. Take a look at that."

Gwen spoke again. "I urge you to accept what has been said, Sandy. I don't see you making any progress toward accepting the disease concept and the fact that you are powerless over alcohol—which tells me that you are not working on your First Step. You will not really get into treatment until you begin focusing on you, your addiction, and how it has affected you."

At the close of the session I hurried away to an isolated chair in the second-floor lounge. I replayed the last exchange—Gwen's voice zapping me for that joke. I felt marooned in a hot funk of embarrassment, like a little girl caught red-handed.

Max's voice broke into my trance. "Sandy, don't look so down. It happens to the best of us."

Looking up, I smiled ruefully. "It's always darkest before it's totally black." Max shrugged and left me alone.

I felt a flush like a prickly rash spreading up my throat and across my face. I had just done it again, made a quip to keep someone at arm's length.

My time came as it did for everyone in our group to read aloud the first homework assignment: a comprehensive look at how addiction had affected every area of my life. Afterward, I waited confidently for the group's approval. No one could accuse me now of covering up: I'd bared my very soul!

But the others disagreed. Some thought I had minimized the effects on my family and myself; others thought that I had "skated away" from talking about real issues.

And I was totally unprepared for Gwen's response. She told me calmly that I was one of the angriest women she had ever had in her group and that I'd better get in touch with that anger or it would surely sabotage my recovery. "When you finish your treatment here," she said, "I think you should consider going to a women's halfway house for continuing recovery."

She added that I'd been so ill for the past twenty years, I hardly knew what planet I was on, and that going to Billings could be disastrous. "And from now on," she concluded, "I want your outsides to match your insides! No more hiding behind your smile."

I was stunned that she detected such anger in me. I hadn't lost my cool even once in the group. Was I really so angry? I wasn't sure I wanted to find out.

After this session, I slipped down to the chapel on the second floor of the treatment center. It was my special place of peace and refuge, an eye of calm in the storm all around me. Kneeling in the serenity of that place, I started to search my life for clues to my aborted anger.

As I meditated, I saw I was indeed angry, and that it had begun when I was very young. I had picked up people's feelings and moods, known what was acceptable behavior and what was not. Observing adult responses to my actions, I'd discovered it was not all right to be angry. My home was not a healthy emotional climate where feelings were expressed frankly. So I learned to mask anger and annoyance, smile sweetly and say nothing. I felt one way and acted another. Pretty soon I didn't know how I felt. Apparently this pattern was still in effect, refined by years of practice. My denial system protected me like a bulletproof vest.

What Gwen said, then, was true. Beneath the placid exterior I was angry. In fact, I was mad as hell! A childhood episode came back to me. Once when I was angry with my grandmother I'd covered my whole body with big, white adhesive-tape Band-Aids. Then I had stood in the lawn sprinkler so the Mercurochrome on the pads would run down my body like blood. It was a pathetic attempt to get people to notice my feelings—and won me no attention at all.

As an adult I became a door-slammer. On three occasions, when angry at my husband, I'd thrown pots through a kitchen window. The man at the glass repair shop chuckled the third time he replaced the pane: "It's be cheaper to kick a tire, lady."

I had never learned to express feelings appropriately. I knew I couldn't blame my parents. They were victims of victims, and I realized that I too had made victims of my children.

Was it this pattern of denied emotions, I wondered, generation after generation, that had made me such a ready receptor for those "angry little men" who had tormented me so long? I only knew there was an avalanche of rage inside that wanted to come out.

A similar pattern of repressed anger shows up again and again in compulsive individuals like me—smiling people-pleasers who are covering up years of suppressed anger and hurt.

"No matter how 'grown-up' one acts in therapy or in life," wrote Arthur Janov, "it must be an act which has little bearing on one's maturity until the 'little girl' is felt…We must feel the anger fully in order to eradicate it. When a person can feel himself, instead of acting out his feelings symbolically, he will be unlikely to act either impulsively or aggressively. The dialectic of anger, as with pain, is that when it is felt, it disappears, when it is not felt, it remains waiting to be felt."[3]

As the days passed and I opened up haltingly to the group, some of the long-buried feelings came out. Memories surfaced that had festered unacknowledged for years. But always, it seemed, more pain lay underneath.

The third week of my treatment was called "family week," made memorable for me by a visit from my son Brent, at nineteen a handsome six-footer. My middle child, Brent has always been creative, athletic and popular with his peers. The day he joined our group, Gwen placed our two chairs in the center of the circle face to face, and then asked Brent to describe how it felt to grow up in an alcoholic home.

He shifted about uncomfortably and said he hadn't noticed anything was wrong until he had visited the homes of his friends and had seen that their mothers didn't drink as I did.

Gwen explained to him that children of alcoholics blank out the pain and have almost an amnesia about their parents' drinking.

As Brent talked, I looked into his guileless eyes and felt such a wrenching pain in my stomach that I thought I would be sick. The sense of lost years with him, Brad and Lisa was almost unbearable.

"Stop crying, Sandy," Gwen ordered. "You're manipulating him with your tears."

It was a hard time, I know, for Brent as it was for me—yet so very good to have him there. After kissing him goodbye as he left for the airport, I returned to my room and found a note propped up against my pillow. It was neatly printed with a black felt-tip pen on a paper towel:

> Dear Mom, I am sorry that my stay had to be so short. I hope that we have cleared up some problems that you have had! I learned a lot while I was here. The people are beautiful. I want you to know I love you very much, and I don't use the term loosely. I'm sure Brad and Lisa feel the same. Please give my best wishes to all the nice friends of yours. I send them all the will power in the world and my very best wishes. Take care, and if you ever have a problem, just give us a call. We will help.
>
> LOVE, BRENT & GOD BLESS

I weep years later upon reading this. The message has been framed and matted in sunny yellow and hangs on my kitchen wall. It's a precious prized treasure from the heart of my son.

During treatment I was served with divorce papers. Though I knew they were coming, the reality devastated me. More guilt, remorse and defeat. For two days I barely functioned. The lecture by a counselor named Jessica was life restoring.

Jessica had been a Roman Catholic nun, then an alcoholic. She had found sobriety through the AA program and was now dedicated to carrying the message of restoration to others. Her very presence inspired confidence. The serenity of her spirit washed over me as she began to speak.

"An alcoholic can be sober," Jessica was saying, "but still the most miserable, God-forsaken person on two feet. There has to be some rebuilding of the spiritual values destroyed by the chemicals: honesty, humility, forgiveness, trust, love, courage. This process begins with surrender. It is saying 'I give up! I surrender to the powerlessness and unmanageability of my life. The chemical controlled me. I said and did things while drunk that were hurtful, painful, devastating and destructive.'

"In recovery," she continued, "the hardest thing for me to accept was the fact that kind, gentle, caring Jessica, while drunk, was capable of doing terrible things. I knew I could be forgiven for those things. But as long as I was unable or unwilling to forgive myself, it was difficult to feel their forgiveness in my gut. I still carried the burden of my past around like a big boulder on my back."

As Jessica spoke my thoughts went back to that night at the Methodist church. The words of the woman minister rang in my head: "If God has forgiven all your sins, how dare you not forgive yourself?" It sounded so simple, but I saw now that a lack of self-forgiveness had continued to be the biggest stumbling block in my recovery.

Jessica continued: "So I finally faced the reality that I was a failure at running my own affairs. Then the question: Where am I going to get help outside myself? Is there anything in this program that I can grab hold of and hang on to very, very tightly that will make me become a healthier, happier person? Is there anything that will give me a deep sense of forgiveness? That brought me to a further stage of surrender—surrender to God as I understood Him—which, surprisingly, I had never really done.

"I know now," Jessica concluded, "that God will give me the grace, the strength, the courage, the people that I need to get through today without drinking. For that I am very grateful."

Powerlessness. Acceptance. Surrender. Gratitude. Great words to say, but how to own them, to integrate them into my life? I suddenly saw with new eyes the unmanageability of my life.

I could take Step One of our recovery program and put any number of things where the world *alcohol* appeared: cigarettes, food, relationships, shopping sprees, the occult, caffeine, anger...* The list seemed endless. I was powerless over my whole life. That was what was unmanageable.

Step Two was equally crucial: "Came to believe that a power greater than myself could restore me to sanity."

Robin Norwood wrote:

> Developing your spirituality, no matter what your religious orientation, basically means *letting go of self-will,* of the determination to make things happen the way you think they should...believing that you alone have all the answers...becoming willing to hold still, be open, and wait for guidance for yourself. It means learning to let go

---

* The Twelve Steps can be applied to any self-help group or program.

of fear (all of the "what ifs") and despair (all of the "if onlys") and replacing them with positive thoughts and statements about your life."[4]

At the end of her talk, Jessica instructed us to stand and grasp the hands of the people next to us while we sang "Amazing Grace." At my right was a ruddy-faced young man whose mother, Carol, was in my treatment group. At my left was Veronica, a tiny, birdlike woman in treatment for her ninth time. I was struck by the difference of handclasps. One so powerful, the other so tremulous. The words we sang pierced my soul: "I once was lost, but now am found, was blind, but now I see."[5]

Soon people were sobbing openly. Veronica leaned against me, her tears wetting the sleeve of my blue cotton shirt. I doubt there was a person in that room who was not grappling with that reality. There was new purpose in faces that before had been vacant. The air was charged with electricity. I felt safe, cared for and loved. But most of all, I felt forgiven.

Lewis Smedes wrote that self-forgiveness without honesty "is psychological hocus-pocus. The rule is: We cannot really forgive ourselves unless we look at the failure in our past and call it by its right name. When you forgive yourself, you rewrite your script. What you are in your present scene is not tied down to what you did in an earlier scene...You release yourself today from yesterday's scenario. You walk into tomorrow, guilt gone."

AT OUR WORST we women who love too much are relationship addicts, "man junkies" strung out in pain, fear, and yearning…We use relationships in the same way that we use our addictive substance: to take our pain away…As long as we are bent on escaping ourselves and avoiding our pain, we stay sick. The harder we try and the more avenues of escape we pursue, the sicker we get as we compound addictions with obsessions.

—ROBIN NORWOOD
Women Who Love Too Much

12

Anger and Male Dependency

As more and more is learned about addictive behavior, therapists are urging patients to continue their recovery programs beyond the twenty-eight-day average stay at a treatment center, preferably in a halfway house. If for one reason or another, often financial, this is impossible, the alternative is a support group in the patient's hometown using the Twelve-Step program.

At the suggestion of Gwen, my counselor at the treatment center, I agreed to enter a halfway house. Twenty years of addictive behavior, she said, could not be changed in a month's program. I hated to be away still longer from Billings where I could see my children several times a week, but my prime responsibility to my family was to get well.

My interview at the Jane Dickman House (about twenty miles outside of St. Paul) was a surprise. The words *halfway house* had always conjured up a vision of cracked plaster walls, leaky ceilings and dead flies on the windowsills. In contrast, the ride up to Dickman House coursed along a winding driveway, past a tennis court and manicured lawn, and came to a halt beneath the portico of a sprawling wood-and-stone structure. It looked more like a country vacation resort than a facility for chemically dependent women.

Inside I was led past groups of women talking over coffee around small tables and into a dining room with a chalet window that offered a panoramic view of a lake. My interviewer asked me probing questions about my life and my goals for recovery, noting my answers on a yellow pad. At the end of our time, she offered a treatment plan for me: I needed to work on building trust levels, improving family relationships and understanding my feelings and emotions. The cost of living there came to about $1,100 a month. All participants were encouraged to find jobs locally in nearby St. Paul, not only to help pay expenses, but to build a new life of independence.

The first few weeks were spent in "Feelings Groups," large and small house meetings, one-on-one counseling, exercise periods and alcohol support group meetings. There were kitchen duties, special weekend projects and social events with our brother halfway house, Team House, in nearby St. Paul.

Each woman at Jane Dickman was given a "verbal" by her counselor. Before we were allowed to speak, we had to use our special verbal and say how we felt. Mine, for example, was, "I need to share with you on a meaningful level. I feel sad (or embarrassed, or angry, or whatever)." By doing this, I would be forced to get in touch with my feelings.

After one group session my counselor, a no-nonsense, authoritative woman named Betsy, called me into her office for a one-on-one. "Sandy, your steady smile tells me that you're a good-natured person. Are you that happy on the inside, or have you gone through life in a smiling depression?"

"Perhaps."

"Then that happy smile must be a mask to cover up how you're really feeling."

I nodded, recalling how my group at St. Mary's had called me on this.

"Some of your smiles seem spontaneous and natural. Others I suspect are cover-ups."

"Cover-ups for what?" I asked, half-afraid to hear her response.

"Your deep-rooted anger. We're going to deal with that in the next few weeks."

With that, Betsy instructed the other women to confront me every time I smiled and ask what I was smiling about. As an exercise to get my insides to match my outsides, I was to pay a small fine whenever I used my smile as a defense. I was also to be penalized if I employed exaggerated words like *itsy-bitsy, teeny, humongous, gigantic.* Such words distorted communication, Betsy said. It was a shock to discover how often these exaggerations popped out in my everyday conversation.

Anger and Male Dependency

Betsy also assigned me individual "anger work." I was to spend five minutes a day in the indoor racquetball court "screaming." At first this exercise seemed ridiculous. Self-conscious at first, my screams were little more than squeaks, but as I got into the routine, the emotion poured out. Using the ball as the object of my anger, I blasted at it with my racquet. Soon the squeaks became roars. I discovered I was not merely angry, but as Gwen had predicted, I was full of buried rage.

If the resident had an automobile, as I did, those of us with anger work were encouraged to use driving time for screaming. Once, on my way back to Dickman House from doing an errand, I was idling at a stoplight and decided it would be a good place to let out some feelings. I didn't realize my car window was open until a woman in the lane next to me scrambled from her car to come to my aid. That cured me from screaming at stoplights, but not on interstates.

Betsy suggested I make an anger diary going back as far as I could remember, noting events, people and situations that made me angry. What revelation that was! I'd had emotional gangrene most of my life and never realized it.

I'd always been one of those "don't-make-waves" people who shied away from confrontations. In our sexual abuse group one day I was urged to deal with my unexpressed anger against Uncle Ralph for his molestation of me when I was five.

"Go back to that place and that episode," the counselor instructed. "Tell your uncle how it was for you. You are not the helpless little girl now. Tell him whatever you need to." She gave me several pillows to use.

Closing my eyes for concentration, I went back in time to Uncle Ralph's living room. I could smell the Sir Walter Raleigh tobacco he rolled into homemade cigarettes...hear the sound of ticking clocks from the hallway.

Then I saw Uncle Ralph sitting in his squeaky wooden rocker. Felt his hands on me, heard him wheezing, clicking his teeth. I started to sob and beat my thighs.

"Use the pillows," the counselor ordered.

"I loved and trusted you, Uncle Ralph, and you took advantage of me. I was little and couldn't fight back. You hurt me! You scared me! I hate you for that!" I was shouting now, my voice high and shrill. The five-year-old Sandy was doubled over, pounding the pillows with both fists.

141

During these sessions I realized that in the past my anger had erupted all right, only in indirect, inappropriate ways. Example: *overeating.* You could never have convinced me when I was bingeing on chocolate that I was really acting out my inner rage. Not just at Uncle Ralph, but at all the times I'd swallowed my feelings and said nothing. It made no difference that my dress size was headed for the twenties, that I was totally repulsed at myself and nauseated physically by food. The raging dragon inside demanded to be fed. Or placated with cigarettes. Or booze. Or a new outfit.

One day the staff counselor at Dickman House jolted me by saying, "Sandy, do you realize how male-dependent you are?"

Anger in me was now very near the surface; *available* was the staff's approving term. It welled up in me. "You make me sound like a street-walker!" I flared.

"I'm not talking about that kind of dependency. Your thoughts, your actions, your needs are centered on men. You require their approval to be fulfilled."

"How can you say that?" I argued. "I've been hurt by men all my life. Now at long last I'm free of them."

The counselor shook her head. "You only think you're free. Let me explain what I mean." She tapped a paper on her desk.

"The results of your psychological testing confirm your hostility and dependency on men. You have probably been dependent on every man in your life, starting with your father. The problem with being male-dependent is that a woman ties all her feelings of self-worth into what men think about her, what they do and say. You need to begin to become responsive to yourself and your own needs. You are a 'people-pleaser' like most alcoholics—and the people you try hardest to please are men."

For several moments I was silent, devastated by this appraisal that I knew deep down to be true. "How do I get free?" I finally asked.

"For the next four weeks you will be on a 'male restriction' program. This means you will not have anything to do with men. You can write or call one male member of your family once a week, but you're to avoid conversations with men, even eye contact with men on the street. You need to learn to trust women and the feedback they have for you."

At first this program seemed peculiar and unfair. Four weeks without talking to a man except my father, Brent or Brad once every week or so? Impossible.

Anger and Male Dependency

But it wasn't. I discovered how automatically I sought to make eye contact with men—in restaurants, at meetings, anywhere—even with total strangers. Somehow the approval of these nameless strangers mattered. I'd be buoyed by the flicker of interest, dejected by indifference. It was a searing discovery.

"The notion that men are absolutely vital to any value we may have," writes Nancy Friday in *My Mother/My Self,* "is so woven into feminine reality that most women think to reject it would be like trying to reject the law of gravity."

Friday recalls in her book that "it was the promise of men, that around each corner there was yet another man, more wonderful than the last that sustained me. You see, I had men confused with life…It was a religion of a god who gave and took away life…"

Psychologist Sonya Friedman in her book *Men Are Just Desserts* points out one of the most deeply ingrained messages that daughters receive from their mothers: *A man is the measure of your worth.*

To break the cycle of male dependency, then, it was apparent that I needed to enhance my sense of self-worth completely apart from men. And, in fact, after the first few days of my male restriction program, it became a little easier. Each time I resisted looking at a man for approval represented a victory. I was greatly encouraged. My self-esteem was growing in little flutters, but growing. By the end of the four weeks, I sensed a new strength in this area.

Other revelations: Male dependence had strangled my development as a person, kept my maturing process on hold. I'd often given up decision making and goal setting to comply with what the "he" in my life dictated. I had not learned to make responsible choices.

It was disconcerting to realize how early I'd begun to depend on male approval of my behavior, my appearance and my plans. An occasional desire for this kind of approval is normal and good, of course, but needing it constantly had long since become an unhealthy way of life.

Robin Norwood explains that:

> A woman who uses her relationships as a drug will have fully as much denial about that fact as any chemically addictive individual, and fully as much resistance and fear concerning letting go of her obsessive thinking and high emotionally charged way of interacting with men. But usually, if she is gently but firmly confronted, she will

at some level recognize the power of her relationship addiction and know she is in the grip of a pattern over which she has lost control.[1]

You can test yourself for "Male Dependency" with the quiz on page 242.

An important aspect of my halfway house program was to reach a point where I could go out into the world and not only acquire a job, but succeed in it. Before I was ready for this step, my counselor felt I needed special preparation.

"Sandy, it's time for you to attend the assertiveness class," Betsy told me one day. She explained that the recovering addict needs to learn how better to handle confrontational situations without waffling or being dishonest—these four everyday situations, for example:

1. A sales clerk won't refund your money.

2. You ordered a steak medium-rare, and it comes to the table well-done.

3. Your car wasn't repaired the way you specified.

4. A door-to-door salesman persists in trying to sell you something you don't want.

In the assertiveness class we were taught to "hang in there" for our viewpoint. Here is a typical role-play:

Clerk: May I help you?

Me: Yes. I'd like a refund of $85.99 on this vacuum cleaner.

Clerk: We don't give refunds.

Me: I understood that if I brought in the receipt, you would refund my money. Here is my receipt. I'd like my money back.

Clerk: I'm not supposed to give refunds. I'll get in trouble.

Me: I'm sorry for you if that happens, but I still want my $85.99 refunded.

Clerk: Why don't you take the vacuum cleaner home and try it out for another week? Get used to it.

Me: I want my $85.99 or your name and the name of your supervisor.

Clerk: I'm not supposed to do this, you know [as he takes the receipt and refunds the money].

Anger and Male Dependency

In the above exchange I was instructed to state persistently what I wanted and avoid being sidetracked onto irrelevant issues. (The person playing the clerk was told to resist in every possible way.) My ace in the hole was what I had been told initially about the store's general policy regarding refunds.

Learning such basic life skills was essential before we recovering alcoholics were ready to enter the rough-and-tumble of the job market. Even with this training, the thought of having to interview for employment paralyzed me. My work as an artist at Disneyland and my public relations position with Pepsi Cola had been over twenty years ago. Who would want to hire a forty-four-year-old-has-been? Was I employable?

For two days at the Office of the Civilian Employment Training Agency (CETA), five of us from Jane Dickman House underwent intensive schooling on how to conduct ourselves at a job interview. Then weeks passed, and the only work that became available for me was through an office temporary service. Stuffing envelopes for mailings didn't pay much, and at the end of the day my fingers were covered with Band-Aids to cover the paper cuts. "I'll never get a decent job," I moaned. "How am I ever going to support myself?"

Then CETA phoned. "The Minnesota Museum of Art is looking for an assistant preparator of exhibitions. Call and set up an interview…and good luck!"

What do you wear for an interview with three museum directors? I had visions of three dour faces peering at me from behind a mahogany, skating-rink-sized conference table. What a shock to find three laid-back, obviously creative, no-nonsense professionals in tweeds and corduroys chatting merrily and drinking coffee.

The business administrator asked most of the questions. I liked her immediately. Her pale blue eyes danced in a thin, angular face. She'd be enjoyable to work with. "Do you have any carpentry skills?" she asked. "You'll need to be able to do a little bit of everything around here."

"My father taught me how to build, paint and wallpaper," I offered. "Even how to do simple plumbing and electrical work."

The director's eyes lit up. "I had pictured giving this job to a man," he said, "but if you think you could handle the physical demands, you might be the one for it. We have a number of others to interview today before we decide. Thanks for your time."

I was waiting for him to say, "Don't call us; we'll call you," but he didn't.

Back at the halfway house I lunged for the phone each time it rang. Hours later the administrator called, "We've reviewed all the applications and have narrowed it down to two. I need to ask you a crucial question: do you know how to drive a truck?"

My mind was racing. I really wanted that job. Could I drive a truck? Of course! But my conscience was saying, *You've driven only a pickup truck.* Clearing my throat, as if to convince myself first, I replied, "I can drive a truck just so long as it isn't an eighteen-wheeler."

"Great," she responded. "The job is yours."

I held the job for seven months until my counselor felt I was ready to go back home to Billings. It was a valuable experience, bolstering my sense of self-worth and rekindling my creativity. It felt so good to be productive again.

A sign of my walk toward wholeness was the interest I began taking in other women and their problems. A seed of love for people was growing inside me. The capacity to reach out had withered during twenty years of addiction, only to sprout anew that night in the Warm Springs Hospital when I comforted Karen.

One of the patients at the halfway house with whom I developed an almost mother-daughter relationship was a seventeen-year-old named Sophia. She was a pretty girl with brown hair and a face that didn't show her drug and alcohol abuse. Sophia had started drinking when she was in the third grade. In the sixth grade she was introduced to marijuana; two years later she began using hashish, speed and LSD.

At fifteen Sophia moved out from her family and in with a boyfriend, got a cleaning job at a bar and was soon drunk morning, noon and night. She'd recently spent a month in treatment, and then entered Jane Dickman House.

I was attracted to Sophia because she was close to the age of my daughter, Lisa (then eighteen), and so needy for love and attention. Treatment had given her some handles on her disease, but her counselor and friends wondered if these would be broken when she returned to her old environment and faced both chemically active friends and a male-dependent relationship.

The issue came to a climax one March afternoon. Her boyfriend—I'll call him Nick—rolled into the parking lot on his motorcycle and bellowed for his "woman." Sophia hadn't seen Nick in six months.

Her roommate and I went outside to talk with him. Nick measured about six-two and looked at us with sullen, half-closed eyes. "Where's Sophia?" he demanded.

"She says she doesn't want to see you," her roommate told him.

"I want *her* to tell me that."

Reluctantly Sophia came outside and faced the past. Several of us formed a protective semicircle behind her while Sophia stared at Nick in silence. We could all feel the power he held over her. Bluntly he ordered her to come with him.

I knew well what was going on inside of Sophia. On the one side, a pull toward sex, drugs and alcohol; on the other hand, freedom from the cravings, the beginning of a new self-worth. The choice: Hop onto Nick's bike and return to her old life, or stay with us and continue being healed.

She turned and looked at us, the people who had befriended her. No one spoke, but something clicked. A decision. She turned to the biker: "No, I don't want to see you ever again." His eyes intensified, bore hard into hers to test her resolve. Then, with a shrug, he got onto his bike and roared away.

Each woman who goes through the program at Jane Dickman has a personal graduation ceremony. Mine was highlighted by a visit from Lisa, generous tributes from the staff, other patients and friends I'd made in the area. First steps had been taken in leaving anger and male dependency behind. It was time, as Sonya Friedman writes in *Men Are Just Desserts*, to reassess my skills, my personality and my self-esteem.

> The more you are, the more you possess yourself without getting caught up with pleasing others and the more you can understand that no one's going to make you happy, or complete, but yourself. The more you *are*, the more you will realize that a man can detract from or enhance your happiness, but he can never be responsible for answering all your needs.[2]

THE KEY WORD IN [SELF-CURE] IS SELF: taking charge of your own problem. Some psychologists call this self-mastery; others, self-efficacy; others, the belief in free will. It translates into three components necessary for change: an urge to quit, the belief that you can quit and the realization that you must quit—no one can do it for you.

—STANTON PEELE, Ph.D.
"Out of the Habit Trap," American Health

13

Deception and Other Little Monsters

Recovery is not only a process; it's a process that takes time. A lot of time. Treatment programs—whether they last a month or a year—are only a beginning, turnaround. The compulsive person is given a temporary sanctuary, a direction to go and guidelines to follow. He is then released into the world, at which point the real battle begins. One chemical dependency specialist estimates that 15 percent of recovery occurs in treatment, the other 85 percent in the outside world.

When I came out of nearly eight months of treatment at Jane Dickman I asked myself, "What have you learned?"

A great deal. I knew, for example, that one drink—just one—could start an avalanche inside me that would propel me down, down, down to destruction. This was not theory. When I emerged from twenty-eight days of treatment in Minneapolis that first time, back in 1977, I abstained for two months, then decided to have a single drink. What followed was a disaster.

Later I had well-meaning church friends tell me I was now free of my bondage and that an occasional drink would not trigger a relapse. I consider that deadly advice.

Besides, even if it were true that I could take a drink without ill consequences, I wouldn't do it. I've come to love the way I feel alcohol-free. I like the clear head, the aliveness. One drink would bring on the dullness I remember too well. What I thought was stimulation was the very reverse. The seduction of alcohol is that you feel you are getting sharper and wittier while the exact opposite is occurring. You are getting duller, more sluggish—merely silly. I want no part of that second-class existence now that I've lived first-class Valentine's Day 1980.

I'd also learned that *recovery means civil war*. Back home I would literally be going to war with myself and my old destructive habit patterns. After nine months of treatment the battleground was clear to me. It involved change—change across the board.

Fortunately, most treatment centers offer an "aftercare" plan. Mine covered the obvious things I'd already been working on:

- Anger
- Male dependency
- Food issues
- Shopping/spending
- Perfectionistic behavior

To help me abstain from chemicals, I was to be involved with a continuing alcohol support group.

- I was to talk about and express my feelings with someone daily.
- I was to get regular exercise.
- I was to watch my nutrition carefully.

As I picked up the routines of living, I discovered that the danger was not going to be so much from the big monsters that had nearly destroyed me, as from a lot of little ones. Reentry into Billings, Montana, where I had been so sick, was painful. There were old relationships to sort through and mend, new ones to contemplate. Most importantly, my grown children lived and worked there. My dearest wish was to reestablish warm, healthy relationships with them. They were so mature in some ways, self-reliant from years of fending for themselves. Yet also hurting and vulnerable, watching me with guarded enthusiasm. Is this really Mom? Is she going to be OK? In some ways we were almost strangers.

Deception and Other Little Monsters

Sometimes at night as I lay sleepless in the small apartment I'd moved into, I tried to piece together the fragments of lost years with them. What had happened during their junior and senior high school years? Those were the years I was mostly out of it. I felt robbed of so many milestones in their lives. In my remorse I tried to think of ways to make up these losses to my children. It wasn't possible, of course. The damage done was real and could not be erased by guilty efforts at compensation. In fact, my counselor had warned me that if I focused too much on trying to undo the past, it would not only sabotage my recovery, but also confuse my children in unhealthy ways.

So each day I tried to deal with the little monster of *if only*. If only I hadn't…whatever. The best method was to focus on today and be grateful for how far I had come. I tried to start each day in this frame of mind, dressing quickly before 6:00 A.M., bounding down the stairs of my small third-floor apartment and walking a three-mile route I'd laid out around the city before digging into my work of costume-and-doll designing for a Boston firm.

There was something therapeutic about being out in the crisp morning air—more so than the compulsive morning exercising at the Y that had been so unproductive. I'd read that walking was good for patients suffering from depression, and now I understood why. All body systems seem to tune up when you're walking. The senses expand to enfold everything about you.

As I passed the Deaconess Hospital on my route, I offered prayers for the patients on the psych ward where I had spent several "drying-out" periods back in the mid-1970s. Looking up at the fluorescent-lit ceilings on the second floor, I recalled the countless hours I stared at those very light fixtures and watched forlornly out the window at people bustling up and down the same streets I now walked in health and growing freedom.

Another of the little monsters I sought to overcome was the monster of *lying*. This was an especially difficult part of my recovery program— to change my deceitful nature into an honest one. The problem is that lying becomes a way of life for the addict. We start by lying to ourselves: "I couldn't have done that. I just *wouldn't* behave that way."

Later my behavior in blackouts had to be covered with lies because I couldn't remember what I'd said or where I'd been. I lived in a constant state of fear because I couldn't remember large blocks of time—what I'd done, how I'd gotten home. The blood spattered on our white Jeep, for example, that had caused me such apprehension. Many were the mornings I raced to the garage to see if my car was in its usual spot.

All of life thus becomes a lie. Even my sober times were colored with various shades of truth. I was wound about like a mummy with layers and layers of deception. My ears were deaf to the truth; my eyes saw only a miniscule slice of reality.

When I started working my recovery program, I knew I had to get honest with both myself and other people—*especially* with myself. My conscience became newly activated. As soon as I told a lie, a searing stab of conviction would hit me.

Once, counting my change outside the grocery store, I realized that the checker had mistaken a ten-dollar bill I'd given her for a twenty. This came at a time when I was short of funds. But I went back into the store to return the money. It was a small act, but it represented growth.

Cash-register honesty came more easily than more subtle challenges. At the beginning of my rehabilitation, I promised myself I wouldn't lie for one whole day. It was interesting to see how quickly little fibs and exaggerations tended to creep into my conversation. A friend asked me over the phone how I liked the book she had loaned me. "I'm getting a lot out of it," slipped off my tongue. A white lie, but still deceptive. The truthful reply should have been, "I'm looking forward to reading it this weekend."

I was interested much later to note a similar push toward honesty in an article by Dr. Sirgay Sanger in the newsletter of the National Council on Compulsive Gambling (Winter 1985). He identified even accepting too much change in a store as a serious ethical problem that often leads to behavioral relapse.

> I have yet to see compulsive gamblers who have been lying and cheating not fall back into gambling. What I usually recommend is a complete dedication to honesty and integrity in as many areas as possible.

My own daily effort at truthfulness showed me how inclined I was to deny unpleasantness, always to paint the rosy picture. The most staggering realization was how I minimized or lied about my feelings. As my time of sobriety lengthened, real feelings that I had medicated for years started emerging. Unwrapping those endless layers of cover-up was agony. Lies had been my armor, my protection. Now I stood shivering in naked vulnerability with no place to escape.

An especially nasty little monster was *profanity*. I had started swearing in high school because it seemed sophisticated, and I progressed to the point where bad language was an automatic knee-jerk reaction to things that went wrong—or even right. Once I overheard a woman tell her husband in hushed tones what a foul mouth I had. I dismissed it as the utterance of a prude.

Now I felt uncomfortable saying, or even hearing, four-letter words. Yet they still slipped out—sometimes at the most inopportune times. Though I've begun to make progress in this area, I don't kid myself. Lurking in my compulsivity is a little monster that has been exposed, rebuked and reduced to a whimper. But it hasn't left the premises. My behavior is often at war with my will. I want to be disciplined, but it's as though my desire world has metastasized, with each tiny fragment capable of spawning a cancerous growth of its own.

Another monster with which I've had to deal is *shopping*. Like so many hurting women, I used spending binges to fill the emptiness in my life. In 1976, for example, my work as sales clerk in Billings' largest department store was a disastrous experience economically. Each day I bought at least one item, rationalizing I was saving money with my employee's discount. At month's end my store bill far exceeded my salary.

Somehow loading my arms with bundles and boxes relieved my sense of low self-worth and made me feel important and cared for. What I didn't realize was that this is addictive behavior as surely as drinking and drug taking.

"It is well known," wrote Erich Fromm in *The Anatomy of Human Destructiveness*, "that...compulsive buying is one attempt to escape from a depressed mood...a symbolic act of filling the inner void and, thus, overcoming the depressed feeling for the moment."[1]

After the well-publicized spending excesses of Imelda Marcos, it is interesting that Tammy Faye Bakker (now Tammy Faye Messner), in the height of the so-called "holy war" among television evangelists, confessed on ABC's *Nightline* to prodigious shopping and bargain-hunting because it "helps my nerves. It's cheaper than a psychiatrist."

During my recovery period I saw my own shopping binges for what they were—I saw the shallowness of them, the disastrous outcome in domestic strife and economic setbacks.

Back in Billings I put myself on a budget. I'd always moaned that this was too hard, that I couldn't do figures. I found, of course, that anyone can do figures if she tries. But I still have to be careful when I'm tired or upset; at such moments shopping can become my fix.

Today when I pass stores advertising a sale, I ask myself, "Do I need this?" If I start to enter a store, I ask, "Why am I going in here?" The temptation to spend always begins with the thought *I want this*. I'm gradually learning to counteract this thought with the question of need. If the desire won't stand cold, hard scrutiny, then I don't really want it at all.

In fact, all my problems, it seems, begin in my thought life: *I'll eat just this one cookie. I'll just browse at this sale and not buy anything. I'll take just one drink.* These thoughts and a myriad of others have to be brought under control.

Procrastination was another little monster that threatened the recovery process. "I'll do it tomorrow" was deeply ingrained. I'd rail at my daily schedule, want to stare out the window or chat on the phone. The *Do it now!* philosophy was helpful in this area. Slowly but surely I watched my life taking on healthy structure.

Each morning I made a list of things that needed to be accomplished that day, trying to prioritize the three most important items and get them done before noon. I also included in my schedule times for recreation and rest. As one who had wasted so much time, rest was hard for me to take. I felt I needed to make every waking count until I realized my body couldn't physically meet those kinds of demands.

Whenever I attacked a compulsive pattern in my life, the little creepy crawler monsters would start to undermine my progress. *Food* and *shopping* continued to be booby traps, probably because I couldn't simply eliminate these areas of my life. Unlike alcohol or cigarettes, where the best—the only—answer for the compulsive woman is total abstinence, we all have to eat, and we all have to go into stores. For the compulsive personality, moderation is the hardest achievement of all.

For a while I'd do fine on a reasonable regimen of eating. Then—most often in the late afternoon—I'd be attacked by what I called the "hungry horrors." Stricken, I'd dash to the refrigerator or out to a nearby convenience store for a pound bag of chocolate-covered peanuts, one of my choice binge foods. This would turn trigger a desire for more sugar, more pastry, anything with white flour. I'd been warned at Dickman House that I was a "wheataholic." (*Why not,* I had thought. *I seem to have been every other kind of "aholic" there is.*)

The tendency to rush to the refrigerator when things go wrong can be compulsivity at its worst. Fortunately, I had friends now to help me face down the food monster. They steered me to a group of singles in Billings who met for meals and fellowship often during the week. This accomplished three things. It made me: 1) eat on schedule; 2) choose nutritious foods; and 3) retain the companionship I needed to strengthen my self-discipline.

Several of us in the singles group who had similar eating problems benefited from a list of alternatives to food bingeing. Here are some steps we learned to take when the urge to binge was overpowering:[2]

1. Call a group member or friend. Keep calling until you reach someone.

2. Take a bath or shower.

3. Take a walk; go running or jogging.

4. Do a non-food-related activity outside the kitchen. Stay out of the kitchen.

5. Go to an eating disorder support group meeting.

6. Do a relaxation exercise.

7. Distract yourself with a craft project, book or TV program.

8. Read something inspirational or positive.

9. Take a power nap.

10. Go to a concert, play, etc.

11. Think the binge through—"what I'll get out of it."

12. Put the binge off five minutes at a time.

13. Write down the things you want out of life.

14. Write down the things you have missed because of bingeing.

It was helpful to remember that it takes twenty minutes for our stomachs to register a "full" feeling. I tried to stop eating *before* I felt full. The best defense I found against the hungry horrors and other assaults was to begin each day with an admission of my helplessness and dependence on God.

My religious faith has played a growing role in my overcoming these and other "monsters." A verse from the New Testament Book of Romans is interesting in this regard: "I do not understand what I do. For what I want to do I do not do, but what I hate I do."[3] This internal warring describes the compulsive woman to a T, and I am as dependent as the writer of these words in finding success by turning to Jesus Christ, my Higher Power, when I am overwhelmed by the temptation to succumb to one of my former compulsions.

The same biblical writer talks in another place about taking "captive every thought" to Christ.[4] Is this God's suggestion to those of us who are dealing with compulsivity?

Many women, of course, do not choose this way of dealing with it. I understand. Regardless of a person's religious orientation, it is imperative only that she practice some form of quieting herself, of centering down, of broadening her perspective on life.

> Develop your spirituality through daily practice. Whether or not you have a belief in God, and if you do, whether or not you're on speaking terms with Him, you can still practice this step…Even if you are a 100 percent atheist, perhaps you get pleasure and solace from a quiet walk, or contemplating a sunset or some aspect of nature. Whatever takes you beyond yourself and into a broader perspective on things is what this step is all about.[5]

Along the way to recovery I found it necessary to break off relationships with old drinking friends or those who had "enabled" me when I was ill. As I expected, some heaped scorn on me as "self-righteous" or "judgmental" or "a lousy friend." Later, when I'm stronger, perhaps I can seek them out and try to establish relationships on a new basis.

Other good advice came to me along the way: Stay in the present! Yesterday is a canceled check. Tomorrow is a promissory note. Today is ready cash. Spend it wisely. Enjoy life where you are right now.

Whenever I forgot and started to dwell on the past, I was dragged down into a numbing state of depression. Actually, I thought of it as a "depressionetta," a mere niggle compared to the crashing, bottoming-out of the past. What helped me was having a meditation time while I walked in the morning and a prayer time when I took my personal inventory before retiring for the night. As I struggled through a succession of difficult choices day by day, I was chasing the little monsters of my life.

"It takes time, effort, and faith to mature out of an addictive disposition," declares Stanton Peele, one of the foremost authorities on addiction. "…Therapy or no, the ultimate responsibility is still our own."[6]

In taking responsibility for my own recovery, I am breaking the pattern of negative thinking I've engaged in for most of my life, I'm learning to get my feelings out on the table, look them over and realize they can be changed.

LEARNING TO FULFILL OUR NEEDS must begin early in infancy and continue all our lives. If we fail to learn we will suffer, and this suffering always dries us to try unrealistic means to fulfill our needs. A person who does not learn as a little child to give and receive love may spend the rest of his life unsuccessfully trying to love.

—WILLIAM GLASSER, M.D.
Reality Therapy

LEARNING TO LIKE YOURSELF

For years I've asked myself why some people carry around such a low self-image when they're as richly endowed with gifts and talents as anyone else.

In my case I've identified some partial answers dating to childhood. An early episode of sexual abuse produced in me a sense of shame because I felt somehow it was my fault that it happened. The silent, unhappy home where emotions were not acknowledged soon made me ashamed of any strong feelings. When eventually my parents divorced, I felt still more shame, believing that undoubtedly this was my fault, too.

The root of compulsive behavior, as we have already seen, is shame. To compensate for my own shame, I became an overachiever and people-pleaser. This way I didn't have to face my own pain, anger, fear and guilt. My constant attempts to win approval led me into a pattern of obsession about my appearance and the neatness of my surroundings. If everything looked impeccable on the outside, no one would ever know that inside there was such a mess.

Because I couldn't love myself, I searched for others to love me, especially men, even though subconsciously I didn't trust them. I was desperate for the reassurance that I was lovable. When these relationships didn't work out, I sought my reassurance from alcohol and food. My search for some sense of wroth and meaning led me into a cult that left me haunted with more self-hate and condemnation than before. Soon all my compulsive behaviors and dependencies became woven together in a spider-web trap. I'd break through in one area only to be strangled in another.

In thinking back to when my suicidally low self-image began a turn-around, I've identified some early steps:

1. Karen singling me out in the hospital as her friend. Her need compelled me to give instead of take.

2. Making a list of simple things to do my first day at home from the hospital—and then getting them done.

3. Making the successful case before the staff for my discharge from the hospital.

4. Stopped smoking.

5. Stopped drinking.

These action steps may not even have been as important as the corresponding changes that took place in my mind and spirit. These changes, harder to trace, began at that magical moment in the hospital when I remembered a Scripture verse learned as a child: "By his stripes we are healed…" I knew then my mind was not damaged beyond recall. The changes that followed revolved around the fundamental—and astonishing—awareness that I didn't have to prove anything to God. To my amazement He loved me unconditionally.

Despite my insights into the origins of a poor self-image and how this can change, developing a sense of self-worth was a painfully slow process. It's a strange thing to encounter the real you for the first time in middle-age. Strange and frightening. What if I didn't like me, let alone love me?

I did love the new freedom—freedom not to have secrets any longer. Freedom to be open and honest. Being able to share in groups, learning to have my own opinions instead of parroting those around me, helped self-esteem grow. Gradually I began to feel more comfortable with myself. For years I had been running and hiding from myself, searching for answers everywhere but inside.

At the four-year mark of my sobriety I felt a sense of peace, of being on target. In Marcy 1984 I had moved back to my home state of Vermont, taking a small house in Montpelier next to my mother's even smaller one. (My stepfather had died the previous spring.) I hadn't wanted to move so far from my children, but they were all in their twenties, out in the working world, driving their own cars, busy with their own friends. We had loving relationships, though not intimate.

So I settled into my little house in Vermont quick to commit to an alcohol support group. I also converted the raised hearth of my living room fireplace into a makeshift altar. I laid a white lace cloth on the bricks and placed on it a pair of my Aunt Ethel's candleholders with white candles. It was here I spent much time in quiet prayer and reflection.

Sometimes my mind went back to the people I'd hurt—used and abused—and to situations I had tried to forget. As I repented of my sins against husbands, children, parents and friends, I asked God to show me where amends were possible and where restoration had to lie with Him alone; where trying to clear my own conscience publicly would only lay further burdens on those I had injured.

Still other times I thought of people I needed to forgive, of anyone against whom I had nursed a grievance, starting with Uncle Ralph. I'd write the name on a scrap of paper, saying a prayer releasing that person from my judgment, and ask God's blessing on his or her life. Then I'd touch the paper to the nearest candle and watch old resentments turn to ashes in the fireplace.

What lightness and exhilaration of the spirit followed! One by one the closed doors of my life were being opened as I did what in effect amounted to a personal housecleaning.

Along the way I discovered six disciplines that have helped me begin to find the creativity I had lost. Since people recovering from addictive behavior have to face up to their need for personal disciplines, I offer these suggestions to you:

1. Be completely honest for one full day in everything you say or do. If you can't be honest about your boss's expansion plans or your friend's new outfit, for example, say nothing.

2. For one hour think or pray on one subject. Or divide the hour into two separate periods, each devoted to one concern.

3. Express a heartfelt regret or ask forgiveness for something negative you have said or done fairly recently to a friend,

coworker, relative, etc. Do this through a letter or telephone call.

4. Make it a point to be concerned about other people. This can be accomplished through volunteer work, through visits to a hospital, through helping a friend, through intercessory prayer.

5. For a set period of time—at least a day, perhaps a week or longer—keep your conversations with close friends or acquaintances or chance encounters on his or her interests solely. Focus on drawing the other person out. Learn what he or she thinks, feels or is experiencing.

6. Set aside one day for obedience. As best you can, let God and/or others determine what you do (within reason, of course, when letting others determine your actions). Consider yourself a total servant for this day. See yourself as a willing tool or instrument to bring joy and encouragement to others.

In the course of my own recovery, I decided the single life must be what I was now called to. I had attended a number of retreats and workshops on how to find fulfillment as a single. I discovered I could help hurting single women, especially the ones with alcohol or drug problems, and felt drawn toward this work.

Sometimes I thought about marrying again, but I always dismissed the thought. Two failures there had battered my self-image as a desirable person. And yet…something deep within me yearned to be a genuine partner. Not the needy, confused Sandy of the past compulsively seeking a man to solve my problems, but a real wife, able to give as well as take. Could I hope to believe I had become, in a real sense, a new woman, clean and pure as the freshly fallen snow on my Vermont rooftop? I thought about this often that first winter back East.

As I began telling my story here and there, a publisher contacted me and suggested I write a book. My newly won self-confidence quailed before such an assignment. I borrowed a typewriter and spent long, frustrating hours in front of it. When it was obvious I didn't know what I was doing, the publisher suggested I attend the *Decision* Magazine Writer's School to be held in St. Paul, Minnesota in August 1984.

Learning to Like Yourself

Once out there, I pored over the week's schedule, wondering what courses to take. On Monday afternoon there was to be a workshop on creative ideas by a longtime *Guideposts* editor named Leonard LeSourd. Hmmm. I needed creative ideas for sure.

Monday morning there was talk at breakfast about the LeSourd workshop and about the death of his wife, Catherine. "He must be awfully lonely," one woman said. "They were so close." Everyone seemed to know this Catherine and said her name with reverence.

Catherine *who?* I wondered to myself, not wanting to show my ignorance. "I've read *Christy* seven times!" someone gushed. Finally someone said Catherine Marshall.

Beyond Our Selves! I'd carried her book around for weeks at the Warm Springs Hospital. I had flipped through the pages thinking, "This woman has it too put together for me." Several times I had stopped at the dedication page—*To Len*—wondering who he could be.

That afternoon I arrived at the auditorium early and found a seat directly in front of the speaker's podium. Soon a handsome gray-haired man wearing a blue-and-white striped seersucker jacket and light blue trousers stepped up to it. Why, as Len LeSourd began to speak, did my heart do a ridiculous flip-flop? I didn't know this man at all.

With so many people crowding around him after the talk, I felt shy about introducing myself. I walked out of the lecture hall regretting that I would never exchange even a word with him.

At dinner, however, Len chanced to sit at the same family-style table where I was. Somehow I found myself telling him about my struggle with alcoholism. To my amazement, tears formed in his slate-blue eyes. "I have a niece who is battling that problem," he said. "Would you be willing to write to her?"

He gave me her address and took mine. Noting that I lived in Vermont, he mentioned that he would be driving through New England later that month. "Maybe I'll give you a call."

Three weeks later in Vermont, my telephone rang. Len was in the area; could I make a room reservation for him somewhere nearby for Saturday night? He'd become such a workaholic since Catherine's death, he explained, that his family had needled him into taking this vacation trip through New England. "I'm supposed to stop regularly and smell the flowers."

I took that as a personal mission. I reserved a room at the Montpelier Tavern Inn, an historic spot where stagecoaches used to stop. Now for a surprise welcome.

Margaret Guilmette, a creative friend of mine, and I borrowed the key to his room. We pinned a newsprint banner—*Welcome to Montpelier, Len!*—to the top of the drapes. On one of the twin beds, we placed a large black teddy bear, decked out in an antique lace collar and black hat trimmed with violets. Nestled next to the bear was a straw basket labeled *First-Aid Kit for the Weary Traveler.* In it was a box of Vermont maple candy, a clump of red grapes, imported cheese, crackers and a bottle of aspirin.

On the small table by the picture window was a bouquet of black-eyed Susans. I smiled recalling how I'd picked them the day before in a drenching rain. Was my compulsive nature showing? Well, Len had admitted to a compulsive side, too.

Late in the afternoon the telephone rang again. Len was chuckling. "There seems to be a bear in my room. Does she have a name?"

"Yes. 'Golly.'"

"I see." A pause. "Is she a good romantic?"

"Oh, yes. She almost never snores."

After our first dinner date at the Trapp Family Lodge in nearby Stowe, Vermont, Len and I began to see a lot of one another. As the weeks passed and he kept discovering reasons to come to Vermont, we acknowledged that we were falling in love. At the same time, both of us were impressed by a principle we chose to govern our relationship: *The best comes out of self-denial.*

I'd known that with my mind all my life. Even as my compulsivity drove me to indulge every passion—whether for chocolate, clothes, booze or cigarettes—I'd known that a saner, healthier existence meant saying *no* to these things. What I'd never been able to do was make my *no* stick.

Now, because of the psychological, chemical and spiritual healing taking place in me, I found a bracing kind of joy in self-denial. By forgoing a sexual relationship, Len and I became friends first. We learned how to laugh together, we got to know each other at a deeper level.

As weeks turned into months and the desire for marriage grew in us both, we set out to visit all members of our two families. The visit that showed me much about my recovery was when I joined Len for a weekend at his farm in Virginia, forty-five miles west of Washington. Living with him in her own wing at Evergreen Farm was his mother-in-law, Leonora Wood, whose exploits as an eighteen-year-old schoolteacher in the Great Smoky Mountains back in 1912 formed the basics for Catherine's novel *Christy*. Mother Wood, now ninety-three, was the beloved and respected family matriarch. How would she receive me? And how would Len's friends and business associates respond to the new woman in his life?

After the Sunday morning service at Len's church, one woman with piercing gray eyes grilled me in a polite way, drawing out that I had been twice married and twice divorced and was presently unemployed because I was trying to write a book. Hardly a success story.

Nor was my time with Mother Wood encouraging. Through frail and bent in body, Mrs. Wood was a towering personage with an active mind mixed with the loneliness of a mother and grandmother who had said premature good-byes to a husband, two children and three grandchildren. She was kind and courteous to me, but I sensed underneath a steely opposition. And why not? To her I must have seemed a brash outsider with designs on taking Catherine's place.

Wherever I went in the nineteen-room farmhouse, Catherine's presence preceded me. She smiled at me from dozens of photos about the home and office. Her serene gaze from a magnificent oil portrait in Evergreen's formal parlor met my own each time I came through the front door.

Only a few years earlier, I would have fallen into the trap of comparing myself with her. Shame-ridden people—compulsive people—do that. Finding no worth in themselves, they make other people the standard. Other people's achievements, other people's virtues.

I learned, happily, that I was far enough along in my recovery to realize that of course I could not take Catherine's place, or the place of anyone else. I was me. I had spent the past few years getting to know me—and, wonder of wonder, I was beginning to like me.

Still, there came a bleak moment when I just wanted to flee. Clearly I didn't belong among these productive, successful people. In my despair I sought out Len and suggested I return early to Vermont. He looked at me, smiled and shook his head.

"It's rough for you, Sandy, but you'll make it."

"But your family is so…put together. I'm still struggling, and I'm a failure as a wife and parent."

"You are not a failure. You're an overcomer. That's even better than being a success."

I knew for sure at that moment why I loved this man.

Other family get-togethers followed over the next few months—with Len's three children and their two spouses, his stepsons and family, my three children and my parents.

The final green light for me came after the Mother's Day church service one May Sunday in Virginia. Len and I had taken Mother Wood there, packing her wheelchair into the trunk of the car. When I leaned down to release the brake before wheeling her out, she drew my face very close to her own and looked into my eyes with incredibly intense blue ones. "I love you, Sandy," she said softly. "I'm so grateful you're going to be part of our family."

Len and I were married on June 22, 1985 at the Trapp Family Lodge, in Stowe, Vermont—ten months after our first date there the previous August. As we began to adjust to each other in marriage, we both took a hard look at compulsive behavior persisting into the present—mine and his. Len had been a workaholic and a sportsaholic. Forty years of meeting publication deadlines, often working past midnight and over the weekend, had produced an imbalance in his life. Often his change of pace came through a more-than-casual involvement in televised sports, especially professional football.

Len's emotional involvement with the Dallas Cowboys was a revelation. "To root for a team you need to read up on the players and coaches and get all the local color," he told me by way of explaining the pile of sports magazines by his chair.

"But why does losing a game take on more importance than a nuclear accident or a disastrous earthquake?" I asked.

Len looked reflective. "I'm powerless over my sports addiction, and my life has become unmanageable," he said with a grin. Then, more seriously, he confessed to disturbance over the intensity, even destructiveness, of fans absorbed with a team, the ridiculous salaries of the players (which often led to drug use) and the obsession with winning.

He admitted that involvement in a late-night game on television often rendered him sleepless for hours afterwards, wiping him out for most of the next day. Sunday afternoon games often assumed such importance, he further revealed, that he would duck social engagements, even family responsibilities, to watch his team play.

Next Sunday afternoon we did go out for a couple of hours. Upon our return he fidgeted miserably about the living room, then switched on the TV. Soon he was glued to the action. I watched him with bemused understanding.

For I'm still battling certain compulsions in my life. Shopping, for one. Sometimes I still come out of stores with more items than I planned buy, and then I rail at myself later.

Then there was the time I made a special greeting card to celebrate the birth of one of the Len's grandchildren. It started out as a simple card. Four hours later it had grown into a huge eight-color poster announcing *The First Annual Mary Catherine Lader Golf Classic.* The following day, playing golf with friends, Len and I displayed the poster on the back of our golf cart and sent photos of the "event" to Len's daughter and son-in-law.

It was this spontaneous "golf classic," silly but fun, that helped me understand something about compulsive behavior.

It's not all bad!

Along with certain native gifts and abilities, we often have an inner drive that helps us channel gifts into a successful career. We need the tenacity, determination and focused energy to achieve worthwhile things. Len's compulsion for work made him a topflight editor; my compulsion for quality—whether in dress design or floral displays—is an exercise of my gift. The all-out effort poured into a project can make that project shine.

This was an important discovery for me. I'm not to crush my zealous nature or scorn it. It's a part of me, a kind of inner dynamo given me for a purpose. Only for years I misused it. I let this driving quality inside, the "I-want-what-I-want-when-I-want-it" part or nature, take over my life.

Now I'm striving to bring this compulsive part of me, like the rest of my being, under control. There are times when I try to take charge again, which we're all free to do. But I'm learning to catch myself.

In my early morning, for example. As soon as we got married, Len and I began praying first thing in the day that God would take the inner drive we both have and guide it—and it seemed to happen for us.

I also find continuous healing as I shift my attention away from myself to other people, focusing on the words *serve, give, teach, share.* As parents and grandparents, this involved Len and me with more than forty people in our family alone. But it didn't stop there.

Len and I began conducting team workshops on the subject of compulsive behavior. Researching the subject took us to treatment centers around the country. What troubled me is that medical and religious programs do not work more closely together, since I received such solid help from both disciplines. The main differences stem from definition. The scientific world regards compulsive behavior as a disease—chemical or psychological or both. Christians consider it a sin.

It was a lift to find one treatment center that combined both approaches.

When we drove into the Dunklin Memorial Camp, thirty miles west of Stuart, Florida, the spacious grounds were alive with activity: men on tractors, or wielding shovels, or hoisting furniture into the back of a mud-spattered pickup truck. This alcohol and drug treatment center was clearly a busy place.

We parked and entered a low stucco office building to receive a warm welcome from Mickey Evans, who over a twenty-three-year period had built a sizable complex out of eight hundred acres of Florida swamp. He eased his powerful frame into a desk swivel chair and got quickly to the facts:

"This is a center for male alcoholics and drug addicts," he began. "We can house about thirty. Most of the men are poly-addicted; we don't get 'simple' alcoholics today except a few older men. We don't detox here. That's done down at the center in Fort Pierce. The men come to us sober. They're here to work and learn. I tell each man, 'There's a waiting list to get into this place. If you want to stay here, you must earn the right. If you don't, I'll give your bed to someone who'll make better use of it.'"

Mickey went on to describe excruciating difficulties with cocaine-users, calling this drug "deadly beyond our understanding; it can stay in the system for up to ten months."

Then came word that elated me: "Some Christian programs treat addiction as a sin, which it obviously is. Sin simply means 'off the mark'—and these men's lives are certainly that. But some of these places go further and take the stand that alcoholism and drug addiction are *not* physical diseases. They shun all medical helps, including the Twelve-Step program. After twenty-three years, I've concluded that chemical dependence is both sin and sickness. We treat addictions as a disease and use the Twelve-Step program that stresses commitment to a Higher Power. Here the Higher Power is Jesus Christ.

"We insist each man have a quiet time first thing in the morning," Mickey continued. "He also must make a daily moral inventory of the past twenty-four hours. This helps him get in touch with the attitudes that are motivating him. Addicts have to change their attitudes before they can change their behavior. All the men keep a journal to record their insights into themselves. Also, some of them never knew prayer is a two-way street. I feel the quiet time—learning to listen as well as to speak—is the key to the whole program."

The work program is also crucial to the addict's recovery, Mickey explained. This includes kitchen duty, laundry, painting, ranch work, gardening and caring for the horses. Residents grow most of their food and raise their own beef.

Weekends are devoted to family programs, when wives and children come out to participate in various activities. Even spouses are asked to do a daily moral inventory. Mickey considers addiction a family disease: "Sometimes the wife and children are sicker than the addict himself."

The Dunklin Camp has seen some remarkable improvements in families on these weekends. "Often it's the first time they've been able to sit down and be honest with each other," says Mickey. "Also, the first time the patient has been thinking clearly enough to hear what his family has to say to him. We won't take a man unless his family will agree to be part of every weekend program."

At first addicts were taken in without charge. But as time passed Mickey became aware of the human tendency to take lightly what we get for nothing. Though the program is still financed largely by contributions, the fee is now set at a thousand dollars for each three months of treatment. Each family pays fifteen dollars for the weekend program.

If a man is too poor to pay but does have a television set, a gun or some garden tools, Mickey will accept these as payment. He is convinced that unless a man has some kind of material investment in his treatment, he tends to drift through it. For those who stay in treatment for one year, there is a 90 percent recovery rate.

When I asked Mickey about a comparable program for women, he said that one Dunklin graduate and his wife had recently started a program in the Orlando area, based on Dunklin procedures.

People helping people. That's the message I receive as I look back on all I've learned over the years. Karen; my Filipino doctor at Warm Springs; my friend Lois Ann; Dirk, who intervened when I was flying without chemicals; my counselor Gwen...the list goes on and on.

July 9, 1986 was an extraordinary day as well as a traumatic one. Len and I had traveled to Billings, Montana to visit my children and meet with certain groups. But I was apprehensive about a speech I was to give before two hundred women at the Warbonnet Inn.

As our hostess for the week drove me to the meeting, I looked at my old hometown with new eyes. So many familiar landmarks, most filled with painful memories. The Warbonnet Inn itself: Twelve years before I had come to this same hotel ballroom for that first International Serenity Society conference. How dazed, confused and frightened I had been back then! And how much worse after my involvement with that cult. Now I felt alive, filled with enthusiasm.

As the audience started arriving, my excitement—and nervousness—mounted. Many of the women had been dear friends during the twenty-one years I had lived in Billings.

- Kathy, my former neighbor, who had led me tot he seminar and church where I received my healing

- Hilda, the women who had been more of a mother to my children as our housecleaner for twenty years than I had

- Shelly, the grocery store clerk who had helped me with my grocery list when I could barely function—who had loved me when I couldn't love myself

I was delighted to greet my former mother-in-law who had visited me faithfully when I was in state mental institution and encouraged me during my dark years.

Best of all, my daughter, Lisa, had taken the afternoon off from her work at a video store.

Never before had there been assembled in one room so many people

Learning to Like Yourself

I loved, so many who had touched my life: the women from the Thursday prayer group, some of my tennis and bridge club friends, friends from the singles group, even former babysitters.

After the introduction I moved up to the podium before these people, opened my mouth to speak…and instead broke down and wept. When I regained my composure, I told the story of my compulsive behavior, addictions, hospitalization and recovery, having a strange sense of being at one point or another *every woman* in the room.

Looking back on my life, I was overwhelmed with gratitude for the patience, love and support of so many people: family members who always believed in me somehow during the darkest of times; close friends who never quit praying that a miracle would occur in my life; and a loving and forgiving God who brought me back from the pit of hopelessness. Now I could say with total conviction that there are no hopeless situations. A helping hand awaits anyone, everyone who reaches out for it.

For I knew only too well the frustration, the pain, the sense of failure, the depression and the desire to self-destruct that compulsive women feel at one time or another. I had been through it all and discovered there are no hopeless cases. There is a way through the darkness into the light. We compulsive women can be freed from our bondage.

The way is long, but it is possible. It begins with a frank acknowledgment of the areas of our addiction, all of them—a surrender to the reality of the problem. The steps to self-forgiveness and forgiving others, going back as far as we can remember, are critical. A "feelings journal," like my anger diary, may be helpful in this. A support group is invaluable. Developing a relationship with a Higher Power is crucial.

Then come the building-up steps. Set a succession of reachable goals. Maybe the admonition *Do it now* will be as helpful to you as it is to me. Every small victory raises our self-esteem, lets us know we can succeed, that we can do something even better. At last we will be ready to move beyond focusing primarily on ourselves and reach out toward those around us.

What a great feeling it is to know we have stopped being takers—that at last we have something to give!

PART TWO

HANDBOOK OF
SPECIAL HELPS

15

HELP FOR THE COMPULSIVE WOMAN AND HER FAMILY

W hile both men and women are prone to compulsive behavior, the problems of women especially concern me—because I have been there.

The good news, for me, having been on the recovery road, is that I know what I have to do to keep on that trek. I can't do it on my own power; primarily it is surrender to the Higher Power that keeps me on track. But there are other guideposts that give me direction every day of my life.

This Handbook of Special Helps, the result of months of research, is a compilation of some of the resources and tools available for additive/compulsive people. Though far from being a complete listing, it can chart a course of where to go in finding the recovery road that is right for you. Suggested action: Go through the listing of helps on the contents page and focus on the areas of compulsivity to which you relate.

I have also included two sections at the beginning of this chapter that will help you and your family—the Twenty Recovery Principles and a section on Families Anonymous, which is helpful for any family who has a member engaged in unhealthy compulsive behavior.

My hope for you is that if you are being defeated by behavior you can't control, as I was for so many years, you will decide today that it is time to do something about it.

TWENTY RECOVERY PRINCIPLES

1. Seek the prayers of others.

2. Say *no* and mean it!

3. Trust God's love for you.

4. Accept yourself just the way you, not the way you think you should be.

5. Stop and smell the flowers.

6. Obey the inner voice.

7. Be selfless and help others.

8. Be open and honest.

9. Be reconciled to God, others and yourself.

10. Identify your real needs.

11. Expect the best.

12. Seize the moment.

13. Forgive those who have hurt you.

14. Keep communications open.

15. Take care of your body, and your body will take care of you.

16. Make a friend…namely yourself.

17. Keep short accounts of oughts against others.

18. You are loved…believe it!

19. Don't let the sun go down on your anger.

20. There is a time to mourn and a time to dance.

Families Anonymous

Families Anonymous is a fellowship of relatives and friends of people who are involved in the abuse of mind-altering substances or exhibiting related behavioral problems such as running away, delinquency, under-achieving, etc. Any concerned person is encouraged to attend meetings—even if there is only a suspicion of a problem. It is a self-help organization whose program is based upon an adaptation of the Twelve Steps and the Twelve Traditions first formulated by Alcoholics Anonymous.

Group discussions are built upon a specific theme such as expecta-tions, anxiety, overprotection or better communications. As members share their own experiences—successes and failures—those going through a particular crisis find understanding and emotional support. Attention is focused upon the feelings, attitudes, actions and reactions of family members, not upon trying to change the person involved in the unacceptable behavior. Experience has shown that help for the family means important help for the chemically dependent individual.

Those wishing to obtain information about the Families Anonymous group in their area or to start a new group may contact:

> Families Anonymous, Inc.
> P. O. Box 3475
> Culver City, CA 90231-3475
> 800-736-9805
> 310-815-9682 (fax)
> www.familiesanonymous.org
> famanon@familiesanonymous.org

Alcohol Addiction

Alcohol and drug dependence are America's number one health prob-lem. Nearly 4 million American women ages 18 and older can be classi-fied as alcoholic or problem drinkers. More than several million women need treatment for drug problems.

The cost and consequences of alcoholism and drug dependence place an enormous burden on American society. As the nation's number one health problem, addictions strain the healthcare system and the economy, they harm family life, and they threaten public safety. If alcohol were to be discovered today, it could only be dispensed by prescription because it is such a powerful drug.

Alcohol and drug abuse cost the American economy an estimated 276 billion dollars per year in loss productivity, healthcare expenditures, crime, motor vehicle crashes and other conditions. Every American adult pays nearly $1000 per year for the damages of addictions.

Substance abuse crosses all societal boundaries; it affects males and females alike, every ethnic group and people in every tax bracket. Scientific documentation defines alcoholism and drug dependence as a disease that has roots in both genetic susceptibility and personal behavior. There are more deaths and disability each year in the US from substance abuse than any other cause.

More than half of the adults in the U.S. have a family history of alcoholism or problem drinking. More than 9 million live with a parent dependent on alcohol and/or illicit drugs. One quarter of all emergency admissions, one-third of all suicides and more than half of all homicides and incidents of domestic violence are alcohol-related. Compared with men, women with drinking problems also are at increased risk of depression, low self-esteem, alcohol-related physical problems, marital discord or divorce, spouses with alcohol problems and a history of sexual abuse. Seventy percent report having been abused sexually before the age of sixteen and are drinking in response to life crises.[1]

The Twelve-Step Program of Alcoholics Anonymous (AA)

Step One: We admitted we were powerless over alcohol—that our lives had become unmanageable.

Step Two: We came to believe that a power greater than ourselves could restore us to sanity.

Step Three: We made a decision to turn our will and our lives over to the care of God as we understand Him.

Step Four: We made a searching and fearless moral inventory of ourselves.

Step Five: We admitted to God, to ourselves and to another human being the exact nature of our wrongs.

Step Six: We were entirely ready to have God remove all these defects of character.

Help for the Compulsive Woman and Her Family

Step Seven: We humbly asked Him to remove our shortcomings.

Step Eight: We made a list of persons we had harmed and became willing to make amends to them all.

Step Nine: We made direct amends to such people wherever possible, except when to do so would injure them or others.

Step Ten: We continued to take personal inventory, and when we were wrong we promptly admitted it.

Step Eleven: We sought through prayer and meditation to improve our conscious contact with God as we understood Him, praying only for knowledge of His will for us and the power to carry that out.

Step Twelve: Having had a spiritual awakening as the result of these steps, we tried to carry this message to alcoholics and to practice these principles in all our affairs.2

These steps are the cornerstone of most treatment programs. Alcoholics Anonymous (AA) is the pioneering group that established the basic principles to guide the addict back to health.

AA was found in Akron, Ohio by two men, publicly identified as Bill W., a New York stockbroker, and Dr. Bob S., a surgeon. Both had long histories of irresponsible drinking. Both had been considered hopeless alcoholics.

In the fall of 1934, Bill W., hospitalized for alcoholism, experienced a sudden spiritual "awakening" that seemed to free him of the desire to drink. He tried to persuade other alcoholics that they could experience the same transformation, but none recovered.

The following spring in Akron, after the collapse of a business venture, Bill was seriously tempted to drink again. Fearful of the inevitable consequences of taking the first drink, Bill recalled that he had had no desire for liquor during the preceding months while he had been working with alcoholics in New York. In desperation, he sought a similar contact in Akron and was led to Dr. Bob. The latter, impressed by Bill's recovery story and by the opportunity to share his own drinking problems with an admitted alcoholic, achieved sobriety shortly thereafter.

More importantly, the two men discovered that their own sobriety was strengthened when they offered to share it with others, stressing their own practical experience as recovered alcoholics. By the fall of 1935, a small group of sober alcoholics was meeting regularly in Akron, known as the Fellowship of Alcoholics Anonymous.

How you can apply the Twelve Steps

Here are suggested guidelines for adapting the Twelve-Step program to your compulsion/addiction. These comments are observations of the author and not of Alcoholics Anonymous.

STEP ONE: This is perhaps the most difficult step for the addict who does not want to concede weakness and helplessness, who says, "I can stop any time I choose to." Taking this first step means conceding that there has been a long period of self-deception. But for progress to begin, the ego must topple off the throne. Then the addict can admit, "I'm no longer in control."

STEP TWO: The addict is faced with a second momentous decision. Previously she admitted her life was out of control; now she needs help, not from a husband or friend, but from the area of a mysterious Higher Power. Most addicts have trouble acknowledging this Higher Power because self has been their higher power for years. Now comes an agonizing shift—a transferal from a power that's broken down to a power that's new and different, a threat to all that was comfortable and familiar.

STEP THREE: The progression of decisions the addict must make continues. First, an admission of powerlessness; second, an acknowledgement of strength greater than our own; third, a decision to surrender to the greater strength. How one resists that idea! Yet inner release comes through giving up that hard-core area of self-reliance. Letting go brings peace. You give up something that's been destructive to get something that promises health.

STEP FOUR: This is a most painful step for the addict who would prefer to blot out from her consciousness all the terrible things she has done to herself and others. Making a searching, fearless moral inventory *means writing* down people, places, events and dates with brutal candor and incisiveness. Spare nothing. This is the way toward recovery.

STEP FIVE: Looking on paper at the specifics for our mal inventory has to raise the question "What can I do about all this?"

Try to forget it? That's the road back to chemical dependency.

Confession? Yes. To God and to another person.

What person?

Someone you trust, someone who will keep what you say in confidence.

Step Six: After confessing their wrongdoing, many women leave it there, figuring they've done all that's necessary. God does forgive, doesn't He? Now we can go on with our lives.

But wait! What about those character defects—pride, anger, lust, jealousy, resentment and so on? They have become "old friends." Are we ready for God to change these things? Are we willing to do what He asks to bring about the change?

We need to make a conscious act of setting our wills in a state of readiness so that we can receive any instructions.

Step Seven: After an act of the will that says to God, "I'm ready for you to change me," then comes the next step, asking God to take action. We have moved ahead steadily from unbelief or indifference to a relationship with God. Now comes the expectation of a miracle! Those who see their Higher Power as human destiny, nature or some other impersonal force may struggle with these steps. If so, they may want to rethink what or who the Higher Power for them really is.

Step Eight: They key words here are *became* willing. The act of making a list will be difficult because of painful memories, some of which may have been blotted out. A good procedure is:

1. Take pencil and paper, go back in time and write down in some chronological order with dates, the names of people harmed and what the offenses were.

2. Pray that God will unblock your mind and reveal the people and events He wants you to include.

3. Ask Him to help you *become willing* to make amends.

Step Nine: In this crucial and painful step of the recovery process, there is need for sensitivity and discernment as to whom we contact. At an alcohol family support meeting one man whose problem was lust admitted that attempts to make restitution to women with whom he had had sexual encounters years before backfired on his current marital situation. Consider each person on your list, seeking wisdom about what action to take.

STEP TEN: The addict has lived in a world of self-indulgence for so long that a formidable defense system separates her from the rest of the world. The road to recovery involves tearing down this defense system. Coming to the point where the addict can admit a mistake, which also may mean an apology, is a big step toward healing. "I was wrong. I am sorry. I made a mistake. Please forgive me." There's healing every time these words are uttered.

STEP ELEVEN: Moving into prayer and meditation is a major step for the addict because it means the building of a relationship with God, a process that could take months, even years. On top of that the addict is to pray for power to follow God's will. For some, Bible study classes and prayer are essential to make Step Eleven work.

STEP TWELVE: This last step is a clarion call to reach out to other addicts. Unlike the previous steps, most of which involve pain, this one flows almost irresistibly from the newfound joy and purpose of our lives. The transition from compulsive self-centeredness to being "others-centered" releases undreamed-of energy into daily living.

Twelve rewards of the Twelve-Step program

1. Hope instead of desperation

2. Faith instead of despair

3. Courage instead of fear

4. Peace of mind instead of confusion

5. Self-respect instead of helplessness

6. Self-confidence instead of helplessness

7. The respect of others instead of their pity and contempt

8. A clean conscience instead of a sense of guilt

9. Real relationships instead of loneliness

10. A clean pattern of life instead of a purposeless existence

11. The love and understanding of our families instead of their doubts and fears

12. The freedom of a happy life instead of the bondage of a drugged obsession

Help for the Compulsive Woman and Her Family

Remember, the task ahead of us is never as great as the power behind us.

Danger signals for women

There are numerous checklists of danger signals—most of them based on what is known about male drinkers. This one, prepared by the National Council on Alcoholism and Drug Dependence, is one of the few aimed specifically at women.

- Do you drink because you are shy with other people?

- Is drinking affecting your reputation?

- Have you gotten into financial difficulties as a result of drinking?

- Do you turn to lower companions and an inferior environment when drinking?

- Does your drinking make you careless of your family's welfare?

- Do you regularly use alcohol as medicine—to relieve menstrual cramps, help calm your nerves or help you sleep?

- Do you take an extra drink or two before leaving for a party, though you know liquor will be served?

- Do you invent social occasions for drinking, such as inviting friends for lunch, cocktails or dinner, or arranging business appointments around mealtimes or after work?

- Do you drink when you're feeling depressed in the hope that it will make you feel better?

- Do you need a drink to feel sociable?

- Do you feel more witty or attractive when you are drinking?

- Do you drink under pressure or after an argument?

- Do you drink to drown out angry feelings or to relax?

◆ Do you try to get someone to buy liquor for you because you are ashamed to buy it yourself?

◆ Do you hide empty bottles and dispose of them secretly?

◆ Do you plan in advance to reward yourself with drinking after you have worked hard in the house or on the job?

◆ Do you have "blackouts"—periods about which you remember nothing?

◆ Do you feel panicky when faced with nondrinking days or when you are without money to purchase alcohol?

◆ Do you ever carry liquor in your purse?

◆ Do you become defensive when someone mentions your drinking?

◆ Do you cover up when you can't remember promises and feel ashamed when you misplace or lose things?

◆ Do you drive your car although you've been drinking, feeling certain you are in complete control of yourself?

◆ Do you use alcohol to engage in sexual activity?

Any woman who answers *yes* to more than five of these questions may have an alcohol problem—but even a few affirmative answers may be a sign of serious trouble.

Which one describes you?

Woman to Woman, a women's alcohol-awareness group, defines three levels of alcohol consumption.

◆ Light drinker: one or two drinks a month
◆ Moderate drinker: one or two drinks a few times a week
◆ Heavy drinker: two or more drinks every day

A drink is defined as five ounces of wine, a twelve-ounce can of beer or one and one-half ounces of liquor.[3]

Help for the Compulsive Woman and Her Family

The Dry Drunk

Below is a checklist of symptoms to watch out for in the case of a dry drunk:[4]

1. *Exhaustion,* or allowing yourself to become overly tired or be in poor health. Some alcoholics are also prone to work addictions; perhaps they are in a hurry to make up for lost time. Good health and enough rest are important. If you feel good, you are more apt to think well. If you feel bad, your thinking is apt to deteriorate. Feel bad enough, and you might begin thinking a drink couldn't make it any worse.

2. *Dishonesty.* This begins with a pattern of unnecessary little lies and deceits with fellow workers, friends and family. Then come important lies to yourself. This is called rationalizing—making excuses for not doing what you do not want to do, or for doing what you should not do.

3. *Impatience.* Things are not happening fast enough, or others are not doing what they should or what you do not want them to.

4. *Argumentativeness.* Arguing small and ridiculous points of view indicates a need to always be right. "Why don't you be reasonable and agree with me?" Looking for an excuse to drink?

5. *Depression.* Unreasonable and unaccountable despair may occur in cycles and should be dealt with—talked about.

6. *Frustration* at people and also because things may not be going your way. Remember, everything is not going to go just the way you want it.

7. *Self-pity.* "Why do these things happen to me?" "Why must I be alcoholic?" "Nobody appreciates all I am doing."

8. *Cockiness*...got it made...no longer fear alcoholism... going into drinking situations to prove to others you have no problem. Do this often enough, and it will wear down your defenses.

185

9.	*Complacency.* "Drinking was the farthest thing from my mind." Not drinking was no longer a conscious thought either. It is dangerous to let up on disciplines because everything is going well. Always to have a little fear is a good thing. More relapses occur when things are going well than others.

10.	*Expecting too much from others.* "I've changed; why hasn't everyone else?" It's a plus if they do—but it is still not your problem if they do not. They may not trust you yet; they may still be looking for further proof. You cannot expect others to change their lifestyles just because you have.

11.	*Letting up on disciplines,* such as prayer, meditation, daily inventory, alcohol support group attendance. This can stem from either complacency or boredom. You cannot afford to be bored with your program. The cost of relapse is always too great.

12.	*Use of mood-altering chemicals.* You may feel the need to ease things with a pill, and your doctor may go along with you. You may never have had a problem with chemicals other than alcohol, but you can easily lose sobriety starting this way—about the most subtle way to have a relapse. Remember, you will be cheating! The reverse of this is true for drug-dependent persons who start to drink.

13.	*Wanting too much.* Do not set goals you cannot reach with normal effort. Do not expect too much. It's always great when good things you were not expecting happen. You will get what you are entitled to as long as you do your best, but maybe not as soon as you think you should. "Happiness is not having what you want, but wanting what you have."

14.	*Forgetting gratitude.* You may be looking negatively on your life, concentrating on problems that still are not totally corrected. Nobody wants to be a Pollyanna, but it is good to remember where you started from—and how much better life is now.

15. *"It can't happen to me."* This is dangerous thinking. Almost anything can happen to you and is more likely to if you get careless. Remember, you have a progressive disease, and you will be in worse shape if you relapse.

16. *Omnipotence.* This is a feeling that results from a combination of many of the above. You now have all the answers for yourself and others. No one can tell you anything. You ignore suggestions or advice from others. Relapse is probably imminent unless drastic change takes place.

Al-Anon

Al-Anon is a fellowship for the families and friends of alcoholics who need help in understanding and dealing with the alcoholic person. Al-Anon meetings are held weekly in most communities throughout the country. Participants give and receive comfort and encouragement through an honest and open exchange of experiences, strength and hope. Such groups are bonded together by a policy of anonymity.

In Al-Anon sessions people learn:

- Not to suffer because of the actions or reactions of other people

- Not to allow themselves to be used or abused in the interest of another's recovery

- Not to do for others what they should do for themselves

- Not to manipulate situations so others will eat, go to bed, get up, pay bills, etc.

- Not to cover up for another's mistakes or misdeeds

- Not to create a crisis

- Not to prevent a crisis if it is in the natural course of events

This kind of detachment is neither kind nor unkind. It does not imply evaluation of the person or situation from which one is detaching. It is simply a means for individuals to recover from the adverse affects on their lives of living with someone afflicted with the disease of alcoholism.

Detachment helps families look at their situations realistically and objectively, thereby making an intelligent decision possible. For further information, write to:

Al-Anon Family Group Headquarters, Inc.
P. O. Box 682, Mid-Town Station
New York, NY 10018-0862
212-302-7240
800-356-9996
www.al-anon.org

For an intervention specialist, write:

Families in Crisis, Inc.
P. O. Box 25
Killeen, TX 76540
254-634-1184 or 254-773-7765
254-526-6111 (fax)
24-hour hotline: 888-799-SAFE
www.familiesincrisis.net

Adult Children of Alcoholics (ACOA)

Following are questions for family members of alcoholics:

1. Do you lose sleep because of a problem drinker?

2. Do most of your thoughts revolve around the problem drinker or problems that arise because of him or her?

3. Do you exact promises about the drinking that are not kept?

4. Do you make threats to a drinker in the family and not follow through on them?

5. Has your attitude fluctuated toward this problem drinker (alternating between love and hate)?

6. Do you mark, hide, dilute and/or empty bottles of liquor or medication?

7. Do you think that everything would be OK if only the problem drinker would stop or control the drinking?

8. Do you feel alone, fearful, anxious, angry or frustrated most of the time? Are you beginning to feel dislike for yourself and to wonder about your sanity?

9. Do you feel responsible and guilty about the drinking problem?

10. Do you find *your* moods fluctuating widely as a direct result of the problem drinker's moods and actions?

11. Do you try to conceal, deny or protect the drinking problem?

12. Have you withdrawn from outside activities and friends because of embarrassment and shame over the drinking problem?

13. Have you taken over many chores and duties that you would normally expect the problem drinker to assume?

14. Do you feel forced to try to exert tight control over the family expenses with less and less success? Are financial problems increasing?

15. Do you feel the need to justify your actions and attitudes and, at the same time, feel somewhat smug and self-righteous when you compare yourself to the drinker?

16. If there are children in the house, do they often take sides with either the problem drinker or the spouse?

17. Are the children showing signs of emotional stress, such as withdrawal, having trouble with authority figures or rebelling?

18. Have you noticed physical symptoms in yourself, such as nausea, a knot in the stomach, ulcers, shakiness, sweating palms or bitten fingernails?

19. Do you feel utterly defeated, that nothing you can say or do will move the problem drinker?

20. Where this applies, is your sexual relationship with a problem drinker affected by the feelings of revulsion? Do you "use" sex to manipulate, or refuse sex to punish him or her?

A *yes* to any five of these questions probably indicates that alcoholism exists in the family and is producing negative changes in the person answering them.

The Bill of Rights for Adult Children of Alcoholics

I have the right…

1. To make other choices besides the choice merely to run away

2. To say *no* when I feel unready or unsafe

3. Not to be molested by fear

4. To feel all feelings

5. To believe I'm probably not guilty

6. To make mistakes

7. Not to smile when I cry or feel hurt

8. To terminate conversations with those who put me down or humiliate me

9. To be healthier than those around me

10. To change and grow

11. To be relaxed, playful and frivolous

12. To set limits and to be selfish

13. To get angry, even at someone I love, without fearing that I, the other person or the relationship will dissolve

14. To do stupid things without believing I am a stupid person

15. Not to be ashamed for what I don't know or can't do

Help for the Compulsive Woman and Her Family

Adult children of alcoholics can obtain help by attending Al-Anon and ACOA (Adult Children of Alcoholics) meetings if they need to understand more about their relationship to alcoholics. A telephone directory or local newspaper can provide local numbers to call for further information.

Drug Dependency

There are nine substances that have destroyed the lives of millions of people. Here are some of the facts about them:[5]

Cocaine

- Causes heart palpitations, which can become chronic and can cause death by cardiac arrest. Increases the pulse rate and blood pressure by constricting the blood vessels and accelerating the heart. This can result in stroke.

- Causes epileptic seizures.

- Causes chronic fatigue and exhaustion resulting in mood swings, depression, paranoia, irritability and suicidal tendencies.

- Brings on a hard-hitting "crash" as the drug's effect wears off, causing a strong desire to take more cocaine for relief.

- Invites other addictions. Cocaine abuses often depend on alcohol, marijuana or heroin to help them sleep or to combat the jittery feeling that characterizes the cocaine high.

- Causes sexual problems. Habitual cocaine use causes a chronic loss of interest in sex as well as impairment of sexual performance.

Alcohol

- Causes birth defects. Babies of mothers who drink during pregnancy are likely to be small and have facial deformities

◈ Causes damage to both the liver and pancreas, which hinders digestion and upsets blood sugar balance.

◈ Changes the metabolism of some heart cells, which can cause fibrillation (uncontrolled fluttering of the heart), arrhythmia (disturbance in the heart's rhythm) and possibly heart attack.

◈ Enlarges red blood cells, causing high blood pressure.

◈ Alters the hormone balance so that the body is in a state of permanent stress; disrupts the menstrual cycle.

◈ Causes slurred speech, disorientation, lack of coordination and impaired memory, perception and judgment.

LSD

◈ Alters perception and can cause sensory distortions.

◈ Impairs judgment.

◈ With long-term use, can cause "flashbacks": periodic distortions of vision or time perception, as well as period of emotional imbalance and the intrusion of dreamlike states while awake; presumed to be due to permanent damage to certain brain systems.

Club drugs

◈ Club drugs such as Ecstasy, Herbal Ecstasy, Rohypnol, GHB and Ketamine are among the drugs used by teens and young adults who are part of club, bar, rave or trance scene.

◈ Many who attend raves or trances do not use drugs, but those who do may be attracted to the generally low cost, seemingly increased stamina and intoxicating highs that are said to deepen the rave or trance experience.

◈ Recent scientific evidence shows serious damage to several parts of the brain from use of these drugs.

◈ Psychological difficulties can include confusion, depression, sleep deprivation, severe anxiety and paranoia.

- Physical problems can include muscle tension, teeth clenching, nausea, blurred vision, faintness, chills and sweating.

- Heart problems may occur later on from heavy usage.

- Recent research also links Ecstasy use to long-term damage to areas of the brain critical to thought, memory and pleasure.[6]

PCP

- PCP (phenylcyclohexyl piperidine) may cause, in large doses, permanent impairment of brain function, including motor control, memory, concentration and the ability to think clearly. The possibility of permanent brain damage may result.

- Causes visual, auditory and motor disturbances in babies born to mothers who have used PCP. Damage is permanent.

- Brings on a psychotic state resembling schizophrenia, characterized by delusions and hallucinations. Behavior is unpredictable and often violent.

- Decreases sensitivity to pain. Users run the risk of serious and sometimes fatal injuries (such as by sticking a hand in a fire) because they don't feel the pain.

- Induces a catatonic state in which the user stares mutely into space, seeming oblivious to others and unable to communicate.

Marijuana

- Causes behavior and reproducing problems, delayed puberty and birth defects in the offspring of parents who smoke it.

- Weakens the immune system. Researchers are now investigating whether those who smoke marijuana may be more vulnerable to AIDS if exposed to the virus.

◆ Causes lung damage similar to that from cigarettes; contains powerful carcinogens.

◆ Impairs psychomotor function, such as driving.

◆ Impairs short-term memory, learning and the ability to learn and comprehend.

Heroin

◆ Depresses the central nervous system, causing slurred speech, clumsy movement and drowsiness.

◆ Slows down breathing. In the case of an overdose, this can result in death.

◆ Overdose causes convulsions and coma.

◆ Increase risk of infections such as AIDS, skin abscesses, endocarditis (inflammation of the heart), hepatitis— from contaminated needles (the drug is almost always injected).

Amphetamines

◆ Increase blood pressure and heart rate, which strains the cardiovascular system and could result in heart attack or stroke.

◆ May cause "mini-strokes" on the brain's surface, in which small portions of the brain die—particularly when the drug is injected.

◆ Cause a condition known as "amphetamine psychosis," similar to paranoid schizophrenia. It's a result of over-stimulation of the same brain systems that cause insomnia. The person may hear imaginary threatening voices and can commit violent acts to defend himself.

◆ Bring on a severe crash when the drug's effects wear off, characterized by depression and irritability.

Barbiturates

◆ Combine synergistically with both alcohol and antihistamines, causing a loss of concentration, coordination and control, and increasing the chance of overdose death.

- Cause anemia, probably because of toxic effects on the liver.

- Prompt rapid tolerance, requiring larger and larger doses to get the same effect, though the lethal does remains constant. Cause lethargy and sleep in mild doses; overdoses lower body temperature, cause lungs to fill with fluid and can bring about coma and death.

- Result in serious addiction. Withdrawal from barbiturates can be fatal, probably because barbiturates interfere with the brain's ability to coordinate many different functions.

Seven dos and don'ts for parents of children on drugs[7]

1. *Be passive.* Don't enter into one-on-one confrontations and conflicts with the youngster. You are dealing with a competitor that can't be beat.

2. *Don't feel compelled to act as a parent should.* Parent/child rules don't apply during this time. You are dealing with a sick person who is in a frenzied emotional state. Normal parental rules and patterns can't work.

3. *Don't use or listen to negative messages.* Detach yourself. Don't participate in name-calling. It's destructive and weakens everyone's self-image. Resist the normal impulse to defend yourself against accusations the teen makes about you.

4. *Don't be angry when your child doesn't show love and concern.* During this time, your child is incapable of displaying genuine emotions. Be responsible first for your own behavior. Don't return useless anger, judgmental resentment and name-calling. Show concern and sympathy, but don't try to cover up or aid the drug-user's addiction. The individual is sick. Don't become sick along with him. Remember your child needs your

unconditional love and support when he or she is the least lovable.

5. *Don't give the teenager anything destructive.* Don't give financial or emotional support if it will be used in a negative way. Be tough in your loving.

6. *Take care of yourself.* Set goals and achieve them. Don't let your teenager be an excuse for your own poor achievement and laziness. Maintain your own health and mental and spiritual well-being.

7. *Go outside the family for help.* City, township and country groups, your local hospital or substance-abuse treatment center, schools and clergy can provide information and support.

For further information, you can contact the following:

The National Institute on Drug Abuse
6001 Executive Boulevard, Room 5213
Bethesda, MD 20892-9561
800-662-HELP
www.drugabuse.gov

Partnership for a Drug-Free America
405 Lexington Ave., Suite 1601
New York, NY 10174
212-922-1560
212-922-1570 (fax)
www.drugfreeamerica.org

Narcotics Anonymous (NA)

This fellowship of men and women is for those for whom drugs have become a major problem. It is a program of complete abstinence from all drugs. There is only one requirement for membership: the desire to stop using. Those who enroll in the NA program make the following admissions:

We admit we could not manage our own lives. We could not live and enjoy life as other people do. We had to have something different, and we thought we had found it in drugs. We placed their use ahead of the welfare of our families, our wives, husbands and our children. We had to have drugs at all costs. We did many people great harm, but most of all we harmed ourselves. Through our inability to accept personal responsibilities, we were actually creating our own problems. We seemed to be incapable of facing life on its own terms.

Most of us realized that in our addiction we were slowly committing suicide, but addiction is such a cunning enemy of life that we had lost the power to do anything about it. May of us ended up in jail, or sought help through medicine, religions and psychiatry. None of these methods was sufficient for us. Our disease always resurfaced or continued to progress; until in desperation, we sought help from each other in Narcotics Anonymous.

After coming to NA we realized we were sick people. We suffered from a disease from which there is no known cure. It can, however, be arrested at some point, and recovery is then possible.

If you want what we have to offer, and are willing to make the effort to get it, then you are ready to come to grips with the Twelve-Step program used by Alcoholics Anonymous.

What can defeat us in our recovery is an attitude of indifference or intolerance toward spiritual principles. Three of these that are indispensable are honesty, open-mindedness and willingness. With these we are well on our way.

Anonymity is the spiritual fountain of all our traditions, ever reminding us to place principles before personalities.[8]

For further information contact:

Narcotics Anonymous, World Service Office, Inc.
P. O. Box 9999
Van Nuys, CA 91409
818-773-9999
818-700-0700 (fax)
www.narcoticsanonymous.com

U.S. Department of Health and Human Services
Substance Abuse and Mental Health Services Administration
National Drug and Alcohol Treatment Referral Service of the
    Center for Substance Abuse Treatment

800-662-HELP (4357)
www.drughelp.org

Cocaine Anonymous, World Services Office
3740 Overland Ave., Suite C
Los Angeles, CA 90034
310-559-5833
www.ca.org
cawso@ca.org

Eating Disorders

My problem with overeating and eating the wrong foods (especially too many sweets) began in childhood and continues to this day. When I wrote an article on compulsive behavior for *Charisma* magazine in 1985, I included in it my struggle to control my food intake.

Anorexia nervosa

The name literally means "nervous loss of appetite," but it is a misnomer. People with anorexia are, in fact, suppressing a constant desire to eat for fear of becoming fat. In anorexia, food and weight are not the issue, but merely symptoms of an underlying problem or problems: low self-esteem, poor conflict resolution skills, overwhelming feelings of body dissatisfaction and extreme perfectionism.

Anorexia is a dangerous eating disorder in that in can result in death, as in the case of singer Karen Carpenter. Other adverse physical effects include loss of menstruation, constipation, low sex drive, low blood sugar, receding gums and rotting teeth, dizziness, lack of protein (leading to loss of hair), intestinal infection, hypoglycemia, ruptured stomach and esophagus, chronic sinusitis, kidney damage, severe dehydration, bleeding and infection of the throat, gastritis, ulcers, abnormal metabolism, vaginal nerve block, rupturing of internal membranes, bowel tumors, rupture of facial blood vessels, severe electrolyte imbalance (which can lead to neuromuscular problems, including muscle spasms and cardiac arrest) and depression.[9]

Bulimia

A variation of anorexia, bulimia ranges from excessive food intake to an out-of-control, compulsive cycle of binge eating where extraordinary amounts of any available food, usually with a high carbohydrate content, may be consumed. It is usually accompanied with purging the food from the system by use of diuretics or laxatives of by vomiting.[10]

Danger signals for eating disorders

- Changes in eating habits
- Changes in general behavior
- Physical changes
- Psychological changes
- Constant talk about food
- Development of rituals around eating
- Consumption of diet soda
- Compulsive exercise
- Increasing social isolation

Survival tips for families

Here are some things that you can do to help a loved one who is suffering from an eating disorder. We have also included a list of things that you should avoid doing.[11]

- Asking yourself "What have I done wrong?" is natural for parents; however, remember there are no perfect parents. You have done the very best you can under the circumstances. Once you have taken the steps for her to take recovery (i.e., medical and psychological help) getting well is her responsibility.

- Educate yourself and other family members about eating disorders.

- Attend a support group; get advice from others who care and can help.

- Remember, that families neither cause nor cure eating disorders.

- Write down specific instances of disordered eating you have noticed.

- Communicate directly to the person the seriousness of your concern, your conviction that treatment is necessary and your willingness to provide emotional, financial and other practical support.

◆ You may say that she needs to eat, rather than if she eats she will look better.

◆ Be aware of the perfectionist tendencies of the individual with the eating disorder.

◆ Keep your regular schedule as much as possible (i.e., eating times, going out as a couple or with friends).

◆ Remember that anyone can feel worthwhile when they are loved; make sure this is evident to your child or friend.

◆ Realize the importance of patience; recovery is a gradual process.

Overeaters Anonymous (OA)

Overeaters Anonymous is a fellowship of men and women from all walks of life who meet in order to help solve a common problem— compulsive overeating. The only requirement for membership is a desire to stop eating compulsively.

Variants of the disorder include the food abuser who has no apparent weight problem and is often quite underweight, but who maintains this by eating and vomiting, a practice called bulimia. Another extreme is a form of self-starvation, which results in anorexia.

Overeaters Anonymous has no religious requirement, affiliation or orientation. The Twelve-Step program of recovery is considered "spiritual" because it deals with inner change. OA has members of many different religious beliefs as well as some atheists and agnostics.[12]

To contact Overeaters Anonymous or other eating disorder support groups, look in your local telephone directory and/or your local newspaper's social or calendar section. Or write:

Overeaters Anonymous, Inc.
World Service Office
P. O. Box 44020
Rio Rancho, NM 87174-4020
505-891-2664

505-891-4320 (fax)

www.oa.org

info@overeatersanonymous.org

Domestic Violence

What is domestic violence?

The terminology can sometimes be confusing. *Domestic violence, family violence, spouse abuse, wife abuse, wife assault and woman battering* are all often used to mean the same thing. *Family violence* includes all forms of violence within families: children being harmed by their parents or caregivers, children being harmed by older siblings or members of extended family networks, women being harmed by women, and older family members being harmed by their offspring. In fact, it includes any type of violence occurring in any type of family.

Domestic violence is commonly used to describe the abuse women suffer at the hands of their male partners. Sometimes, however, *domestic violence* is also used to mean family violence. Because of this confusion, *spouse abuse* and *wife assault* are used to define more clearly the exact nature of the violence.[13]

What kinds of behavior does domestic violence include?

- **Physical abuse:** This can range from pushing and slapping to punching, hitting, shoving, pulling hair, twisting limbs, choking, breaking bones, etc. It can also include killing family pets, breaking household goods and causing property damage. It involves the use of weapons/firearms, denial of basic human needs such as food, sleep, medical care and money and any acts of violence that are designed to control, hurt, harm or otherwise physically assault a partner.

- **Verbal/emotional abuse:** Any action that is intended to degrade, humiliate and demean, both in pubic or private, including threats to injure or otherwise harm the partner or the children, is considered abuse. This includes blackmail; putting one's partner down and making them feel bad about themselves and their abilities; treating one's partner like a servant; abuser making

201

decisions regarding partner's financial status, free time, friendship, work and leisure activities.

◆ **ECONOMIC ABUSE:** Economic abuse occurs when the abusive partner controls and limits access to the family income, thus forcing the abused partner to be dependent on the abuser for money and survival.

◆ **SEXUAL ABUSE:** This includes any attempt to force a partner to have sex or perform sexual acts against their will. Physically attacking the sexual parts of a partner's body; treating a partner like a sexual object; making demeaning and humiliating sexual comments or jokes; threatening physical violence should partner not comply with sexual demands—these all comprise sexual abuse.

◆ **SOCIAL ABUSE:** This occurs when the abuser enforces social isolation or social control, preventing the abused partner from having any social contact with friends and/or relatives. The abuser limits what the partner does, whom they see, what they read, where they go, etc.

Violence-related injuries treated in hospital emergency departments

A study of violence-related injuries treated in hospital emergency departments was conducted in 1994 using the Consumer Product Safety Commission's National Electronic Injury Surveillance System (NEISS) program. The study found that 1.4 million persons were treated in hospital emergency departments in 1994 for injuries inflicted in confirmed or suspected interpersonal violence. Of these, 243,000 were afflicted by someone with whom the victim had an intimate relationship (spouse, ex-spouse, current or former boyfriend or girlfriend), an estimate four times higher than the equivalent estimate from the National Crime Victimization Survey.[14]

Are you or is someone you know being emotionally or physically abused? If you answer *yes* to several of the following questions, we urge you to call and get help.[15]

◆ Does your partner shove, hit, shake or slap you?

◆ Does your partner make light of the abuse, insist that it didn't happen or shift the responsibility for his/her abusive behavior, blaming you for it?

- Does your partner continually put you down, call you names or humiliate you?

- Does your partner intimidate you through looks or actions, destroy your property or display weapons?

- Does your partner control what you do, whom you see and talk to, and where you go, limiting your involvement outside the relationship?

- Are you made to feel guilty about the children, or has your partner threatened to take the children away?

For family and friends....

- Does she appear anxious, depressed, withdrawn and reluctant to talk?

- Does her partner criticize her in front of you, making remarks that make you feel uncomfortable when you're around the two of them?

- Do you see or hear about repeated bruises, broken bones or other injuries that reportedly result from "accidents"?

- Does her partner try to control her every move, make her account for her time and accuse her of having affairs?

- Is she often late or absent from work? Has she quit a job altogether, or does she leave social engagements early because her partner is waiting for her?

The National Domestic Violence Hotline answers about ten thousand calls each month from those experiencing domestic violence, as well as their family and friends. They provide callers with intervention, information about domestic violence and referrals to local programs twenty-four hours a day, seven days a week in many languages.

You can contact the National Domestic Violence Hotline at:

National Domestic Violence Hotline
P. O. Box 16180
Austin, TX 78716
800-799-SAFE (7233); 800-787-3224 (TDD)
www.ndvh.org

Bipolar Disorder/Manic Depression

Bipolar disorder, often called manic depression, is one of the major mood disorders and is distinguished by behavior that fluctuates from extreme highs (mania) to serious lows (depression) interspersed with periods of "normal" mood. Mania is a term used a lot these days (like "basketball mania"), but in medicine, mania refers to behavior that includes profuse and rapidly changing ideas, exaggerated sexuality, extreme gaiety, intense irritability and decreased sleep.

In 1994 I was diagnosed with bipolar disorder. Medications were prescribed at that time. They were effective, and my recovery was going well. But, like many manic-depressives, when I started to feel really well, I arbitrarily took myself off my medications. Not a good idea! The subsequent emotional spiral was horrendous. As one who has had to pay the price for being my own physician, all I can say is, "I had a fool for a patient." Stay on your medications until such time as your doctor releases you to discontinue their use.

The word *depression* is used frequently to describe a feeling of sadness. With bipolar disorder, however, the lows of depression are characterized by extreme hopelessness and a feeling of worthlessness accompanied by thoughts of suicide.

Manic depression typically begins in adolescence or early adulthood and continues throughout life. Because manic and depressive episodes may be less extreme in the early stages, or if a person has periods of mild mania, the disorder, unfortunately, is often not recognized for years or even decades.

Becoming familiar with the facts of this disorder will help you or someone you love from suffering needlessly. Effective treatments greatly alleviate the suffering caused manic depression and can usually prevent its devastating complications.

◆   Two million Americans suffer from manic depression.

- Bipolar disorder affects women and men almost equally.

- Bipolar disorder tends to run in families and may be inherited.

- Family members of people with bipolar disorder also suffer.

- Bipolar disorder is characterized by extreme highs and lows.

- Only about one-third of those suffering with bipolar disorder seek treatment.[16]

DEPRESSION

Depression is the most common mental health concern in our country today. Depression is considered the world's number one health problem. Statistics indicate that depression affects more than 19 million Americans each year, with a significant increase since September 11, 2001.[17] If you are one of those statistics, be encouraged and know that there is hope and help!

All of a sudden you wake up one morning, and it's there. Those feelings of sadness and anxiety seem overwhelming. Your sleep patterns change, and you begin to lose interest in everything; consequently you either gain weight rapidly due to lack of exercise or you loose weight because even food does not sound good to you. You can't concentrate or make decisions, and you are always tired and run down. If left unchecked, you may start thinking that tell you're worthless and the world would be better off without you. You don't have to stay there any longer.

Women experience depression at roughly twice the rate of men.[18] Girls fourteen to eighteen years of age have consistently higher rates of depression than boys in this age group.[19] Contributing factors to depression in women include:

- Developmental, reproductive, hormonal, genetic and other biological differences (e.g., premenstrual syndrome, childbirth, infertility and menopause)

- Social factors may also lead to higher rates of clinical

depression among women, including stress from work, family responsibilities, the roles and expectations of women and increased rates of sexual abuse and poverty.

Marriage and childbirth can affect depression. Married people have a lower rate of depression than those living alone. However, unhappily married people have the highest rates of depression; happily married men have the lowest rates.[20]

Postpartum depression affects approximately 10 to 15 percent of new mothers, most frequently occurring within the first year after the birth of a child.[21]

According to a National Mental Health Association survey on public attitudes and beliefs about clinical depression:

- More than one-half of women believe it is normal for a woman to be depressed during menopause and that treatment is not necessary.

- More than one-half of women believe depression is a normal part of aging.

- More than one-half believe it is normal for a mother to feel depressed for at least two weeks after giving birth.

- More than one-half of women cited denial as a barrier to treatment, while 41 percent of women surveyed cited embarrassment or shame as barriers to treatment.

- In general, over one-half of the women said they "know" more about depression than men do.

Here are some informational statistics about depression:

- Approximately 12 million women in the United States experience clinical depression each year.[22]

- About one in every eight women can expect to develop clinical depression during her lifetime.[23]

- Depression occurs most frequently in women aged twenty-five to forty-four.[24]

- Depression in women is misdiagnosed approximately 30 to 50 percent of the time.[25]

Help for the Compulsive Woman and Her Family

- Fewer than half of the women who experience clinical depression will ever seek help.[26]

Don't be embarrassed or afraid to ask for help! Here is a list of suggestions that you can implement into your daily life to help yourself.

- Live in the present and leave the past in the past.

- Don't compare yourself to anyone else. You are you.

- Replace those negative scenarios with positive thoughts.

- Accept all basic parts of yourself.

- Rent some comedies and get some good belly laughs going.

- Take care of your own needs and stop putting yourself on hold.

- Make reality a focus every single day.

- Fill up your time with good deeds for other people.

- Keep up the maintenance when the depression lifts.

The best way to climb out of depression is to give yourself away to others. Even when you don't feel like it, send a card to someone who is seriously ill, take a "positive" friend out to lunch, go to the circus or carnival with your niece or nephew or bake a cake for your neighbor. Get out of yourself and invest yourself in someone else. The more you do it, the better you will feel.

How you take care of your depression is totally up to you. But you need to know that with the wide variety of options in the professional field of mental health today, your recovery is almost 100 percent guaranteed. Whether you choose a psychiatrist, psychologist, family doctor, clinical social worker, pastoral counselor, psychiatric nurse or licensed counselor, you can be smiling again in no time.

POSTPARTUM DEPRESSION

Having a baby changes everything. A woman's body changes drastically. Her personal history and feelings about parenting can bring up very powerful emotions. The family may be financially strained. Social pressures may be mounting.

The majority of research into the condition shows that, for about 10 to 15 percent of women and more than a fourth of all adolescent mothers, childbirth results in postnatal depression.[27]

Characteristics of postpartum depression:

- It lasts more than two or three weeks.

- It begins weeks or months after the new baby arrives.

- It is more than anxiety. A woman with postnatal depression may believe that there is something truly wrong with her abilities as a mother. She may start to distance herself from the baby. A woman who suffers from postpartum psychosis may completely lose touch with reality, experiencing hallucinations and delusions.

- Usually, symptoms are evident the first four to twelve weeks after postpartum, but they can appear up to ninety days after delivery, and in some cases, eighteen to twenty-four months after the baby comes.

- The postpartum psychosis frequently includes hallucinations and delusions, usually with a focus on the basis or being divine or demonic. Some may hear voices telling her to hurt herself or others. This is the point of the highest risk for committing infanticide and/or suicide.

Postpartum psychosis symptoms include:

- Hyperactivity
- An increased rate of speech
- Delusions
- Paranoia
- Extreme confusion
- Hallucinations
- Extreme depression

This level of disorder often includes bipolar brain disorder. Please consult a physician if your are experiencing any of the above symptoms.[28]

Post-Abortion Stress Syndrome

According to reports of the Department of Education and the Alan Guttmacher Institute, By the age of forty-five, 43 percent of women in the United States have had at least one abortion. Ninety-one percent suffer from post-abortion trauma. As many as 91 percent of all abortions cause severe psychological problems, both immediate and long-term.

Anxiety, depression, regret, anger, a deep sense of loss, guilt, crying, nightmares, marital problems, difficulty sleeping, flashbacks, hopelessness, psychotic reactions and loss of self-image were all cited as directly resulting from abortion.

Women who have had an abortion claimed they were misinformed of the long-term affects of the possibility of miscarriages, sterility or post-abortion trauma. Almost one out of four women study specifically complained that they had been either misled or misinformed about abortion by clinic personnel. In one case a woman was told, "Don't think of it as killing but as taking blood out of your uterus to get your periods going again."[29]

Please read through the survey below to see if you are suffering from post-abortion stress syndrome. If you are, please seek professional help.

- Are you affected by physical reminders of your abortion (babies, pregnant women, etc.)? Are you uncomfortable around pregnant women or children?

- Does the sight of blood bother you more than it might have in the past?

- Did you or would you lie about having an abortion or the number of abortions you've had to a doctor, or to family or friends? For example, not telling or denying you've had abortion, or saying it was a "miscarriage," or saying it was for "medical reasons," when it wasn't?

- Are you bothered by certain sounds, like vacuum cleaners or other machinery that make loud noises?

- Are there certain times of the year you find yourself depressed, sick or accident-prone, especially around the anniversary date of the abortion or would-be birth date?

- Are you resentful and unforgiving toward anyone because of his/her involvement or lack of involvement in your abortion—husband, parents, other friends, the medical personnel who performed your abortion?

- Do you have trouble with emotional intimacy or relationships since your abortion? With physical intimacy?

- Do you avoid sex now, or have you had trouble with sex (pain, difficulty with orgasm or enjoyment of sex) since the abortion?

- Do you think about having a "replacement baby," especially with the same man, and think that all the guilt will go away if you get pregnant again and "keep it" this time?

- Are you still in a relationship with the partner you had the abortion with and unwilling to end it because then it would feel like the abortion was "for nothing"?

- Did you marry, or rush into marriage with the man you had the abortion with, to "justify" your abortion?

- Have you experienced periods of prolonged depression since your abortion?

- Have you had any suicidal thoughts or attempts?

- Do you find yourself crying more easily and more frequently than usual?

- Has any drug or alcohol use occurred or become more frequent since the abortion?

- Have you started or increased any self-harming behaviors (cutting, anorexia-bulimia) since the abortion?

- Do you have sleeping problems?

- Do you have trouble with anxiety and/or panic attacks?

- If you have children now, do you smother them with your love or overprotect them, or worry about them being harmed or hurt?

- Do you notice other babies/children, and think that they are "the same age as your aborted child would be right now"?

- (If your abortion was recent) Do you notice pregnant women and judge where they are in their pregnancy, as related to where you would be in yours right now?

- Has your self-concept or self-esteem changed since your abortion?

- Do you have trouble making decisions since the abortion?

- Did your relationship to or concept of "God" change after your abortion?[30]

Teen Depression

Because most depressed teens do no seek help on their own, parents, teachers, school counselors and coaches have to recognize the symptoms and know something about teen suicide facts and signs. Without treatment, the illness can last for weeks, months, years or a lifetime and can have an impact on all aspects of your life.

Yes, teen stress is real. You are physically, emotionally and mentally developing at a very rapid rate; hormones kick in. Parents expect you to make decisions about your future. Pressure to do well in school, to excel at athletics or to put a lot of time into studying and community activities comes from your parents, your teachers and your peers. Social pressures can be intense. Teen stress can cause sleep disturbance, anger, inability to concentrate, nervousness, headaches, nausea, social withdrawal and depression.

Did you know that…

- Each year 500,000 young adults aged fifteen to twenty-five attempt suicide. Each year 5,000 young adults succeed.

- Suicide is the third leading cause of death among fifteen- to twenty-five-year-olds.

- Suicide is the sixth leading cause of death among five- to fourteen-year-olds.

◆ Young adult males succeed at suicide almost two times more as any other group.

◆ Without treatment, of the young adults who attempt suicide, 80 percent will try again.

◆ Teen depression almost always leads to thoughts of suicide.

The following situations indicate that you may be at risk:

◆ Traumatic events or changes in your life (an abusive parent, divorce, death of a loved one, breaking up with a longtime girlfriend or boyfriend, for example)

◆ Difficulty coping with your anger, problems in school

◆ Lifestyle changes such as weight loss, weight gain or difficulty sleeping

◆ A desire to drink alcohol or use drugs

◆ An interest in violence or a growing fear of violence

◆ Cult activity

While teen suicide facts are astounding, here are some positive facts about teen depression and suicide.

◆ The number one cause of suicide is untreated depression.

◆ Most suicidal teens respond positively to psychotherapy and medication.

◆ Nearly 90 percent of depression benefits from medication.

◆ Those contemplating suicide can be "talked out of it."[31]

CLINICAL DEPRESSION/PANIC DISORDER

The onset of panic disorder usually occurs in young adults in their thirties and is more common among women. The first panic attack often occurs in the context of a life-threatening illness/accident, loss of a close relationship or during family separation. Even when these conditions are resolved, the attacks continue. They usually occur when a patient is engaged in a routine activity; they will experience a sudden onset of fear, terror, apprehension and a sense of impending doom. They usually peak at ten minutes and last from five to twenty minutes, rarely lasting more than an hour with the several of the following symptoms:

- Palpitations
- Choking/smothering
- Hot/cold flashes
- Dizziness
- Sweating
- Feeling of unreality
- Faintness
- Fear of dying/going out of control

Anxiety/Panic Disorders

Anxiety disorders are serious medical illnesses that affect approximately 19 million American adults.[32] These disorders fill people's lives with overwhelming anxiety and dear. Unlike the relatively mild, brief anxiety caused by a stressful event such as a business presentation or a first date, anxiety disorders are chronic, relentless and grow progressively worse if not treated.

Effective treatments for anxiety disorders are available, and research is yielding new, improved therapies that can help most people with anxiety disorders lead productive, fulfilling lives. If you think you have an anxiety disorder, you should seek information and treatment.

People with anxiety/panic disorder have feelings of terror that strike suddenly and repeatedly with no warning. They can't predict when an attack will occur, and many develop intense anxiety between episodes, worrying when and where the next one will strike.

If you are having an anxiety/panic attack, most likely your heart will pound; you may feel sweaty, weak, faint or dizzy. Your hands may tingle or feel numb, and you might feel flushed or chilled. You may have nausea, chest pain or smothering sensations, a sense of unreality or fear of impending doom or loss of control.

You may genuinely believe you are having a heart attack or losing your mind, or on the verge of death. Some people's lives become so restricted that they avoid normal, everyday activities such as grocery shopping or driving. In some cases they become house bound.

Anxiety/panic disorder is one of the most treatable of the anxiety disorders, responding to most medications and or psychotherapy.

Obsessive-Compulsive Disorder (OCD)

OCD involves anxious thoughts or rituals you feel you can't control. If you have OCD, you may be plagued by persistent, unwelcome thoughts or images, or by an urgent need to engage in certain rituals. You may be obsessed with germs or dirt, so you wash your hands over and over. You may be filled with doubt and feel the need to check things repeatedly. You may have frequent thoughts of violence and fear you will harm people close to you. You may spend long periods of touching things or counting. You may be preoccupied by order or symmetry, or you may be troubled by thoughts that are against your religious beliefs.

The OCD person is not likely to be addicted to alcohol, sex, gambling or food—which all include an element of real enjoyment. In contrast, the OCD gets no pleasure from the dreary, often despised rituals he's driven senselessly to perform.

The disturbing thoughts or images are called "obsessions," and the rituals that are performed to try to prevent or get rid of them are called "compulsions." There is no pleasure in carrying out the rituals you are drawn to, only temporary relief from the anxiety that grows when you don't perform them. OCD affects about 3.3 million adult Americans. Research evidence suggests OCD might ruin families. OCD generally responds well to treatment or medications and carefully targeted psychotherapy.

If you think that you have OCD, you should seek the help of a mental health professional. Family physicians, clinics and health maintenance organizations may be able to provide a treatment or make referrals to mental health centers and specialists. Also, the department of psychiatry at a major medical center or the department of psychology at a university may have specialists who are knowledgeable about the treatment of OCD and are able to provide therapy or recommend another doctor in the area.

Here are twelve signals to help you recognize that a person is having problems. Remember, it is not "just their personality." Changes are gradual yet significant.

1. Withdrawal

214

2. Doing things again and again—repetitive behaviors

3. Constant questioning of own judgement, need for constant reassurance

4. Simple tasks taking longer than usual

5. Increased fatigue

6. Perpetual tardiness

7. Increased concern for minor things and details

8. Severe and extreme emotional reactions to small things

9. Inability to sleep properly

10. Significant change in eating patterns

11. Daily life becomes a struggle

12. Avoidance[33]

For further information on obsessive-compulsive disorder and its treatment, contact:

Obsessive-Compulsive Foundation, Inc.
337 Notch Hill Road
North Branford, CT 06471
203-315-2193
203-315-2196 (fax)
www.ocfoundation.org
info@ocfoundation.org

Posttraumatic Stress Disorder

Posttraumatic stress disorder (PTSD) is a psychiatric disorder that can occur following a tragic event such as what happened on September 11, 2001, or witnessing life-threatening events such as military combat, natural disasters, terrorist incidents, serious accidents, abuse (sexual, physical, emotional, ritual) and violent personal assaults like rape. Often people with PTSD have persistent frightening nightmares and flashbacks, have difficulty sleeping, and feel detached or estranged; these symptoms can be severe enough and last long enough to significantly impair the person's daily life.

PTSD is marked by clear biological changes as well as psychological changes and symptoms. It is complicated by the fact that it frequently occurs in conjunction with related disorders such as depression, substance abuse, problems of memory and cognition, and other problems of physical and mental health. Many suffering from this disorder have difficulty functioning in a social or family life. These difficulties may include occupational instability, marital problems and divorces, family discord and difficulties in parenting.

About 3.6 percent of U.S. adults ages eighteen to fifty-four (5.2 million people) have PTSD during the course of a given year. Thirty percent of the men and women who have spent time in war zones experience PTSD. One million war veterans developed PTSD after serving in Vietnam. PTSD has also been detected among veterans of the Persian Gulf War some estimates running as high as 8 percent.

PTSD can develop at any age, including childhood. Symptoms typically begin within three months of a traumatic event, although occasionally they do not begin until years later. If you believe you are suffering from posttraumatic stress disorder, see your doctor or a clinical psychologist for help.[34]

For more information about posttraumatic stress disorder and other anxiety disorders, contact:

> National Institute of Mental Health
> NIMH Public Inquiries
> 6001 Executive Blvd., Room 8184, MSC 9663
> Bethesda, MD 20892-9663
> 301-443-4513
> 301-443-4279 (fax)
> www.nimh.nih.gov
> nimhinfo@nih.gov

Managing traumatic stress: Tips for recovering from disasters and other traumatic events

The terrorist attacks on September 11, 2001 were the type of events we thought could never happen. Like other types of disasters, they were unexpected, sudden and overwhelming. In some cases, there were no outwardly visible signs of physical injury, but there is nonetheless a serious emotional toll. It is common for people who have experienced traumatic situations to have very strong emotional reactions. Understanding normal responses to these abnormal events can assist you in coping effectively with your feelings, thoughts and behaviors. It can also help you along the path to recovery.

Shock and denial are typical responses to terrorism, disasters and other types of trauma, especially shortly after the event. Both shock and denial are normal protective reactions. Shock is a sudden and often-intense disturbance of your emotional state that may leave you feeling stunned or dazed. Denial means that you not acknowledging that something very stressful has happened, or you are not experiencing fully the intensity of the event. You may temporarily feel numb or disconnected from life.

As the initial shock subsides, reactions vary from one person to another. The following, however, are normal responses to a traumatic event:

- Feelings become intense and sometimes are unpredictable. You may be more irritable than usual, and your mood may change dramatically. You might be especially anxious or nervous, or even become depressed.

- Thoughts and behavior patterns are affected by the trauma. You might have repeated and vivid memories of the event. These flashbacks may occur for no apparent reason and lead to physical reactions such as rapid heartbeat or sweating, You may find it difficult to concentrate or make decisions or become more easily confused. Sleep and eating patterns may be disrupted.

- Recurring emotional reactions are common. Anniversaries of the event, such as at one month or one year, as well as reminders such as aftershocks from earthquakes or the sounds of sirens, can trigger upsetting memories of the traumatic experience. These "triggers" may be accompanied by fears that the stressful event will be repeated.

- Interpersonal relationships often become strained. Greater conflict, such as more frequent arguments with family members and coworkers, is common. On the other hand, you might become withdrawn and isolated and avoid your usual activities.

◈ Physical symptoms may accompany the extreme stress. For example, headaches, nausea or chest pain may result and may require medical attention. Preexisting medical conditions may worsen due to the stress.

There are a number of steps you can take to help restore emotional well-being and a sense of control following a terrorist act, a disaster or other traumatic experiences, including the following:

◈ Give yourself time to heal. Anticipate that this will be a difficult time in your life, and allow yourself to mourn the losses you have experienced. Try to be patient with changes in your emotional state.

◈ Ask for support from people who care about you and who will listen and empathize with your situation. But keep in mind that your typical support system may be weakened if those who are close to you also have experienced or witnessed the trauma.

◈ Communicate your experience in whatever ways feel comfortable to you, such as talking with family or close friends or keeping a diary.

◈ Find out about local support groups that are available, such as groups for those who have suffered from natural disasters, for women who are victims of rape. These can be especially helpful with limited personal support systems.

◈ Try to find groups led by trained and experienced professionals. Group discussions can help people realize that other individuals in the same circumstances often have similar reactions and emotions.

◈ Engage in healthy behaviors to enhance your ability to cope with excessive stress. Eat well-balanced meals and get plenty of rest. If you experience ongoing difficulties with sleep, you may be able to find some relief through relaxation techniques. Avoid alcohol and drugs.

◈ Avoid major life decisions such as switching careers or

jobs if possible; these activities tend to be highly stressful.

There are also several things parents and those who care for children
can do to help alleviate the emotional consequences of trauma, including the following:

- Spend quality time with children and let them be more
  dependent on you during the months following the
  trauma—for example, allowing your child to cling to
  you more often than usual. Physical affection is very
  comforting to children who have experienced trauma.

- Provide play experiences to help relieve tension.
  Younger children in particular may find it easier to
  share their ideas and feelings about the event through
  nonverbal activities such as drawing.

- Encourage older children to speak with you and with
  one another about their thoughts and feelings. This
  helps reduce confusion and anxiety related to the
  trauma. Respond to questions in terms they can comprehend. Reassure them repeatedly that you care about
  them and that you understand their fears and concerns.

- Keep regular schedules for activities such as eating,
  playing and going to bed to help restore a sense of
  security and normalcy.

Individuals who experience prolonged reactions that disrupt their
daily functioning should consult a trained and experienced mental
health professional. Psychologists and other appropriate mental health
providers help educate people about normal responses to extreme stress.
These professionals work with individuals affected by trauma to help
them find constructive ways of dealing with the emotional impact.[35]

Shopaholics

Dos for compulsive shoppers

1. Reduce temptation by reducing the number of your
   credit cards; use only cash.

2. Live on a budget, allowing so much each month for spending.

3. Families should discuss spending problems together and agree on what to buy.

4. When you shop, shop alone. Friends tend to encourage each other to buy.

5. Shop with a list and calculator. Buy only what is on the list. This helps to establish some control over your spending. Plan a nonspending reward for sticking to your list.

6. Avoid sales! Many people buy things impulsively at sales they don't need or even want just to get a bargain.

7. Throw out catalogs immediately. Go directly from the mailbox to the trash can. Catalogs have a way of tempting a person in a weak moment, as do the shopping networks on TV. Change the channel!

8. If you go into debt from shopping, don't hide. Communicate with creditors, explain your debt situation and seek a mutually acceptable schedule of payments.

9. Reward yourself by saving. Put aside money for something you really want, and when you have the cash, go buy it.

Don'ts for compulsive shoppers

1. When you see a sale sign, you don't always have to stop.

2. Remember that if you don't need something, it is not a bargain at any price, even if it is on sale.

3. Limit the cash you take with you on trips. If you have more, you may spend it.

4. Don't add new debts.

5. Don't use credit for small purchases. Pay cash for everything if possible.

Help for the Compulsive Woman and Her Family

Answer the following questions to see if you are a "shopaholic":

1. Is shopping your major form of activity?

2. Do you buy new clothes that sit in the close for weeks or even months before you wear them?

3. Do you spend more than 20 percent of your take-home pay to cover your loans and credit cards?

4. Do you ever pay one line of credit with another?

5. Do you pay only the minimum balance on your charge accounts each month?

6. Do you ever hide your purchases in the car or lie about them so your spouse doesn't know you were shopping?

7. Do you ever lie about how much something cost so your spouse or friends think you were just after a great bargain?

8. Do you buy something just because it's on sale even though you have no use for it?

9. When out with friends for dinner, do you offer to put the check on your credit card so you can collect the cash?

10. Do you feel nervous and guilty after a shopping spree?

11. Is your paycheck often gone on Tuesday when the next payday isn't until Friday?

12. Do you borrow money from friends, even though you know you'll have a hard time paying it back?

13. Do you frequently have to charge small purchases, such as toiletry items and groceries, because you don't have enough in your pocket?

14. Do you think others would be horrified if they knew how much money you spent?

15. Do you often feel hopeless and depressed after spending money?

If you answered *yes* to five or more of these questions, the experts say you have a spending problem and should seek help. Several cities have chapters of *Debtors Anonymous,* an organization for compulsive spenders modeled after Alcoholics Anonymous. You can contact them to see if there is a local chapter in your area at:

Debtors Anonymous
P. O. Box 920888
Needham, MA 02492
781-453-2743
www.debtorsanonymous.org

PERFECTIONISM

Do you feel you must give more than 100 percent on everything you do or else you will be mediocre or even a failure?

If you are a perfectionist, it is likely that you learned early in life that other people valued you because of how much you accomplished or achieved. As a result you may have learned to value yourself only on the basis of other people's approval. Thus your self-esteem may have come to be based primarily on external standards. This often leaves a person vulnerable and excessively sensitive to the opinions and criticism of others. In attempting to protect yourself from such criticism, you may decide that being perfect is your only defense.

A number of the following negative feelings, thoughts and beliefs may be associated with perfectionism:

- Fear of failure. Perfectionists often equate failure to achieve their goals with a lack of personal worth or value.

- Fear of making mistakes. Perfectionists often equate mistakes with failure.

- Fear of disapproval. If they let others see their flaws, perfectionists often fear that they will no longer be accepted. Trying to be perfect is a way of trying to protect themselves from criticism, rejection and disapproval.

- All or none thinking. Perfectionists frequently believe that they are worthless if their accomplishments are not perfect.

- Believing that others are easily successful. Perfectionists tend to perceive others as achieving success with minimum effort, few errors, little emotional stress and maximum self-confidence. At the same time, perfectionists view their own efforts as unending and forever inadequate.

If you want to know what you can do about being a perfectionist, challenge your thoughts and behaviors that fuel perfectionism. Some of the following strategies may help:

- Set realistic goals based on your own wants and needs and what you have accomplished in the past. This will enable you to achieve and also will lead to a greater sense of self-esteem.

- Experiment with your standards for success. Choose any activity, and instead of aiming for 100 percent, try for 90 percent, 80 percent or even 60 percent success. This will help you to realize that the world does not end when you are not perfect.

- Focus on the process of doing an activity, not just the end result.

- Use feelings of anxiety and depression as opportunities to ask yourself, "Have I set up impossible expectations for myself in this situation?"

- Confront the fears that may be behind your perfectionism by asking yourself, "What am I afraid of? What is the worst thing that could happen?"

Once you have tried these suggestions, you are likely to realize that perfectionism is not a helpful or necessary influence in your life. There are alternative ways to think that are more beneficial.[36]

Are you a perfectionist?

Check the following statements that apply to you.

_____ If I can't do a thing exactly right, I won't do it at all.

_____ I often start things I don't finish.

_____ It's hard for me to relax even after my work is done.

_____ I am often amazed at the incompetence of others.

_____ I can't stand it when things are out of place.

_____ I find unpredictability vexing, if not intolerable.

_____ I have a burning need to set things right.

_____ I worry a lot about why I haven't done better.

_____ Any kind of personal failure is the worst thing I can think of.

_____ It seems to me that standards are slipping everywhere.

If you checked more than three of the above, you tend to be a perfectionist, which means you are subject to procrastination, problem-filled relationships and low self-esteem. Extremes of perfectionist behavior can lead to anorexia, bulimia and psychosomatic behavior.

An evaluation

Use the following profiles as an evaluation tool. How many "position statements" can you identify with in each of the four categories? Check those statements that apply to you, then take a look at the scoring.

CARETAKER

_____ I generally feel responsible for the happiness of others.

_____ I have often bent the rules to bail people out of trouble that they brought on themselves.

_____ Sometimes I wonder why so many people lean on me without being sensitive to my need to lean once in a while.

_____ I find it easier to take care of others than to take care of myself.

_____ I never have enough time to accomplish all my tasks.

_____ I am more interested in talking about other people's problems than in talking about my own.

Help for the Compulsive Woman and Her Family

PEOPLE PLEASER

_____ I have trouble saying no even when I know I should.

_____ I often say that it doesn't matter when it really does.

_____ I seldom feel angry, but often feel hurt.

_____ In the name of peace, I try to avoid talking about problems.

_____ I usually feel that other people's needs and opinions are more important than my own.

_____ I often apologize.

_____ I would rather give in than make someone mad.

MARTYR

_____ I am usually willing to do without so others can have what they want.

_____ I feel I have terrible luck.

_____ It feels natural to worry a lot about other people.

_____ My first impulse is to say no when something fun comes up.

_____ When life runs smoothly for a while, I begin to anticipate disaster.

_____ I believe life is a struggle, and I accept suffering as my lot.

TAP DANCER

_____ I find it difficult or impossible to tell anyone the whole truth.

_____ I would rather end a primary relationship than make a binding commitment.

_____ Figuring out what I can get away with is exciting to me.

_____ I have an abiding fear of being caught or concerned.

_____ I always have Plan B in mind in case I need to escape.

_____ To avoid feeling lonely, I have to run farther than I used to.

Remember, no one is perfect. Everyone faces some of these obstacles. Even though we may shake our heads and say, "Oh, no, I'm all of it," the issue is that we can deal with anything we can name. This is not an exercise to see how broken we are, but to understand that if we can identify the obstacles and are willing to work through them, we will increase our ability to "soar like eagles."

Understanding ADHD/ADD

ADHD is a condition of the brain that makes it difficult for children and adults to control their behavior. It is one of the most common chronic conditions of childhood. It affects 4 to 12 percent of school-aged children. About three times more boys than girls are diagnosed with ADHD.

What causes ADHD?

ADHD is one of the most studied conditions of childhood. But the cause of ADHD is still not clear at this time. Your family doctor may refer you and your child to a specialist if these areas of concern are evident:

- Mental retardation

- Developmental disorders such as speech problems, motor problems or a learning difficulty.

- Chronic illness being treated with a medication that may interfere with learning

- Trouble seeing and/or learning

- History of abuse

- Major anxiety or major depression

- Severe aggression

- Possible seizure disorder

Help for the Compulsive Woman and Her Family

Treatment

Treatment for ADHD uses the same principles that are used to treat other chronic conditions like asthma or diabetes. Long-term planning is needed because these conditions continue or recur for a long time. Families must manage them on an ongoing basis.

Educating the people involved about ADHD is a key part of treating you or your child. As a parent, you will need to learn about ADHD. Read and talk to others who understand it about the condition. This will help you manage the ways ADHD affects you, your child and your family.[37]

ADHD criteria

If six or more of the following symptoms of inattention have persisted for at least six months to a degree that is maladaptive and inconsistent with development level, you should seek medical help.[38]

INATTENTION

- Often fails to give close attention to detail or makes careless mistakes in schoolwork and/or in home money management

- Often has difficulty sustaining attention in tasks, recreational activities

- Often does not follow through on instruction and fails to finish schoolwork, household chores or duties in the workplace

- Difficulty organizing tasks and activities

- Avoids, dislikes or is reluctant to engage in tasks that require sustained mental effort

- Loses items necessary for task-oriented assignments

- Forgetful in daily activities

RESTLESSNESS

- Easily distracted, tendency to drift

- Restlessness, constant motion, legs moving, fidgety

- An internal sense of anxiety or nervousness

- Impatient, low frustration tolerance
- Frequent traffic violations
- Tendency to embarrass others
- Lying or stealing on impulse

POOR ORGANIZATION

- Poor organization and planning, trouble maintaining an organized work/living space
- Chronically late or chronically in a hurry
- Often has piles of stuff
- Easily overwhelmed by tasks of daily living

PROBLEMS GETTING STARTED AND FOLLOWING THROUGH

- Chronic procrastination or trouble getting started
- Starting and stopping projects
- Enthusiastic beginnings but poor ending
- Spends excessive time at work because of inefficiencies
- Mood swings
- Chronic low self-esteem
- Negativity/sense of impending doom

RELATIONAL DIFFICULTIES

- Trouble with intimacy/sustaining friendships or intimate relationships
- Immaturity
- Self-centeredness
- Non-communication
- Verbally abusive to others/trouble with authority
- Short fuse
- Sleep deprivation vs, coming out of sleep

- Low energy/feeling tired

- Sensitive to touch, easily startled

If more than twenty items were selected, there is a strong tendency toward ADHD. Clinical studies and field experience have shown the cause of ADHD to be nutritional in nature about 62.5 percent of the time. If you are experiencing any of these symptoms, seek professional help.

TV Addiction

Why does a person become drawn into television viewing and isolated from external experiences? TV addiction has the same interactive nature as other addictions—failure at real-world interactions and the need for comfort and reassurance of a safer alternative (the TV). In other words, no addiction can be described simply by the object of the addiction without directly relating the environment of the addict.

General observations

1. TV addiction (along with obesity and seemingly with all addictions) is always rising in our society, because our worlds are portrayed and perceived as increasingly dangerous, whether crime rates actually go up or down.

2. You can set aside time periods for alternative activities or simply limit time on the TV while finding positive alternatives. Or you can take up a whole new enterprise that simply forbids the great amounts of time of TV watching in which you were engaged. Make it a fixed schedule that brooks no backsliding.

3. TV addiction is fundamentally about an active orientation to life. Addiction is passivity, lack of control (and thus a need for artificial control) and consumption; seeking and obtaining real-world activity and reward.

4. There are oodles of ways to treat non-substance addictions in the U.S., only they're for the most part identical to the Twelve-Step ways we treat every other addictive problem—through prayer and self-abnegation. The

229

issue is really not whether treatment exists, but how to get realistic enough about addictions to prevent treatment for them from being a part of the overall addictive-problem.[39]

Internet Addiction Disorder (IAD)

What most people online who think they are addicted are probably suffering from is the desire to not want to deal with other problems in their lives. Those problems may be a mental disorder (depression, anxiety, etc.) a serious health problem or disability, or a relationship problem. It is no different than turning on the TV so you won't have to talk to your spouse, or going "out with the girls" for a few drinks so you don't have to spend time at home. The only different is the modality (or substance used).[40]

Computer and cyberspace addiction

People who spend time online without any other problems present may suffer from compulsive overuse. But compulsive behaviors are already covered by existing diagnostic categories, and treatment would be similar. It's not the technology (whether it is the Internet, a book, the telephone or the television) that is addicting—it's the behavior. And behaviors are easily treatable by traditional cognitive-behavior techniques in psychotherapy.

Perhaps on a broad level, it makes sense to talk to about a "cyberspace addiction"—an addiction to virtual realms of experience created through computer engineering. Within this broad category may be subtypes with distinct differences. The teenager who plays Donkey Kong may be very different person from the middle-aged housewife who spends 500 hours a month in AOL chat rooms.

Some cyberspace addictions are game- and competition-oriented, some fulfill more social needs, and some simply may be an extension of workaholism. Nevertheless, some people are definitely hurting themselves by their addiction to computers and cyberspace. When people lose their jobs, flunk out of school or are divorced by their spouses because they cannot resist devoting all of their time to virtual lands, they are pathologically addicted. These extreme cases are clear-cut. But as in all addictions, the problem is where to draw the line between "normal" enthusiasm and "abnormal" preoccupation.

Help for the Compulsive Woman and Her Family

Almost anything could be the target of a pathological addiction—drugs, eating, exercising, gambling, sex, spending, working and so forth. You name it, someone out there is obsessed with it. Looking at it from a clinical perspective, these pathological addictions usually have their origin early in a person's life, where they can be traced to significant deprivations and conflicts. They may be an attempt to control depression and anxiety and may reflect deep insecurities and feelings of inner emptiness.

As is true of any official diagnosis, an "Internet Addiction Disorder" or any similarly proposed diagnosis must endure the weight of extensive research. It must meet two basic criteria: Is there a consistent, reliably diagnosed set of symptoms that constitutes this disorder? Does the diagnosis correlate with anything—are there similar elements in the histories, personalities and future prognosis of people who are so diagnosed?

Symptoms of the addiction

- Do you feel preoccupied with the Internet or online services and think about it while off line?

- Do you feel a need to spend more and more time online to achieve satisfaction?

- Are you unable to control your online use?

- Do you feel restless or irritable when attempting to cut down or stop online use?

- Do you go online to escape problems or relieve feelings such as helplessness, guilt, anxiety or depression?

- Do you lie to family members or friends to conceal how often and how long you stay online?

- Do you risk the loss of a significant relationship, job or educational or career opportunity because of online use?

- Do you keep returning even after spending too much money on online fees?

- Do you go through withdrawal when off line, such as increased depression, moodiness or irritability?

- Do you stay online longer than originally intended?

231

Other psychologists are debating other possible symptoms of Internet addiction. These symptoms include:

- Drastic lifestyle changes in order to spend more time on the Internet

- General decrease in physical activity

- A disregard for one's health as a result of Internet activity

- Avoiding important life activities in order to spend time on the Internet

- Sleep deprivation or a change in sleep patterns in order to spend time on the Internet

- A decrease in socializing, resulting in loss of friends

- Neglecting family and friends

- Refusing to spend any extended time off the Internet

- A craving for more time on the computer

- Neglecting job and personal obligations

If diagnosis or treatment is desired, we recommend that you consult an appropriate professional.[41]

Internet sex can be harmful

People who spend too much time on the Internet sex sites may be at risk for developing psychology problems like sexual compulsiveness...

About 15 percent of the 57 million Americans logging onto the Internet visit sexually oriented sites, most of them without developing any negative impact. Some 92 percent spend less than one hour a week at on-line sex sites, and most spend less than one hour a week. But another 8 percent spend more than 11 hours weekly and are at risk.

"People don't realize how important the Internet is to sexuality," says Alvin Cooper, co-author of the study and director of the San Jose Marital and Sexuality Center in San Jose, California. "Internet sex sites are accessible, affordable and anonymous."[42]

According to a study appearing in the journal *Professional Psychology: Research and Practice,* women favor the use of chat rooms to interact with other Web users and develop relationships. "According to the study, most people accessed sexual Web sites from home, although 5.8 percent used an office computer and 12.7 percent accessed such sites both from home and the office."[43]

> About 47 percent of people accessing sexual Web sites are married and 17 percent are in a committed relationship. Of the single people, half were dating...
>
> "A big part of overall Internet addiction is probably on-line sex" Cooper says. "Sexually compulsive people can get what they want quickly on the 'Net. The sex has more control over their life than they have over it."[44]

Just as with any other addiction, if you or someone you know is having a problem using the Internet to meet their psychological, physical, emotional or sexual needs, seek professional help.

COMPULSIVE EXERCISING

Exercise is good for you when done under proper guidance and controls. Therapists and physical education people can help you find a balanced program of walking, jogging and/or use of gym equipment.

When you turn exercise from a "want-to" into a "have-to," you take the healthy part and the joy out. Watch out.

It becomes compulsive exercising when you stop listening to your body, how you're feeling, and drive yourself with an urgency that has little to do with reality. Compulsive exercising is when you're afraid that your looks, well-being and relationships all hinge on going to exercise class six days a week.

Warning signs

Watch out for these warning signs:

- You get so used to your exercise routine that even very important events are intrusions. You start fitting your life into your classes instead of fitting your classes into your life.

◆ What you eat or don't eat depends on whether you are exercising or not.

◆ You don't feel "right," "complete" or "good" unless you exercise.

◆ You exercise even when you feel sick or tired.

When all or any of these warning signs apply to you, here are some things to do.

1. Listen to them. They are a sign that something has gone wrong.

2. Don't go to your class for a day or a few days. Take a walk instead, or sit in a rocking chair for about an hour and do nothing, or read a book.

3. The next morning after you skip a class, notice that although you didn't burn off 500 calories the day before, you have not suddenly gained ten pounds. Keep noticing.

4. Remind yourself of all the things you are besides your body. Make a list. Begin it with "I am…" and don't allow any negative judgments about your body to creep in. In case you forget, you are worthwhile, you are caring, you are growing—to name just a few attributes.

5. Eat when you are hungry, eat what you want and stop when you are satisfied. Remember that your body does not want to destroy you and will not go haywire as soon as you let down your guard. Trust that the two of you are working for the same end—your health, your happiness and your peace.[45]

WOMEN AND PROBLEM GAMBLING

For many women, gambling may be an enjoyable, recreational activity— an opportunity for fun, excitement and socializing. Their introduction to gambling often is through another family member.

For some women, gambling progresses into a problem. These women may now gamble for a number of reasons ranging from escaping emotional problems, abuse addiction, trauma, sexual abuse, loneliness, a controlling spouse or to solve financial problems. As these additional problems escalate, so does the frequency in which she gambles.

The Connecticut Council on Problem Gambling reports:

> Women now constitute the fastest-growing group of Connecticut residents seeking help for their gambling problems. Women are also finding themselves increasingly impacted by the gambling problems of their partners, dependent children and elderly parents.
>
> For most women, gambling remains a low-risk activity. But for some, gambling is associated with depression, substance abuse, family conflict and work difficulties. Problem gamblers often are behind in paying household bills and may commit crimes such as embezzlement, insurance fraud and theft. Female gamblers tend to develop problems later in life than male gamblers. The progression of a gambling problem for women is usually shorter than it is for men, and women tend to seek help sooner than men. The Connecticut Council on Problem Gambling reports that half of the callers who sought help from the Problem Gambling Helpline in 1998 were women. About 3 out of 4 (76.5%) were calling about their own gambling problems, and about 1 out of 4 (23.5%) were calling for help for spouses, other family members and friends.[46]

In that same Connecticut report, statistics show for themselves that gambling isn't based on race, creed, religion, sex, financial or social status:[47]

- 78.6% of women gamblers were Caucasian; 12.1% African American, Latino/Hispanic.

- 46.1% were Catholic; 18.9% Protestant

- 62.2% work full time,

- 49.9% of the women gamblers have dependent children at home.

- 29.1% earn less than $25,000; 48.6% earn $25,000–$44,999.

- The women had been gambling for an average of 7.8 years (compared to male gamblers who had been gambling an average of 10.8 years).

The report also listed the top five types of problem gambling reported for women:[48]

- Casino slots, 60.9%
- Lottery scratch-off tickets, 27.8%
- Lottery-daily numbers, 25.8%
- Lotto, 19.7%
- Casino blackjack, 16.8%

Other excessive behaviors in addition to gambling:[49]

- Smoking, 58.7%
- Food, 22.3%
- Alcohol, 10.9%
- Spending/shopping, 12.5%

Problem gambling is gambling behavior that causes disruptions in any area of life: psychological, physical, social or vocational. The term *problem gambling* includes, but is not limited to, a condition known as "pathological" or "compulsive," a progressive addiction characterized by increasing preoccupation with gambling, a need to bet more frequently, restlessness or irritability when attempting to stop "chasing" losses, and loss of control manifested by continuation of the gambling behavior in spite of more serious negative consequences.

Three stages of gambling

WINNING (USUALLY VERY SHORT OR NONEXISTENT)

- Occasional gambling/self-esteem boost
- One large or several small wins/emotional relief from problems
- Gambling as a social event
- Fantasizing about big win/rationalizing losses as bad luck
- Increased wagers
- More time spent gambling or thinking about gambling
- Cycle of winning, losing and breaking even begins

Help for the Compulsive Woman and Her Family

CHASING (RETURNING TO TRY AND RECOUP LOSSES OR INCREASE WINS)

- Losing alone
- Hiding gambling
- Lying to cover money spent
- Family fights over money or time spent gambling
- Borrowing money
- Losing time from work due to gambling
- Negligent of family or family responsibilities
- Heavy borrowing (loans)
- Attempts to stop gambling

HOPELESSNESS (OFTEN REFERRED TO AS THE GAMBLER'S BOTTOM)

- Suicide attempts
- Possible incarceration
- Divorce
- Emotional breakdown
- Financial ruin

Not every woman will experience all of the symptoms or progress through the stages in the same order or at the same rate. Some women may return to a previous stage for a short period of time. This is often seen after a bailout has occurred. If you are concerned about your gambling, if you know a woman who may be experiencing problems related to gambling or if you would like more information on women and problem gambling, please contact:

The National Problem Gambling Help Line
208 G Street NE
Washington, DC 20002
800-522-4700
www.ncpgambling.org

Ten questions about gambling behavior

1. Have you often gambled longer than you had planned?

2. Have you often gambled until your last dollar was gone?

3. Have thoughts of gambling caused you to lose sleep?

4. Have you used your income or savings to gamble while letting bills go unpaid?

5. Have you made repeated, unsuccessful attempts to stop gambling?

6. Have you broken the law or considered breaking the law to finance your gambling?

7. Have you borrowed money to finance your gambling?

8. Have you felt depressed or suicidal because of your gambling losses?

9. Have you been remorseful after gambling?

10. Have you gambled to get money to meet your financial obligations?[50]

If you or someone you know answers yes to any of these questions, consider assistance from a professional regarding this gambling behavior.

The addiction of the millennium

It was soon after October 19, 1987—Black Monday, the day the Dow plunged 508 points—that we first began to notice the severity and extent of stock market gambling.

During the six weeks which followed, 44% of the calls to our 1-800 GAMBLER Helpline were from persons who were troubled or devastated by the October 19 market correction. Previous to that, calls about compulsive gambling problems associated with stocks, bonds, commodities and options rarely reached two percent of a month's total calls...

The recent meteoric rise in stock prices, coupled with the availability of online trading, has made the stock market gambling problem bigger than ever. Hundreds of men and women have become addicted to stock market gambling for two reasons—because of the "action" caused by wildly-gyrating prices...and the possibility of making a big financial return in a very short period of time.

Many stock market investors are "day-traders"...people who buy and hold stocks for only a matter of hours or minutes, gambling that they will go up (or down) a few points in a short period of time.

Some day-traders have quit their regular jobs so they can be at home to monitor the market—and place their orders at just the right time …These day traders are, basically a new breed of "investor": they trade on-line using computers rather than brokers for their buying and selling.

In 1997 there were 4.1 million on-line trading accounts; last year there were 7.5 million…and by the year-end there are expected to be ten million plus. Right now…many of those who are day-trading are making money in this wildly-ecstatic bull market. Unfortunately, the bull market is luring them in…giving them a false sense of security …and not preparing them for the inevitable—a market correction later on this year, next year or two years from now.

Among other things, we have proposed a comprehensive education and awareness program which will make brokerage houses and their employees more aware of compulsive gambling…and steps which might be taken to provide advice to some of their customers who may be showing a pattern of compulsive gambling activity…

Others also are working to make certain that there is a more of an "internal early warning signal" at brokerage houses…something that would alert brokerage employees about gambling-type activity with stocks…

The securities industry can no longer keep its head in the sand. On-line trading will continue to grow and with it more compulsive gamblers who go over the line. It's time for the brokerage industry to implement responsible trading programs on compulsive gambling awareness as part of Series 7 Licensing and in continuing education programs for brokers.[51]

A fascination with speculation

Let's face it—gambling and speculating are fun. Both attempt to increase wealth dramatically. Gambling actually creates a risk, while speculating usually involves taking over an existing risk. Not that it makes much difference. Compulsive gambling is a sickness in parts of our society, and speculating may be just a more sophisticated expression of the disease.

Investing, on the other hand, is an attempt to generate ongoing income and to protect against the downside. It is less concerned with trading assets than with owning and nurturing them.[52]

Gambling and homelessness

Eighteen percent of men and women at America's Rescue Missions cite gambling as a cause of their homelessness. That is one of the key findings from a newly released nationwide survey of more than 1,100 Rescue Mission clients.

The survey also found 70 percent of men and women at missions believe that the prevalence of gambling opportunities, including lotteries, makes it difficult for them to put their lives back together. And 37 percent said that, even though they are homeless, they still occasionally gamble or play the lottery.

"Gambling destroys lives, " said Rev. Stephen Berger, executive director of the International Union of Gospel Missions. "State lotteries and casino gambling are creating a new generation of homeless addicts coming to Rescue Missions in need of our help. And it is taking money from the people who desperately need it for other purposes.

"Make no mistake about it: The man or woman stumbling into our mission, addicted to gambling, is just as sick as the person addicted to alcohol or drugs. The addiction may be different, but the shattering of the human spirit is the same."[53]

Adolescent female gamblers

Problem gambling does happen to young people as well. If you are or know an adolescent female where gambling is or may be becoming a problem, then please read the following signs and questions:

- Gambling paraphernalia (bingo daubers, lottery tickets scratch tickets)

- Increased requests for money, borrowing from family and friends

- Lying, cheating and stealing

- Signs of depression or anxiety, such as changes in sleep or eating patterns

- Increased preoccupation, emotional distance and worry

- Withdrawal from social groups or activities not related to gambling

- Coexisting harmful behaviors (eating, alcohol, drugs, shopping/spending, sex)

- Distorted perception or disregard for money

- Preexisting experience with video and computer games

- Influential family members who gamble[54]

Gambling participation among youth

Children routinely gamble. Although private card games and wagering on skill are the most popular forms of gambling for youth, gambling on sporting events and the lottery are also very popular. Approximately 80 percent of youth ages twelve to seventeen have gambled in the last twelve months.

Youth consistently show elevated rates of problem and pathological gambling to adults in the general population. Studies demonstrate that youth with gambling problems have family, academic, peer and legal problems.

- Recent studies suggests between 9 and 14 percent of youth are at risk for a gambling problem, with 4 to 7 percent exhibiting criteria of pathological gamblers.

- Several studies have shown adolescent pathological gambling is associated with alcohol and drug use, truancy, low grades and problematic gambling in illegal activities to finance gambling.

- Youth whose parents gambled excessively had twice the number of problems with the law and twice the attempted suicide rate than their classmates.

A recent review of U.S. and Canadian adolescent gambling students found that in the past ten years the number of teenagers ages twelve to seventeen reporting gambling problems has increased from 10 to 15 percent. The age of gambling has dropped so that now, throughout America, the majority of twelve-year-olds are already gambling.[55]

Where to go for help

The National Council on Gambling and its thirty-five state affiliates offer services for problem gamblers and their loved ones. You can call the twenty-four-hour, toll-free National Problem Gambling Help Line at 800-522-4700. (See page 237 for their address.)

RELATIONSHIP DEPENDENCIES

If you feel you have a tendency toward unhealthy relationships, *Codependents Anonymous* is a self-help organization that uses the Twelve-Step recovery program of Alcoholics Anonymous to break the pattern of addictive and destructive relationships. Support is provided during painful breakups. The meetings emphasize the importance of confidentiality; only first names are used. For further information, contact:

Codependents Anonymous, World Services, Inc.
P. O. Box 7051
Thomaston, GA 30286
706-648-6868
706-647-1755 (fax)
www.codependents.org
info@codependents.org

How male dependent are you?

If you wonder to what degree you are dependent on men to satisfy your emotional needs, the following test will give you some clues. Answer by checking Yes or No in the designated spot.[56]

1. You come from a dysfunctional home in which your emotional needs were not met. ___Yes ___No

2. Having received little real nurturing yourself, you try to fill this unmet need vicariously by becoming a caregiver, especially to men who appear, in some way, needy. ___Yes ___No

3. Because you were never able to change your parent(s) into the warm, loving caretaker(s) you longed for, you respond deeply to emotionally unavailable men whom you can again try to change through your love. ___Yes ___No

4. Terrified of abandonment, you will do anything to keep a male relationship from dissolving. ___Yes ___No

5. Almost nothing is too much trouble, takes too much time or is too expensive if it will "help" the man you are involved with. ___Yes ___No

6. Accustomed to lack of love in personal relationships, you are willing to wait, hope and try harder to please. ___Yes ___No

7. You are willing to take far more than 50 percent of the responsibility, guilt and blame in any relationship. ___Yes ___No

8. Your self-esteem is critically low, and deep inside you do not believe you deserve to be happy. Rather, you believe you must earn the right to enjoy life. ___Yes ___No

9. You have a desperate need to control your men and your relationships, having experienced little security in childhood. You mask your efforts to control people and situations under the guise of "being helpful." ___Yes ___No

10. In a relationship, you are much more in touch with your dream of how it could be than with the reality of your situation. ___Yes ___No

11. You are addicted to men and to emotional pain. ___Yes ___No

12. You are predisposed emotionally and often biochemically to becoming dependent on drugs, alcohol and/or certain foods, particularly sugary ones. ___Yes ___No

13. By being drawn to people with problems that need fixing, or by being enmeshed in situations that are chaotic, uncertain and emotionally painful, you avoid focusing on your responsibility to yourself. ___Yes ___No

14. You may have a tendency toward episodes of depression, which you try to forestall through the excitement provided by an unstable relationship. ___Yes ___No

15. You are not attracted to men who are kind, stable, reliable

and interested in you. You find such "nice" men boring.
___Yes ___No

If you answered *yes* to twelve to fifteen of the questions, you are strongly male addicted; nine to twelve, you have a definite problem; six to nine, there is instability in your life; five or less, watch out—you could be in the early stage of a self-defeating male dependency.

What women want most

A recent survey of three hundred women of all ages revealed that it's not sex, not money, not good looks that women want most—it's *intimacy*. A similar survey of men was done the previous year. Here are the comparisons:[57]

- In their twenties, women want love and romance, but also want to be respected for their brains and talent. Men want a beautiful, sexy woman.

- In their thirties, women want helpmates. They would rather have someone who will take the kids to the orthodontist than have a candlelight dinner once a week. Men want a woman with outside interests and a good income.

- In their forties, women want it all—men who are cooperative, caring, attentive and sexy. Men focus again on beauty, sex—and younger women.

- In their fifties and sixties, women and men want companionship. They do more things together.

SEXUAL ADDICTION

Sex addiction refers to the thinking and behavior patterns of a person who uses sex to cope with life and to defend against low self-worth and a shameful identity. For the addict, sex is not a fulfilling experience that enhances a primary relationship and life itself, but a compulsive, often highly ritualized activity that ultimately adds to the pain and loneliness the addict is already battling.

The term *sexual addiction* is used to describe the behavior of a person who has an unusually intense sex drive or obsession with sex. Sex and thoughts of sex tend to dominate the sex addict's thinking, making it difficult to work or engage in healthy personal relationships.

Sex addicts engage in distorted thinking, often rationalizing and justifying their behavior and blaming others for problems. They generally deny they have a problem and make excuses for their actions.

Sexual addiction also is associated with risk-taking. A person with a sex addiction engages in various forms of sexual activity, despite the potential for negative and/or dangerous consequences. In addition to damaging the addict's relationships and interfering with his/her work and social life, a sexual addiction also puts the person at risk for emotional and physical injury.

Behaviors associated with sexual addiction include:

- Compulsive masturbation (self-stimulation)
- Multiple affairs (extramarital affairs)
- Multiple or anonymous sexual partners and/or one-night-stands
- Consistent use of pornography
- Unsafe sex
- Phone or computer sex (cybersex)
- Prostitution or use of prostitutes
- Exhibitionism
- Obsessive dating through personal ads
- Voyeurism (watching others) and/or stalking
- Sexual harassment
- Molestation/rape

How is sexual addiction treated?

Most sex addicts live in denial of their addiction, and treating an addiction is dependent on the person accepting and admitting that he or she has a problem. In many cases, it takes a significant event—such as the loss of a job, the breakup of a marriage, an arrest or health crisis—to force the addict to admit to his or her problem.

Treatment of sexual addiction focuses on controlling the addictive behavior and helping the person develop a healthy sexuality. Treatment also includes education about healthy sexuality, individual counseling and marital and/or family therapy. Support groups and Twelve-Step recovery programs for people with sexual addictions (i.e., Sex Addicts

Anonymous) also are available. In some cases, medications used to treat obsessive-compulsive disorder may be used to curb the compulsive nature of the sex addiction.[58]

Ask yourself—a quiz

If you answer *yes* three or more of the following fifteen questions, you may want to seek help for an addiction to sex.

1. Has your sexual behavior caused you either to seek help or made you feel scared or different—somehow alienated from other people?

2. Do you keep secrets about your sexual or romantic activities from those important to you? Do you lead a double life?

3. Have your needs driven you to have sex in places with people you would not normally choose?

4. Do you find yourself looking for sexually arousing articles or scenes in newspapers, magazines or other media?

5. Do you find that romantic or sexual fantasies interfere with your relationships with others or are controlling you?

6. Do you frequently want to get away from a sex partner after having sex? Do you frequently feel remorse, shame or guilt after a sexual encounter?

7. Does each relationship continue to have the same destructive patterns that prompted you to leave the last relationships?

8. Have you ever tried to leave a specific person or a destructive relationship and found yourself returning?

9. Do you obsess about sex or romance even when it interferes with your daily responsibilities or causes emotional discomfort?

10. Does the time you spend reading pornographic magazines or watching films interfere with the demands of your daily activities and relationships with people?

11. Is it taking more variety and frequency of sexual and romantic activities than previous to bring the same levels of excitement and relief?

12. Are you in danger of being arrested because of your practices of voyeurism, exhibitionism, prostitution, sex with minors, indecent phone calls, etc.?

13. Does your pursuit of sex or romantic relationships interfere with your spiritual development?

14. Do your sexual activities include the risk, threat or reality of disease, pregnancy, coercion or violence?

15. Has your sexual or romantic behavior ever made you feel hopeless or suicidal?[59]

You may also call or write:

Sexaholics Anonymous (SA)
P. O. Box 111910
Nashville, TN 37222
615-331-6230
615-331-6901 (fax)
www.sa.org
saico@sa.org

Sex Addicts Anonymous (SAA)
P. O. Box 70949
Houston, TX 77270
713-869-4902
800-477-8190
www.saa-recovery.org
info@saa-recovery.org

For those who are/have been in a relationship with sex addict write:

COSA National Service Organization (Codependents of Sexual Addiction)
P. O. Box 14537
Minneapolis, MN 55414
763-537-6904
info@cosa-recovery.org

HOMOSEXUALITY IN WOMEN

In her book *From a Mess to a Miracle* (Creation House Press, 2002), Dr. Kimberly Daniels exposes the issue of homosexuality and its roots. In chapter two, "The Homosexual Issue in the Church," she describes how homosexual tendencies multiply by contamination and transference of spirits. The manifestation reaches its peak when the victim believes the lie that has been sent his way. Homosexuality is a counterfeit and a lie.

Dr. Daniels bases her information on the biblical text of Romans 1:21–27: "Whatever is in the root will feed the tree."

> Masturbation opens a door to homosexuality. It takes a vain imagination to masturbate, and vain imagination is the root spirit of homosexuality. Masturbation is a type of self-sex in the natural, though the person is never alone in the spirit. Incubus and Succubus (sexual demons) lie in wait for masturbating victims to enter their body and help with the sex act. Genesis 38:9 explains how a male through masturbation corrupted the seed in the eyes of God.[60]

Dr. Daniels confirms that when we deal with homosexuality in the pulpits and on the pianos, the entire body will be open for deliverance. This refers to the maturity of the church in coming together as one faith. Without unity, we cannot obtain this maturity.

> There are two types of homosexual breeders in the church: the people who consciously or unconsciously support homosexuality by not addressing the issue; and second, the molesters and the seed droppers who transfer spirits in various ways. Though God loves the homosexual, the enemy seeks to kill, steal and destroy. He knows that those who commit these acts will reap the repercussion, which is death.[61]

If you or someone you know is struggling with the homosexual lifestyle, there is a God who loves and forgives us of all our iniquities. You can be free. For more information, write or call your local church parish for prayer.

Some thoughts to consider if you are being tempted by homosexual behavior:

1. Seek prayer from trusted individuals in your church.

2. Find a support group who deals with these issues.

3. Don't wait until you have acted out on a fantasy; get help dealing with feelings of sexual frustration.

4. Stay in the Word (Bible).

If you feel like you are drawn to an individual for sexual pleasure or are having fantasy thoughts that are considered vain imaginations, leading to masturbation or other sexual acts, get help!

Deliverance from homosexuality

There is hope for those wanting to leave the lesbian lifestyle. In an article I wrote for *SpiritLed Woman* magazine, a close friend spoke of her conversion from lesbianism to heterosexuality.

> First, she had to come before God on her knees and repent for her sins and rebellion. As she tearfully poured out her heart out to Him, the warmth of His love and forgiveness poured over her like warm, fragrant oil. His sovereign deliverance flooded her with a peace that had eluded her all her life.
>
> Under the discipleship of a mature couple in her local church, Jackie learned to focus her attention on the Lord rather than on the things of this world. After two years, God brought a godly man into her life who eventually became her husband…After 18 months of marriage she found herself a widow, single again—but not alone. Jackie stood on Isaiah 63:4–5.
>
> Through all the stages of her life—single, married, widowed—Jackie learned that Jesus was her all in all.[62]

My friend now serves as a director of a pregnancy service in the New England area helping other woman in crisis.

How do women identify with homosexuality?

> Many women…were brought up with poor masculine role models …in reaction to the negligent or unresponsive father, and coupled with an ambivalence or disdain toward her mother, the daughter assumes masculine functions. She rejects the feminine role model based on her view of her mother, and embraces all that is masculine. The woman focuses on what she can do, rather than on who she can be, and she places emphasis on self-reliance, perfectionism and competition. The woman becomes performance-oriented, and

has a tendency to spend her energies on causes or "rights" in which she believes. So often this is an unspoken cry for final recognition from her dad.[63]

The author of *Out of Egypt* describes her own problem as functioning in the "masculine mode." She had little problem with initiation. She was able to perform and accomplish many things. But she was woefully inept at receiving from anybody.

> To walk in wholeness requires a more balanced approach to life that we have been experiencing. It requires a compatibility between our masculine and feminine sides, which will produce harmony rather than discord.
>
> Similarly, the masculine/feminine equilibrium has often been disturbed in a woman who has suffered abuse. Her thoughts encourage [her to engage in] controlling and manipulative behavior. *No one will ever hurt me again!* Thus keeping everyone at bay, or controls them through seduction...
>
> Many women adopt pseudomasculinity as a form of self-protection. They reject all that is inherently feminine, and strive to obtain "equality" with, or superiority over, men...By attaining "equality" with men, women entomb their gentle, vulnerable and trusting qualities under a guise of toughness, independence and suspicion...
>
> The other end of the spectrum of imbalance manifests itself in women who derive their sense of identity and security from other people. Assuming the role of a child, these women rely on others to define and determine their lives. They often mistake passivity for femininity...Continual grasping from other people obscures the women's understanding of self...[64]

Deep wounds can be attributing to extricating oneself from femininity. As a woman becomes secure in her gender, she automatically opens the door to femininity. Ask yourself pertinent questions like these: *What is my self-talk? Who do I say that I am?* Consciously reject all thoughts that do not measure up with the truth.

Walking through the door to femininity can be awesome. But it takes courage and determination to shed your old image of yourself and to embrace your emerging femininity.

WOMEN AND PORNOGRAPHY

It's true that pornography affects men in greater numbers than women, and part of that is the different way that women approach sex. Generally speaking, women aren't as "visually stimulated" as men.

Romance novels that describe gory sexual details are intended to create sexual arousal in women. They have the same effect on girls that *Playboy* has on guys. It's porn for girls, and women can almost be more easily sucked in because women don't tend to think of romance novels as pornography.

By reading things these explicit romance novels women not only open themselves up to a subtle form of pornography, but they can also create a fantasy romance which is unrealistic. Any form of sex outside of marriage, even imagined, is progressively addictive and destructive. Women can become lustful and develop false expectations when it comes to real relationships.

Studies have shown that pornography can diminish a person's sexual happiness. Instead of feeding the desire for intimacy, which is often the goal for women addicted to pornography, they end up with intensified feelings of loneliness and shame. Girls who personally struggle with pornography or other secret sexual activity often live with the fear that someone may discover their "secret" life.

Just as with men, the power of lust for women is in mind control. Feeding this hunger won't quench it, but it intensifies until a "bigger fix" is needed. Pornography has stages, just the same as a drug addiction. What might start out as a harmless romantic fantasy could end up as an uncontrollable, unrealistic, lustful thought pattern.[65]

Breaking the pornography addiction

I

I walk down the street.
There's a big hole in the sidewalk.
I fall in.
I am lost...I am helpless;
It isn't my fault.
It takes forever to find a way out.

II
I walk down the same street.
There is a deep hole in the sidewalk.
I pretend I don't see it.
I fall in again.
I can't believe I am in the same place;
But it isn't my fault.
It still takes a long time to get out.

III
I walk down the same street.
There is a deep hole in the sidewalk.
I see it is there.
I still fall in…it's a habit.
My eyes are open.
I know where I am.
It is my fault.
I get out immediately.

IV
I walk down the same street.
There is a deep hole in the sidewalk.
I walk around it.
IV
I walk down a different street.[66]

Do women struggle with pornography addiction?

Women are not exempt from pornography addiction. It was once thought to be just an addiction men struggled with, but that's not so anymore. Romance novels, soap operas, male strippers, chat rooms and other avenues have opened the door for women to become addicted to pornography.

Women have become tempted by the glamour, success and riches of being a *Playboy* bunny or centerfold. Some fall for the temptation of large pocket books if they choose stripping as a career. Women have put themselves through college by working as strippers at high-class and or not-so-high-class strip clubs. Some women support themselves financially by becoming Phone Sex Operators, also known as fantasy chat.

Help for the Compulsive Woman and Her Family

Some women have become involved in cybersex. The addiction is definitely growing among women.[67]

Is it possible for a woman to be a sex addict?

Many people cannot accept the reality that women can become sex addicts. One of the greatest problems facing female sexual addicts is convincing others that they have a legitimate problem and not that they are a slut, a whore or promiscuous.

There is very little on the subject of female sexual addicts. Sexual addicts feel tremendous guilt and shame about their out-of-control behavior. Many live in a state of constant fear of being exposed, yet they continually act out to attempt to medicate the pain of their addiction.

Mood-altering drugs like alcohol or fantasy drugs are taken to cope with relational pain. They may suffer from clinical depression or have suicidal tendencies. Women with a "sex-addiction-the-making" have, at an early age, learned to block out all painful feelings of inadequacy or loneliness through sexual fantasy, rituals and an escalation of self-destructive sexual behaviors.

Sexual addiction self-test

Listed below are a few questions to ask yourself to see if you might have a problem with a sexual addiction:

- Do you regularly purchase sexually explicit romance novels or magazines?

- Do you feel that your sexual behavior is abnormal?

- Do you often find yourself preoccupied with sexual thoughts or romantic daydreams?

- Do you have trouble stopping your sexual behavior when you know it is inappropriate?

- Has your sexual behavior ever created problems for you and your family?

- Have you ever worried about people finding out about your sexual activities?

- Have you make efforts to quit a type of sexual activity and failed?

253

◈ Have you ever felt degraded by your sexual behavior?

◈ Has sex or romantic fantasies been a way for you to escape your problems?

◈ Has your sexual activities interfered with your family life?

◈ Do you feel controlled by your sexual desire, fantasy or romance?

If you answered *yes* to any of these questions, you may have a sexual addiction problem.

Signs of sexual addiction

◈ Loss of control: Doing more that you intended or wanted

◈ Compulsive behavior: A pattern of out-of-control behavior over time.

◈ Efforts to stop: Repeated attempts to stop the behavior that fail

◈ Loss of time: Significant amounts of time lost seeking, doing and/or recovering from the behavior

◈ Preoccupation: Obsessing about the behavior or ritual

◈ Inability to fulfill obligations: The acting out behavior interferes with work, school, family and/or friends

◈ Continuation despite consequences: Unable to stop the behavior, despite its self-destructive nature and despite the potential negative consequences

◈ Escalation: Need to make the behavior more intense, more frequent or more risky to get the same "high"

◈ Losses: Giving up hobbies, family, friends, and/or work in order to act out

◈ Withdrawal: When you try to stop the behavior it causes distress, anxiety, restlessness, irritability or physical discomfort. Many people report feeling depressed.

Help for the Compulsive Woman and Her Family

Why does someone become a sexual addict?

Research has shown that a very high correlation exists between childhood abuse and sexual addiction in adulthood. Sexual abuse can be a major influence in both the development and continuation of sexual addiction. A woman addicted to sex often has sexual abuse in her past that she has kept secret from others.

Other sexual abuse victims may feel worthless, like damaged goods, and that it really doesn't matter what happens to them. So they continue to reinforce the lie of their unworthiness or unlovableness by acting out in additional self-destructive behaviors. Another way that unresolved sexual abuse could play a role in sexual addiction is through the process called "trauma bonding." In trauma bond, the sex addict has actually attached herself to the trauma of the past and reenacts the experience in fantasy or in actual relationships. In this case, she will tend to repeat the exact same behavior where she is the victim in the situation. In a majority of cases, women who struggle with sexual addiction admitted that in their fantasy they were mostly submissive.

Can women be addicted to pornography just as men are?

In one study of 932 sex addicts, 90 percent of men and 77 percent of women said that pornography was significant to their addiction. The same study found that childhood sexual abuse and frequent use of pornography accompanied by masturbation are key parts of the formation of sexually addictive behavior.[68]

Most women are less interested in sexual imagery and more interested in romance. Some women prefer relational activities, i.e., chatting online with sexual partners. Some women sexual addicts do use porn as part of their compulsive behaviors.

What is the difference between a female sex addict and a male sex addict?

Women become more shameful and secretive in their addiction. For men, sex is macho; it is a badge. Women are considered sluts and tramps when they pursue sex. Women are more inclined to keep the sexual addiction a secret for fear of being labeled a whore or promiscuous. There is less societal acceptance of women's sexual behaviors.

Eighty percent of women who engage in sexual behavior on the Internet are more likely to meet a person off line. Thirty percent of men who engage in sexual behavior on the Internet will never go off line to meet anyone. Women are more likely to want the relationship, the give-and-take, of a live encounter. There have been numerous reports of women being beat up and left for dead through these liaisons. Many women are too embarrassed and ashamed to report a rape of physical altercation as a result of meeting someone off line. Women are more interested in romance and achieving it through sex. Men are more interested in the sexual encounters and less interested in long-lasting romantic relationships.

What about masturbation?

Masturbation is a common practice and a critical issue for most women addicted to sex. In virtually all cases, masturbation involves some type of fantasy and creates in women a great deal of shame and guilt.

The earliest onset of masturbation is the cornerstone of women addicted to sex. It is usually one of the first consistent sexual behaviors that a very young female can participate in at almost anytime. Sixty percent of female sex addicts admit to masturbating at least two to four times a week. Masturbation fuels the addiction by engaging in submissive fantasy. Many women have admitted that they struggle with masturbation to the point of self-injury.

Masturbation is hard to quit for several reasons:

1. It is always available. You don't have to get into a car and connect with your drug dealer. It is always there and available.

2. The behavior usually starts in childhood and has been reinforced and engrained in your repertoire of behaviors.

3. It has been viewed as less important than other female sex addictions.

4. Masturbation releases a chemical in your body, where your brain becomes "addicted" to the chemicals released during orgasm. The root of addiction can be found in many possible areas.

There is help!

Having acknowledged that there is a problem, many sex addicts have reported that the following have helped them in their recovery process:

- Prayer
- Attend a Twelve-Step all female addiction meeting
- Daily contact with a sponsor or accountability partner and a ninety-day initial abstinence plan
- Making your computer safe
- Reading about sexual addiction[69]

INCEST AND SEXUAL EXPLOITATION BY PROFESSIONALS

In recent years there has been a shocking new awareness of the magnitude and destructiveness of child abuse. As I have revealed my own experience of childhood molestation by an uncle in behavior workshops, workshops, seminars and discussions groups, women have opened up, often with an explosion of tears, to tell how it happened to them. "All these years I've kept it hidden," they almost always say. "I've never been able to tell anyone before."

It is painful for them to open up old wounds, yet many, many healings have resulted when they do. Sexual abuse, incest survivors and battered women support groups are forming all over the country.

Child abuse is often sexual and incestuous. It can be physical, verbal, mental, emotional and spiritual as well. Deprivation abuse occurs when the parent(s) are in the home but are emotionally unavailable to the child. There are more and more cases of parents beating their children to death. As drug abuse has increased, child abuse has increased.

Recent studies reveal that one in three women will be sexually molested before their eighteenth birthday—usually by someone she knows.

When professionals exploit

Psychologists, psychiatrists, counselors, therapists, ministers, priests, doctors, nurses, attorneys, professors, educators, social workers, emergency/crisis/victim services, and law enforcement officers are all entrusted and empowered by society to have authority and power in people's lives.

This power gives them the opportunity, by virtue of their professional role, to serve and help others. If this power is abused, if a client's dependence on a professional is exploited, the client is almost always injured, and the professional has betrayed the trust of the client and society. When a client is sexually exploited, the wounds can be particularly deep. It is a violation that goes beyond physical. It is an emotional and spiritual violation as well. It is the most intimate way a person can be abused.

For someone who has been sexually exploited by a professional, reactions are unique, but the consequences sometimes can be devastating, with many resultant problems, symptoms, and emotions:[70]

Alienation from family	Increased risk of suicide
Changes in appetite	Insomnia
Chronic fatigue	Intense guilt/shame
Depression	Intense rage or anger
Embarrassment	Irritability
Emotional withdrawal	Lowered self-esteem
Extreme fear	Nightmares
Faith and spiritual crisis	Posttraumatic stress
Feelings of betrayal and	disorder
abandonment	Remorse
Grief	Sexual dysfunction
Hatred	Spontaneous crying
Humiliation	Substance abuse

Sexual exploitation by professionals is a serious societal problem with an alarming prevalence. Current estimates are that one-third of all money awarded for medical malpractice is for damages for sexual misconduct.[71] (In some specific professions, such as psychology, this monetary figure is estimated at greater than 50 percent![72]) Sexual exploitation by professionals has come to be recognized as a problem of great magnitude in recent years.

Studies indicate that as many as 10 to 12 percent of male therapists sexually exploit clients at some point in their career.[73] For many, this is not a single incident, but a repeated behavior. For clients abused in this way, as many as 90 percent suffer from serious consequences. Tremendous harm can result from this prevalent form of abuse.

> There is absolutely nothing romantic about it. It is not about love; it is really not even about sex. It is about power and exploitation. It

is about what happens when an unethical professional encounters a psychologically vulnerable patient, client, student, or other and decides to use her trust in him, primarily engendered by his power and position, to his own advantage—with little regard to the consequences for her/him.[74]

The consequences are far-reaching and can cause a damaging or harmful impact on persons close to the victim.[75] Most cases of this abuse are not reported, and the process of going through legal channels sometimes further traumatizes and discourages victims. Tragically, some even attempt suicide. But the good news is that there is hope, and there is help available!

CHILD PORNOGRAPHY

By now, we've all seen or read the stories of abuse, abduction and murder of young children, but the news keeps getting worse. The statistics are horrifying:

- In 1994, Child Protective Services substantiated 1,036,00 children as victims of child abuse. This represented 16 out of every 1,000 U.S. children.

- Currently, about 47 out of every 1,000 children are reported as victims of child abuse. Since 1985, the rate of child abuse fatalities has increased by 48%. Based on current numbers, more than three children die each day as a result of child abuse or neglect.

- According to a report of the Presidential Task Force on Violence and the Family, approximately one-third of all juvenile victims of sexual abuse cases are children younger than 6 years of age.

- According to the Justice Department, one in two rape victims is under age 18, and one in six is under 12.[76]

What is happening here? What is at the root of this horrendous increase in violence against innocent children? For at least two generations now our Western culture, Europe and North America, has fanned the yearning for more and more sensual pleasure and indulgence. Our society has winked at fornication, laughed at adultery, paid for abortions with tax dollars, promoted homosexuality on TV, in movies and now in classrooms—and the Supreme Court majority, supposedly the wisest and most erudite council of citizens, cannot even muster the moral courage to condemn child pornography on the Internet!

THE EFFECTS OF CHILD SEXUAL ABUSE ON AN ADULT SURVIVOR

Any sexual contact between a child and a trusted individual that damaged the child, covert or overt, whether flirtation or sexual intercourse, needs to be dealt with assertively. It scars virtually all facets of the victim's life since she or he is left with little or no self-esteem. At least one of five boys and one out of four girls will be abused before they reach the age of eighteen. The child's emotional growth will be stifled at the age of the first attack, and the victim will probably not begin to recover until adulthood, if ever.

Some of the social maladjustments arising from incest are alcoholism, drug addiction, prostitution and promiscuity. Eating or sleeping disorders, migraines, back or stomach pains are just a few of the physical consequences a victim may suffer. Food, sex, alcohol and/or drugs deaden the painful memories of the abuse and expel reality temporarily. If a victim perceives obesity to be unattractive, and if she believes she was abused because she was pretty, a victim may overeat in a misguided attempt to defend herself from further sexual assault. "I felt like throwing up" is a common response among victims, and bulimia is a way of acting out that feeling. Anorexia is another form of self-punishment, eventually leading to the ultimate self-victimization—suicide.[77]

Emotional problems that emerge from such abuse may not surface until later in life. Here are a few signs that will help you identify with someone you love or even yourself: inability to trust, perfectionism, phobias, avoidance of both intimacy and emotional bonding. Once the denial system has insured a victim's survival, the victim will be robbed of having or enjoying an unencumbered adulthood. Trying to convince that once innocent child that it wasn't their fault takes a lifetime to heal.

Occasionally you will find a parent who, when they do find out about the abuse from the child, is reluctant to believe such atrocity. The steps in recovery begin when a parent begins to believe that it did happen. Here are some important steps to take into consideration:

- Listen. It is vital that you listen carefully and calmly. No matter how upset you are, it is critical you remain calm.

- Do not stand over the child in way that might frighten or intimidate her. Even if you are agitated and feel the need to pace, sit or kneel beside the child and comfort her.

- Do not threaten to hurt or injure the perpetrator. The child may have conflicting feelings and decide to protect the perpetrator as someone she loves or loved.

- Do not ever tell a child that life is ruined forever because of the abuse. Confirm in them the positive.

Marilyn Van Derber Atler, a former Miss America who raised public awareness by disclosing that she was a victim of incest, has become an advocate for children who have been sexually violated and is the host of the video *Once Can Hurt a Lifetime,* in which children and adults tell how sexual abuse affected their lives.[78]

Who Commits Sexual Assaults?

The national Crime Victimization Survey, conducted by the U.S. Department of Justice, found that 76 percent of sexually assaulted women were attacked by a current or former husband, cohabitating partner, friend or date. Strangers only committed 18 percent of the assaults that were reported in this survey.

Early reactions to an assault are nightmares, difficulty concentrating, sleep deprivation or being jumpy or on edge. Highly disruptive symptoms that make it incredibly difficult to function in the first month will disrupt a person's daily life and prevent her from seeking assistance. Symptoms of ASD (Acute Stress Disorder) include feeling numb and detached, like being in a daze or a dream, or feeling that the world is strange and unreal; difficulty remembering important parts of the assault; nightmares; avoidance of things (thoughts, feelings) that remind the woman of the assault; and anxiety or increased arousal.

If you or someone you know, male or female, child or adult, has been sexually assaulted, there is help. Contact your local police, Department of Social Services, and the National Center for Posttraumatic Stress

Disorder at 802-296-6300. Remember you are loved, valued and needed. You are an important fiber of the society in which you live.

GRIEF

Grief is the spiritual reaction to being separated from someone or something for whom you have feeling. The grief process is not an enemy, but a movement toward the restoration of wholeness. Someone once said, "If no man's life were significant enough to cause weeping, if birth and death were unmarked, if the measure of our years on earth were nothing, we might better be house flies rather than human beings, made in God's image." Profound grief is preceded by deep love that gave life meaning. In the deepest sense, our days would be empty and futile if we never grieved.

Grief is experienced psychologically, socially and physically. It is experienced psychologically through your mental thoughts and feelings. It is experienced socially through the interaction you have with those around you and through the health of your body.

Your grief may express itself in many ways, often with disturbing and confusing feelings, emotions never felt before or experienced. These feelings can often overwhelm you and be frightening. They may last long periods of time.

Mourning can best be described as a series of processes that a person goes through in adapting to and accepting the loss of a loved one. In mourning, the person works at gradually undoing the emotional ties that created the loving bond with a loved one who has become separated from them, either permanently through death or through distance. They must work to adapt to the loss and learn to live a new life without the loved one or thing to which they were attached.

The intensity of your grief will more than likely fluctuate over time. You must not set yourself up for disappointment by thinking that grief is based on a sliding scale. Your grief will have many ups and downs. Some may be due to life changes such as birthdays, holidays, anniversaries, etc. The change in the intensity of your grief may last a few minutes to a few days. It is important in your recovery that you learn to accept these fluctuations as a normal part of the grieving process and not as a permanent setback or failure on your part to recover from your loss.

There is no time period for how long your grief will last. Your grief is unique to you and you alone. One thing to remember is this: No two people's experience will be the same. Most people are very surprised to find that the grieving process, which includes all aspects of grief, may take an individual up to six or more years to work through effectively, depending on the type of loss and the factors or complications impacting the process.

You can assume that at some point in time the suffering will ease in its level of intensity. This will occur as you accommodate and integrate the loss into your new life. This does not mean that you will ever stop experiencing periods of sadness, remorse and longing for your loved one. However, it does mean that the intense acute phase of suffering will eventually come to an end as you work your personal grief.[79]

COPING WITH ANGER

From a very young age, girls are told it's "not nice to get angry!"

According to Charles Spielberger, Ph.D., a psychologist who specializes in the study of anger, anger is "an emotional state that varies in intensity from mild irritation to intense fury and rage." Like other emotions, it is accompanied by physiological and biological changes; when you get angry, your heart rate and blood pressure go up, as do the levels of your hormones, adrenaline, and noradrenaline.

Anger can be caused by both external and internal events. You could be angry with a specific person (such as a coworker or supervisor) or event (a traffic jam, a canceled flight), or your anger could be caused by worrying or brooding about your personal problems. Memories of traumatic or enraging events can also trigger angry feelings.

Both professionals and the general population typically view anger as dangerous and unhelpful. But it is an emotion, one of many inherent in human experience, and as such can offer insight power and growth when its energy is harnessed constructively.

The three main approaches to anger are expressing it, suppressing it and calming it. Expressing your anger feelings in an assertive—not aggressive—manner is the healthiest way to express anger. To do this, you have to learn how make clear what your needs are, and how to get them met, without hurting others. Being assertive doesn't mean being pushy or demanding; it means being respectful of yourself and others.[80]

Anger management in recovery

First, you must recognize your angry feelings:

- How do you know when you are angry?
- How does your anger show?
- Do you deny your anger and hide it?
- Do you own your anger and go with it?

Then you must list the signs of your anger:

- Head, stomach and back aches
- Yelling and screaming
- Sarcasm or cynicism
- Denial or rationalism about your behavior
- Revenge fantasies
- Thoughts about drinking or using drugs
- Arguing with others
- Becoming silent or withholding
- Isolating
- Becoming violent
- Compulsive eating, spending, cleaning or sex

Then you can identify the cause of your anger:

- What is the situation?
- Who is involved?
- Is this the first time, or is this a pattern?
- What other feelings are you experiencing?
- Are you stressed? Tired? Hungry? Lonely? Scared?

You can then decide how to behave:

- Reason with your angry self-talk.

- Change your thoughts from "I'm angry at you because you…" to "It's unfortunate this happened, but it's not worth the price I pay."

- Do a physical activity. Walk or jog. Begin some physically demanding work.

Help for the Compulsive Woman and Her Family

 Talk directly to the person involved using a calm and assertive tone. Practice listening, and don't interrupt. If you are too angry, practice first with a third party.

 Avoid behavior that will make the situation worse: artificial stimulants like nicotine and caffeine, ranting and raving, name-calling and compulsive behavior with food, money or sex.

The aim is to inhibit or suppress your anger and convert it into more constructive behavior. The danger in this type of response is that if it isn't allowed outward expression, your anger can turn in on yourself. Anger turned inward may cause hypertension, high blood pressure or depression.

Unexpressed anger can create other problems. It can lead to pathological expressions of anger, such as passive-aggressive behavior (getting back at people indirectly, without telling them why, rather than confronting them head-on) or a personality that seems perpetually cynical and hostile.[81]

Symptoms of hidden anger

 Procrastination in completing imposed tasks

 Habitual tardiness

 A preference for sadistic or ironic humor

 Sarcasm, cynicism or flippancy in conversation

 Effected politeness

 Smiling when hurting

 Laughing when nothing is funny

 Frequent nightmares or disturbing dreams

 Difficulty sleeping, either getting to sleep or awakening the night

 Boredom, apathy, loss of interest in things that once interested you

 Getting tired more easily than usual

265

◆ Excessive irritability over trivialities

◆ Drowsiness at inappropriate times

◆ Sleeping more than usual—using it as an escape

◆ TMJ, soreness in jaws, clenched jaws, grinding teeth—especially while asleep

◆ Stressed-related physical symptoms: sore back and neck muscles, facial ticks, spasmodic foot movements, habitual fist clenching, stomach ulcers, pains in the back, neck and abdomen not related to other biological illnesses

◆ Chronic depression

Strategies to keep anger at bay

Relaxation: Simple relaxation tools, such as deep breathing and relaxing imagery, can help calm down angry feelings. If you are involved in a relationship where both partners are hot-tempered, it might be a good idea for both of you to learn these techniques.

◆ Breathe deeply, from your diaphragm; breathing from your chest won't relax you.

◆ Slowly repeat a calm word or phrase such as "relax," "take it easy."

Problem solving: Sometimes our anger and frustration are caused by very real and inescapable problems in our lives. Not all anger is misplaced, and often it's a healthy natural response to these difficulties. The best attitude to bring to such a situation, then, is not to focus on finding the solution, but rather on how you handle and face the problem.

Make a plan, and check your progress along the way. Resolve to give it your best, but also not to punish yourself if an answer doesn't come right away. If you can approach it with your best intentions and efforts and make a serious attempt to face it head-on, you will be less likely to lose patience and fall into all-or-nothing thinking, even if the problem does not get solved right away.

Better communication: Angry people tend to jump to—and act on—conclusions, and some of those conclusions can be very inaccurate. The first thing to do if you're in a heated discussion is slow down and think through your responses. Don't say the first thing that comes into your head, but slow down and think carefully about what you want to say.

Listen, too, to what is underlying the anger. For instance, you like a certain amount of freedom and personal space, and you find yourself hearing from the person who loves you most that he or she needs more closeness. He or she may start complaining about your activities. But don't retaliate; listen to what is being said. He or she may feel neglected or unloved. Patience is the key. Don't let you or your anger get out of control.

Silly humor can help defuse rage in a number of ways. For one thing, it can help you get a more balanced perspective. When you feel angry and want to call someone a name or refer to them with some imaginative phrase, stop and picture what that word would literally look like.

Changing your environment: Sometimes it's our immediate environment or surroundings that give us cause for irritation. Problems and responsibilities can weigh you down and make you feel trapped. Give yourself a break. Make sure you have some "personal time" scheduled for times of the day that you know are particularly stressful. Bring with you a book on famous quotes or lyrics; a good laugh can cure any tension. Share the laughter with someone else to break the monotony of the day.

If you really feel that your anger is out of control, that it is having an impact on your relationships and on important parts of your life, seek counseling. A good counselor can help you identify the problem areas of your life so that you can walk in wholeness and live in peace with those around you.[82]

Parents Anonymous

Parents Anonymous is a program for parents who already have, or are afraid they might, physically abuse their children because of anger. This is not a Twelve-Step program.

Child Help USA National Headquarters
15757 N. 78th Street
Scottsdale, AZ 85260
800-4-A-CHILD
480-922-8212
www.childhelpusa.com

Suicide

Suicide is a complex behavior. The risk factors for suicide frequently occur in combination. Scientific research has shown that almost all people who kill themselves have a diagnosable mental or substance abuse disorder; the majority have more than one disorder. Before you finish reading this page, someone in the United States will try to kill himself. At least eighty Americans will have taken their own lives by tomorrow. More than thirty thousand people in the United States killed themselves last year, and nine times that many attempted suicide. Many of those who attempted will try again, a number with lethal success. And here's the irony: Except for a very few, all of the people who commit suicide want desperately to live.

No single group, color or class of people is free from self-inflicted death. Rich or poor, male or female, Christian or Jew, black or white, young or old—to some extent every category of man suffers death by suicide. Males are four times likely to die from suicide than are females.

The most typical American suicide is a white Protestant male in his forties, married with two children. He is a breadwinner and a taxpayer. The sorrow his untimely, preventable death brings to his family cannot be totaled, but the financial burden on his family and community is considerable. Costs begin with the city or country ambulance fee. The cost of the coroner's time and facilities soon follows. Widows' and survivors' benefits and insurance must be added. Recent studies indicate that the surviving children of suicide victims frequently require mental health care.

Over the years a suicide can cost his community at least $50,000. Counting all taxes that he would have paid over the next quarter century, in the end, a suicide may cost the community a great deal more.

Suicide by firearms is the most common method for both men and women, accounting for 60 percent of all suicides.

Suicide is the third leading cause of death among young people fifteen to twenty-four years of age, following unintentional injuries and homicide.[83]

Warning signs

As a parent, relative or friend of a troubled loved one, here are some of the warning signals that indicate he or she might be thinking about committing suicide:

Help for the Compulsive Woman and Her Family

- Extreme depression, which could include sadness, anxiety and other behavioral changes

- An unexplained drop in quality of work

- Clear changes in sleeping or eating habits

- The abuse of drugs or alcohol

- Sudden withdrawal from spouse, family and close friends

- Taking unnecessary risks

- Major decline of energy and interests

- Verbal expression of suicidal thoughts or threats

- Beginning to give away prized possessions

- Extreme neglect of appearance

- Preparations for death, such as putting affairs in order, making a will

Ways to help the person who might be considering suicide

- Understand the facts, that most suicide attempts come from intense feelings of loneliness, worthlessness, helplessness, depression or from disease.

- Take his/her feelings and statements seriously.

- Listen and ask concerned questions.

- Don't ever challenge the person to "go ahead." He or she may call your bluff.

- Stay with the depressed person. Do something together.

- Don't analyze motives.

- Don't argue or try to reason.

- Encourage the suicidal person to get professional help. Give him or her a crisis line number to call. Most communities have local crisis line numbers and information listings.

The cardinal rule of suicide prevention is to : DO SOMETHING. If someone you know has attempted suicide and has not received professional care: GET HELP.

If someone threatens to end their own life, GET HELP.

If someone you know has undergone a drastic change in his/her life and begins preparing wills or gives away personal possessions, GET HELP.

Don't wait to see if other signs develop.

Don't decide to consider it for a while. Do it today. Tomorrow may be too late.

Your friendship, concern, and actions could save a life.

Give him/her crisis line numbers and information listings. Other sources of help include suicide prevention centers, crisis intervention centers, mental health clinics, hospitals, family physicians and clergymen.[84]

NICOTINE ADDICTION

The evidence is overwhelming…smoking is dangerous to one's health, to nonsmokers around the smoker and even to persons not yet born. Researchers have found that secondhand smoke is life threatening. Yet the facts are that most smokers are motivated and would like to quit… but have given up to some extent on their ability to succeed and on the value of outside assistance.

100 percent bone density loss for those who smoke

Reporter Janice Billingsley…recorded Dr. [Stephen] Conrad's statistics that nonsmoking women at age 65 have an average bone loss of 33.5 percent, while women of the same age who have smoked for five years or more suffer a loss of bone density at a rate from 40 percent to 60 percent. Supporting these statistics was a Tufts University study finding older men and women smokers to be losing three-quarters of a percent more bone mass per year than nonsmokers.[85]

Smokers more susceptible to injury

After finding that leg fractures took 70 percent longer to heal in people who smoked, compared to their nonsmoking counterparts, Dr. Miguel Schmitz, an orthopedic surgeon, wondered, "Why haven't we figured this out before?" According to HealthScout report Janice

Billingsley, Dr. Schmitz found that the average time for clinical healing for smokers was 276 days compared to 152 days for nonsmokers.

He called the difference remarkable, noting, "I would hypothesize that blood flow to the bone is sluggish and that nutrients and oxygen are not fed to the bone in an expedient fashion. Nicotine is a very powerful constrictor…and decreases the flow of blood to the periphery of the body." Dr. Conrad agreed. "It has been measured and found that there is a 29 percent blood flow decrease to the thumb after smoking two cigarettes."

When there is a decrease of blood flow throughout the body, it follows that there is also less oxygen in its tissues. Oxygen is essential for maximum health. Carbon monoxide is inhaled during the smoking process, which further exacerbates the problem. It replaces the oxygen that should be abounding in the body's red blood cells. "Over time," Dr. Conrad notes, "muscles, tendons, ligaments and bones are all weakened."

Dr. John Gardner, of the U.S. Defense Department, who co-authored a study discovering that young Army recruits who smoked had higher rates of injury during basic training, believes the invasive consequences of smoking are immediate. He concludes, "At least some of the detrimental effects of cigarette smoking may occur at an early age and have immediate consequences." Reporting in the *American Journal of Preventive Medicine,* he found that out of 2,000 recruits, smokers were 1.5 times more likely to be injured during eight weeks of basic training than nonsmokers. Not only that, smokers also suffered more than double the number of ankle sprains and muscle stresses than nonsmokers.[86]

Smokers have a higher rate of impotence

Henry Feldman, a scientist at the New England Research Institutes in Watertown, Massachusetts, found that male smokers had a higher rate of impotence than nonsmokers. Even second-hand smoke raised the rate considerably. Again, the culprit is blood flow, compromised by oxygen depletion.[87]

Guidelines for quitting

1. See yourself as a nonsmoker, enjoying food more, being more congenial, healthier.

2. Set this phrase solidly in your thinking: "Smoking is a threat to my life. I must quit."

3. Set a goal for doing without smoking. If you backslide, don't be depressed. Start over. You can do it!

4. The urge to smoke lasts five to ten minutes. Wait it out by exercising, reading, meditating, etc. The first twenty-four hours without a cigarette are the hardest.

5. Stay in areas and situations where smoking is not allowed.

Smokenders

One avenue of help is Smokenders, the oldest, largest and most successful program of its kind in the world. It has been in operation for over seventeen years, and is taught throughout the United States, Canada, Great Britain, Australia and Japan.

Smokenders is not a quick fix, but a comprehensive six-week program designed to deal with the addiction and to break the psychological connectors. The two-hour sessions are taught by former smokers who have quit successfully with Smokenders, then were trained to become instructors. For further information call or write:

Smokenders
901 NW 133rd Street, #A
Vancouver, WA 98685
800-828-HELP (4357)

Other sources of help are the American Cancer Society and Smokers Anonymous. Check your director and local paper for information.

WORKAHOLISM

Workaholism is an epidemic. Now that it is feasible to work any hour of the day or night, people do. It has been a kind of piety about it, but there's a high price to pay in terms of stress, personal life and health. In Japan, it's reached the point where coroners sometimes record a verdict of *Karoshi* (death from overwork).

The pendulum is beginning to swing back, in some cases to the far side. In Vechta, near Hamburg, civil servants are encouraged to doze for twenty minutes after lunch. Gould Evans Goodman, a company in Kansas City, provides "spent tents," complete with sleeping bags and alarm clocks, for worn-out associates.

Dr. Earnest Rossi advocates twenty-minute breaks every two hours or so, He has identified "ultadian cycles," where we peak and trough over about a two-hour period. We can work through our troughs, but it makes more sense to work at our peaks and use our troughs to refresh ourselves or change to a different type of work. We can check our e-mails, weed the garden-, or sit and look vacant. Whatever we choose to do, it's important to have breaks.

It's not just a question of getting tired. We can only pay attention to one thing for so long before the mind goes sluggish. We can still perform, hour after hour, but we'll become more and more robotic as the hours wear on. It's about time management, stress management and work-life balance.

Have you ever wondered how much of a workaholic you are? We have found the following inventory to be useful in that determination. Complete it as quickly as you can! Your first response is often your most honest answer.[88]

Workaholism inventory

1. Once I start a job I have no peace until I finish.
   ____True ____False

2. Whereas most people are overly conscious of their feelings, I like to deal with facts.
   ____True ____False

3. I sometimes become so preoccupied by a thought that I cannot get it out of my mind. ____True ____False

4. I have periods in which I cannot sit or lie down—I need to be doing something.
   ____True ____False

5. My mind is often occupied by thoughts about what I have done wrong or not completed. ____True ____False

6. I feel irritated when I see another person's messy desk or cluttered room. ____True ____False

7. I am more comfortable in a neat, clean and orderly room than in a messy one.
   ____True ____False

8. I cannot get through a day or week without a schedule or a list of jobs to do. ____True ____False

9. I believe that the man who works the hardest and longest deserves to get ahead.
   ____True ____False

10. If my job/housework demands more time, I will cut out pleasurable activities to see that it gets done. ____True ____False

11. I frequently feel angry without knowing what or who is bothering me. ____True ____False

12. I think talking about feelings to others is a waste of time.
    ____True ____False

13. I like always to be in control of myself and to know as much as possible about things happening around me.
    ____True ____False

14. I feel that the more one can know about future events, the better off he will be.
    ____True ____False

15. I rarely give up until the job has been completely finished. ____True ____False

16. I often expect things of myself that no one else would ask of himself. ____True ____False

17. I sometimes worry about whether I was wrong or made a mistake. ____True ____False

18. I would like others to see me as not having any faults.
    ____True ____False

Now go back and count the number of *trues* you checked. A score of five or less reflects a fairly relaxed person. A score of six to ten is average. A score of ten or more reflects a definite tendency toward workaholism.

Help for the Compulsive Woman and Her Family

For further information contact:

Workaholics Anonymous
World Service Organization
P. O. Box 289
Menlo Park, CA 94026
510-273-9253
www.workaholics-anonymous.org

ALCOHOL AND DRUG TREATMENT CENTERS

For information about the location of alcohol and drug treatment centers contact:

U.S. Journal, Inc.
3201 SW 15th Street
Deerfield Beach, FL 33442
800-851-9100
www.usjt.com

OTHER RESOURCES FOR PUBLICATIONS, FILMS, TAPES, ETC.

COMPCARE PUBLICATIONS
200 S. Hoover Blvd., Bldg. 219, Ste. 200
Tampa, FL 33609
813-288-4808
www.compcare.com

HAZELDEN FOUNDATION
P. O. Box 11
Center City, MN 55012
800-328-9000
www.hazelden.org

JOHNSON INSTITUTE
1273 National Press Building
Washington, DC 20045
888-421-4321
www.johnsoninstitute.com

THOMAS W. PERRIN INC.
P. O. Box 423
Rutherford, NJ 07070

CLEAR LIFE CLINICS
P. O. Box 120148
New Brighton, MN 55112
651-628-0220
www.clearlife.com

16

Help for Families and Friends

This letter could be written by anyone with compulsive/addictive behaviors.

Open Letter to the Family

I am an alcoholic. I need help. Don't allow me to lie to you and have you accept it as the truth, for in doing so you encourage more lies. The truth may be painful, but get at it.

Don't let me outsmart you. This only teaches me to avoid responsibility and to lose respect for you at the same time.

Don't let me exploit you or take advantage of you. In doing so, you become an accomplice to my evasion of responsibility.

Don't lecture, moralize, scold, praise, blame or argue when I'm drunk or sober.

Don't pour out my liquor; you may feel better, but the situation will be worse.

Don't accept my promises. This is my method of postponing pain. If an agreement is made, keep it.

Don't allow your anxiety to tempt you to try to do for me what I must do for myself.

Don't lose your temper with me; it will destroy you and any possibility of helping me.

Don't cover up the consequences of my drinking; it reduces the crisis but perpetuates my illness.

Above all, don't run away from reality as I do. Alcoholism, my illness, gets worse as my drinking continues. Start to learn now. Understand. Plan for my recovery. I need help from professionals who deal with my illness. I cannot help myself. To do nothing is the worst choice you can make for me.[1]

INTERVENTION

During my period of alcoholism I had two experiences where loving people tried to make me face up to my problem. These confrontations now have a specific *name—intervention.* The purpose: to get the sick person to face up to his/her problem and, preferably, go into a treatment center, or if this cannot be financed, to seek help through a local support group.

The first effort on my behalf succeeded in getting me to a treatment center. After coming home from this twenty-eight-day program, I was dry two months before "falling off the wagon." I was one of the small percentage of failures of this particular treatment center.

The second intervention also got me to a treatment center and saved my life.

Careful planning is essential. It can work with serious drug, alcohol, gambling problems and other life- or family-threatening addictions. You can see how carefully the following intervention must have been planned and rehearsed beforehand.

Intervention: A case study

Later one Sunday morning Paul Taylor dragged himself out of bed with a groan. He was sick to his stomach, his head hurt, and his hands were shaking. He wished he hadn't had so much to drink the night before, and he was looking forward to a strong cup of coffee.

When Paul came downstairs, he was surprised to find his wife and children sitting in the living room with the family doctor and the vice president of the insurance company where he was a salesman. The doctor explained to Paul that they wanted to talk with him about his drinking problem, and he asked Paul to take a seat.

It was Paul's wife who spoke first, her voice shaking. "Paul, on our family vacation this summer, you fell asleep while drinking and smoking, and you set our cabin on fire. We paid two thousand dollars in damages, and even though we've been going to that camp for fourteen years, the management asked us not to return."

Paul stared at his wife incredulously, too surprised to respond. "Three weeks ago," she continued, "you came home drunk in the middle of the night, yelling and swearing. You threw my mother's antique china through the window, and the children and I hid in one of their bedrooms. We were so afraid of what you might do that we locked the door."

Paul glared at his wife and shook his head in amazement. He turned to the vice president, who was his immediate supervisor, and explained that his wife was a nervous woman who frequently became hysterical for no reason. "I may have a little too much to drink now and again," Paul admitted with obvious irritation, "but my wife is really sick. Maybe she needs to see a psychiatrist."

"Dad," Paul's oldest son interrupted hesitantly, "when I played football in high school, I was always afraid of how you would act at my games. One time when you were drinking, you ran out on the field and tried to slug the referee. Last month I brought my fiancée home to meet the family, and you were sitting in the rocking chair, drinking. When we were alone you said that you could take her any time you wanted, that she would like an older man."

Paul was furious. "You're a liar!" he shouted at his son. "If I have a few too many drinks once in a while, it's none of your business."

Next to speak was Paul's employer. "You're one of our best salesmen," the vice president said warmly. "And we go back a lot of years. But lately you've cost us three major clients because of your heavy drinking. We want to keep you in the company, but as long as you are drinking, we can't afford to have you with us."

After the vice president listed examples of Paul's inappropriate behavior, Paul grew quiet and grim-faced. He slumped down into his chair and listened impassively while his twelve-year-old son explained how worried he was that his father could no longer follow the story line of television shows. "You can't even tell Charlie's Angels apart. You always ask me to explain what's happening, but when I do, you get angry and say I can't talk right. You say I'm stupid."

Paul's seventeen-year-old daughter was the next to speak. She told her father how much she loved him and how much it hurt that he did not keep his promises. "On my sixteenth birthday, you were going to take me out for dinner, but you came home from work drunk and passed out on the floor. I spend a lot of time at my girlfriend's house, but I never bring her here anymore. I'm afraid she might see you drunk, and I don't know what you will say to her."

The family doctor spoke last. He explained to Paul the physical consequences of his heavy drinking, starting with the damage to his brain and descending to his throat, heart, stomach and liver. "Your high blood pressure makes you a likely candidate for a stroke," he concluded. "And you are fast becoming impotent because of the shrinking of your testicles. If you continue to drink alcohol, your chances of living another five years are not very good."

When the doctor finished speaking, Paul threw up his hands and looked helplessly at his boss. He admitted that he had been drinking a bit too much and that he was worried about his health. "I promise I've had my last drink. You won't see me drunk again."

The doctor reminded Paul of all the previous times that he had promised to quit drinking and had failed. He explained that alcoholism is a disease that does not respond to will power or good intentions. It was highly improbable that Paul would ever stop drinking on his own. But there was a local treatment center that could give him the help he needed. A room was waiting for him, and he could leave in the morning for a twenty-eight-day stay.

Paul admitted that maybe he did need help, but he was offended by the suggestion that he leave immediately. He appealed to his boss to explain that it would take at least a month to find a substitute for his job. The vice president told Paul that his job was covered, and he was not expected back at work until he completed treatment. This news startled Paul, who protested that he was being railroaded. He wouldn't be pushed around by anyone. He would think it over, and if it seemed like a good idea, he would go when he got ready.

There was an uncomfortable moment of silence, and then Paul's youngest child, a thin, shy five-year-old girl, walked over to her father and put her hand in his. "Daddy," she pleaded, "it's now or never." Paul looked at his daughter and without warning burst into tears. By the next morning he was on his way to a treatment center. Note that the core of this intervention was truth. No persuasions, except by the five-year-old at the very end. Medical facts. Facts regarding family events. On such-and-such a date, this happened. Paul's work performance spelled out by his employer. All carefully planned ahead of time.

Codependence

Codependents, also without being aware of it, are in bondage to a drinking or drug-using family member or to a close friend who is an addict. You can measure the degree of your codependency by the number of the following statements that apply to you.

- My good feelings about who I am stem from being liked by you.

- My good feelings about who I am stem from receiving approval from you.

- Your struggles affect my serenity. My mental attention focuses on solving or relieving your pain.

- My mental attention is focused on pleasing you.

- My mental attention is focused on protecting you.

- My mental attention is focused on manipulating you to "do it my way."

- My self-esteem is bolstered by solving your problems.

- My self-esteem is bolstered by relieving your pain.

- My own hobbies and interests are put aside. My time is spent sharing your interests and hobbies.

- Your clothing and personal appearance are dictated by my desires because I feel you are a reflection of me.

- I am not aware of how I feel. I am aware of how you feel. I am not aware of what I want. I ask you what you want. If I am not aware of something, I assume.

- The dreams I have for my future are linked to you.

- My fear of rejection determines what I say or do.

- My fear of your anger determines what I say or do.

- I use giving as a way of feeling safe in our relationship.

- My social circle diminishes as I involve myself with you.

- I put my values aside in order to connect with you.

- I value your opinion and way of doing things more than my own.

- The quality of my life is in relation to the quality of yours.

Freeing oneself from codependency

- To "let go" does not mean to stop caring, but that I can't do it for someone else.

- To "let go" is not to cut myself off, but to realize that I can't control another.

- To "let go" is not to enable, but to allow learning from natural consequences.

- To "let go" is to admit powerlessness, which means the outcome is not in my hands.

- To "let go" is not to try to change or blame another, but to make the most of myself.

- To "let go" is not to care for, but to care about.

- To "let go" is not to fix, but to be supportive.

- To "let go" is not to judge, but to allow another to be a human being.

- To "let go" is not to be in the middle arranging all the outcomes, but to allow others to affect their destinies.

- To "let go" is not to be protective, but to permit another to face reality.

◈ To "let go" is not to deny, but to accept.

◈ To "let go" is not to nag, scold or argue, but instead to search out my own shortcomings and correct them.

◈ To "let go" is not to adjust everything to my desires, but to take each day as it comes, and cherish myself in it.

◈ To "let go" is not to criticize and regulate anybody, but to try to become what I dream I can be.

◈ To "let go" is not to regret the past, but to grow and live for the future.

◈ To "let go" is to fear less and love more.

Codependence: A case history

Then there was Scott, thirtyish, who handled legal matters for our family. He admitted to me that he had become a codependent to his alcoholic father. When Mark, his younger brother, was being married, Scott agreed to try and get their father to the wedding sober. He made the enabler's classic statement: "I'll take care of it," thus assuming the role of the protector. In Scott's own words, here's what happened:

> When I walked into the room, I knew Dad was really "out of it!" I was so angry. My brother and I had made such a point of asking him to lay off the stuff for just this one day.
>
> "Dad, can you make it through the wedding?" I asked.
>
> "Of course. I've only had a couple of drinks. I'm just fine."
>
> How many times have I heard that before! I should have left him in the motel room, but I got him into the car and started parenting him. I told him not to ruin his son's big day.
>
> He got furious at me and said if I couldn't trust him, I should turn the car around and take him back to the motel. That put me completely on the defensive, so I caved in and said, "OK, Dad, let's go to the wedding and have a good time."
>
> He stumbled slightly working his way into the church pew, but nobody noticed but me. Then at the reception he got absolutely ploughed, fell down flat on his face twice. The third time he careened into the gift table and knocked a tray of crystal goblets to the floor. As if this weren't bad enough, when I looked down at his

pants, his fly was open and the tail of his shirt was sticking out of his zipper.

At this point, the bride was in tears. My brother was furious with me, like it all was my fault, and I wanted to strangle Dad, I was so angry. When I got him back to the motel, I unlocked his room, practically carried him out of the car and shoved him through the door. He fell down on the bed face first. Then I felt terrible. He was so helpless. Like a bad little boy. As I looked at him on the bed, I didn't know if I loved him or hated him. Finally I undressed him, as I've done hundreds of times before, and made sure he was securely tucked in bed. He was snoring and hiccuping when I left.

While driving back to the reception, I was grinding my teeth like I used to do at night as a boy when I lay in my bed listening to my father in a drunken rage screaming at my mother. Before my mother died of cancer several years before, she told me one day how much she hated my father.

I said, "But Mom, you've got to forgive him," trying to be the peacemaker.

She looked me straight in the eye and said, "I'll never forgive him for what he's done to me and all of you. Never! Never! Never!"

Today Scott is getting help at Al-Anon and Adult Children of Alcoholics meetings where spouses, families and friends of alcoholics gather weekly to learn how to apply the Twelve-Step program to their situations.

17

The Spiritual Dimension

Alcoholics for Christ

Alcoholics for Christ (AC) is a nondenominational, nonprofit Christian fellowship founded in 1981 for alcoholics and their families. It is dedicated to the propagation of the gospel of Jesus Christ as well as the sharing of His burden for lost and hurting individuals. This fellowship uses the Word of God as its primary source of direction. Its statement:

> We agree that drunkenness is a sin and we believe that alcoholism is a disease with spiritual origins. We rejoice that Jesus forgives us of our sin and heals us of our diseases. Both Scripture and science indicate that there can be an inherited *trait* in the alcoholic.
>
> This "trait" may be triggered in some by persistent rebellious abuse of alcohol (drunkenness) while in others, relatively casual use is all that is needed to set it in motion and, whether we describe it as *predisposition to alcoholism* or the results of *a curse* ("visiting the iniquities of the fathers upon the children to the third and fourth generation"...Exod. 20:5), the cure is to be found in *total abstinence* through Jesus Christ.
>
> We are learning that the Lord delivers some persons immediately from the compulsion and desire to drink, for others He does it gradually. In either case, the requirements for *maintaining* deliverance are total abstinence and an ever-increasing relationship with

the Lord. We believe that God wants us "chemically free" and that is not His purpose to make "social drinkers" out of drunks. God heals us by removing the compulsion and desire and restoring us to Himself.

The alcoholic and family members who attend local AA or Al-Anon groups are encouraged to remain active in them and, where possible, to continue to worship within their own body of believers. However, we do recommend where no strong denominational ties exist, regular attendance in a Bible-believing church of their choice.

While the references deal primarily with alcoholism and the alcoholic, the spiritual principles set forth in AC are applicable to all persons and families who are, or have been, chemically dependent, regardless of the nature of the addiction.

For further information contact:

Alcoholics for Christ, Inc.
1316 North Campbell Road
Royal Oak, MI 48067
248-399-9955
www.alcoholicsforchrist.com

Christian Treatment Centers

As the compulsion/addiction problem reaches crisis proportions in America, more and more Christian churches and groups are setting up treatment centers throughout the country. Specific information can be obtained through local churches. Here are names and addresses of a few treatment centers.

Rapha—a Christ-centered in-hospital counseling care unit, treating psychiatric and substance abuse problems for the Christian community.

Rapha Christian Counseling
3021 Gateway, Suite 290
Irving, TX 75063
800-227-2657
www.raphacare.com

Teen Challenge—a national ministry devoted to "soul saving and life saving." For information about drug and alcohol treatment write to:

The Spiritual Dimension

Teen Challenge, Inc.
444 Clinton Ave.
New York, NY 11238
718-789-1414
www.teenchallenge.com

Dunklin Memorial Camp Assisted Living Facility (see report on page 168)

407 NW 2nd Avenue
Okeechobee, FL 34972
863-763-4524

Hebron Colony and Grace House—a Christian treatment center for both men and women. Eight-week course. Basic approach is that alcoholism is not a disease, but a sin against oneself, one's family, one's neighbor, one's God. Scriptural program.

Hebron Colony/Grace House
Route 3, P.O. Box 4600
Boone, NC 28607
828-580-6806

Faith Farms—threefold recovery program to achieve spiritual maturity, mental awareness, physical discipline.

Faith Farms
9538 Highway 441
Boynton Beach, FL 33436
561-737-2222
www.faithfarm.org

Ephesians Life Ministries, Inc. (Be not drunk with wine which leads to wild living but rather be filled with the Spirit.) For information about programs and treatment, contact:

Ephesians Life Ministries, Inc.
1620 Elton Rd., Suite 204
Silver Spring, MD 20903
301-439-7191
www.ephesians.org

AFTERWORD

To: The person reading this book

From: The person who wrote this book

Re: The rest of the story

This is a new beginning for the *The Compulsive Woman*. Published in 1987, she and her "sister books," *The Not So Compulsive Woman* and the compilation book *A Woman's Journey to Freedom,* have sadly gone out of print.

As I speak and minister to broken women all over the country, one thing became crystal clear; this book is needed more now than ever before. There's a whole new generation of women struggling with life-defeating, life-threatening lifestyles.

It seemed obvious *The Compulsive Woman* needed to be updated and republished. By the volume of mail I received I knew peoples' lives were being changed. Several men wrote me. One in particular said, "I bought your book as a gift for my wife. Before I went to bed I thought I'd just read a couple of pages...It's 5:00 A.M. and I just finished the entire book. It answered so many questions I've struggled with all my life. Thank you for helping me understand myself and my wife better..."

Another from a professional friend "Your book has been tremendously helpful in my practice. It should be in every counselor and pastor's library."

The letter I cherish is from a woman prisoner from Washington state who, after her parole, found her personal life in such chaos she felt the only solution was suicide. She writes, "Sandy, someone gave me a copy of your book. There was no way I wanted to read it. Death seemed the only answer to end the turmoil going on inside…That was many months ago. I read your book from cover to cover. It gave me hope. If you could make it, I could make it. I can honestly say your book saved my life."

If the book had only been written for her it was worth all the effort.

The rewrite of this book has been an interesting continuation of my own healing journey. The world is a much different place than it was in 1987. More hostile, dangerous, challenging. Women's issues too have accelerated in alarming ways. So much so that new subjects have been added at the back of the book: pornography (especially child porn), women's increasing addictions, gambling problems, sexual addiction, post-abortion stress, domestic violence, depression in its many forms, workaholism, power sex abuse by those in positions of authority, perfectionism, computer/Internet/TV addictions, anorexia, bulimia and much, much more.

An undertaking as complex as republishing this book has to be a team effort. My friends Alan and Carroll Maxwell were my most enthusiastic cheerleaders for resurrecting *The Compulsive Woman*. As was Allen Quain at Creation House Press. The time was right, so "Let's roll!"

If I may use an old soap opera technique—the flashback—let's revisit chapter seven, "Breaking the Cycle," and my encounter with a fellow patient, Karen…

The plot thickens. An element of mystery has been added. Now, twenty-three years later I marvel at how that fragile event with Karen had begun a fundamental change in my life. What had happened?

The Billings women had prayed God would send someone to me. I believe today that Karen was was that God-sent person. My holding her in my arms, saying the words she needed to hear, had not only comforted her but had stirred something deep within me.

By assuring her that Jesus loved her I was somehow saying those very words to myself. "Yes, Sandy, Jesus loves you, too." In an instant I had changed from a totally self-centered individual to one with the tiny beginning of a caring heart for others.

Not that in some supernatural way I suddenly became an others-centered person. That had to take place over a period of time. But there had been a supernatural change of attitude in my spirit. A small thing perhaps, but life changing.

Afterword

After publication of *The Compulsive Woman,* I set about making a list of people I wanted to send gift books to. Countless people were used by God along the journey: family, friends, doctors, pastors, priests, counselors. But in thinking about those involved, I realized Karen and the Billings women probably topped the list.

We had no difficulty getting books to most on the list, but how to track down Karen? I got a letter off to the Montana State Hospital with the dates Karen and I had been patients, the ward we'd been on and any other facts I could recall.

Several weeks later a letter arrived from the institution. "Dear Mrs. LeSourd: Thank you for your inquiry. We have no record of the patient you mentioned in your letter."

My first reaction had been one of annoyance at their dismissive attitude. Then, as I reread the letter, absorbing the implications of its terse comments, my body was flooded with chills.

If there was no record of such a patient...could Karen have been...an angel? She had certainly looked like one. At times her physical beauty had taken my breath away.

But it was her love, her grace, her inexhaustible pursuit of Jesus and of me. A hound of heaven? I said to Len, "Do you suppose she could have been an angel?"

"If she isn't, Sandy, you'll hear from her. You've told the Karen story on national television, in your book, in articles, at dozens of conferences. Sooner or later, if she lives on this earth, she'll hear about your recovery and get in touch with you."

I've never heard from her. But I have been touched by the brush of angels' wings.

Our world started to crumble in late summer of 1995 when we received the heart-stopping news that Len had a large cancerous tumor in his intestines. He had ignored all symptoms. The cancer had already spread to his liver.

We prayed and believed for a healing miracle. Chemo was to no avail. The cancer continued to ravage Len's increasing fragile body. At 4:00 A.M. on February 5, 1996, the phone rang. It was "the call."

I lay in our bed, stunned at what I'd just learned. Len had been very ill for several weeks. But he wasn't supposed to die so soon—or at all. We had planned on many more years together.

We'd been blessed with ten great years of marriage and a partnership as editor/author/conference speakers and prayer ministers. A friend's remark about us never failed to rouse a chuckle: "Len taught Sandy how to work, and Sandy taught Len how to play..."

I felt that my life was over, too! My beloved life partner and mentor, my sweetheart and best friend, was suddenly whisked away from me and out of the lives of our blended families. His loss was devastating to all of us.

Unable to face being alone in our bed, I spent many months sleeping on the living room couch wearing Len's pajamas and eating an entire pint of ice cream each evening. My "sleeping pill," I called it.

I gained twenty pounds. The Scriptures were as dry as dust. My prayer life was practically nonexistent. I couldn't concentrate on anything or anyone but Len. What would I do without him?

The most important lesson I learned from my experience as a widow is that our happiness does not stem from a relationship with a man but from a relationship with the living God. He alone loves us completely and offers us everlasting union with Him.

Many widows wrestle as I did, through dark nights of grief and loneliness. But when they emerge into the light of a new day, they find that God never left them. Neither did He forsake them.

When I finally realized that bed could no longer be my hiding place, I had to get on with the business of living. I was learning more and more how to build up my spiritual resources, how to deal with temptations when they assaulted me and always keep my eyes on the One whose name Karen had called from the pit of despair. Circumstances changed. I changed and grew. God was so faithful to answer my prayers and meet me at the point of my deepest need. He is still faithful as my Healer, Provider, Protector and Husband (Isa. 54:5). He loves His widows and holds me tenderly "in His everlasting arms."

As part of my healing journey, I revisited Delray Beach, Florida where Len and I spent our winters. How he loved to walk the beach, drink in the tropical beauty and spar on the tennis court with men half his age. It seemed surreal to return to all the old familiar places: New Covenant Church where we worshiped, the Bar Harbour where lived, our favorite restaurants, and most painful of all, the room where Len died at Bethesda Hospital in Boynton Beach.

Returning to Florida, as emotionally difficult as it was, helped heal me and set me free at a deeper level. My heart felt a stirring of closure. The journey continues. Prayer knits up our raveled hearts so that one day we can say, "Weeping may remain for the night, but joy comes in the morning [mourning]" (Ps. 30:5). What peace it gives us to know that our loved ones who love Jesus have gone on "home" to be with HIM.

After Len had been gone for two years, I felt a new season was to begin, and it was to be in my home state of Vermont. I moved to Montpelier to be close to my eighty-seven-year-old mother who lives in a retirement home.

Len's memory was very much there, too. This is where we fell in love and got married. I pass City Hall where we got our marriage license, the restaurants we frequented, the state capitol steps where we sat and dreamed and planned our lives together. What wonderful surprises the Lord had in store for us.

On our wedding anniversary (June 22) I returned to the Trapp Family Lodge (of *Sound of Music* fame) in Stowe where we'd married in 1985. My heart throbbed as I returned to that place…to the third floor in Maria Von Trapp's parlor, which had been transformed into a beautiful wedding chapel. I could still see our family and friends seated together waiting for the bride and groom to enter.

I could still hear the music and see Len's radiant grin as he gave me the "thumbs-up" sign in the hallway before the ceremony began. It all seems a beautiful dream now. Neither of us could have known how God would used us and bless us as a team in answer to years of prayer or have imagined the joyful purpose and companionship He had for us.

Some years before Len died, I'd found him gazing out the window at the sky. "I wonder what's going on up in heaven today? You know, Sandy, someday I'm going to be the editor of the "Heavenly Gazette."

Not long after 9-11, I visited Len's grave in Lincoln, Virginia. Staring back at me from Len's headstone was the simple sentence: "He served." Kneeling down I planted an American flag on his grave. My mind flooded with the ways Len had served. Countless ways to countless people. He had his list of priorities:

1. God
2. Spouse
3. Family
4. Work/Ministry

…and so on. I used to kid him that his work sometimes got bumped up a notch on the list.

As the little silk flag fluttered in the soft autumn breeze, I was reminded how proud Len had been to serve his country in the Army Air Corps as a pilot/instructor. But he was totally sold out to serving God with every fiber of his being. Very simply, Len lived to serve.

Back home in Vermont, I checked my mail. Still no copy of "The Heavenly Gazette." But nothing is impossible with God.

Notes

Introduction

1. Connell Cowan and Melvyn Kinder, *Smart Women/Foolish Choices*, reissue (n.p.: New American Library, 1991).

Chapter 1: Facing Off

1. Jim Orford, *Excessive Appetites: A Psychological View of Addictions*, 2nd edition (New York: John Wiley and Sons, 2001).

Chapter 2: The Violated Childhood

1. Martha Janssen, *Silent Scream* (Philadelphia, PA: Fortress Press, 1983), 13.
2. Bonnie S. Fisher, Francis T. Cullen and Michael G. Turner, "The Sexual Victimization of College Women" (Bureau of Justice, U.S. Department of Justice, and the National Institute of Justice), quoted in editorial, "Guns effective defense against rape," *Minnesota Daily* (February 20, 2001). Accessed online at www.daily.umn.edu/daily/2001/02/20/editorial_opinions/oo0220 on August 25, 2002.
3. National Crime Victimization Survey, Bureau of Justice statistics, U.S. Department of Justice, 1997.
4. From a lecture by Terry Kellogg at the Compulsivity Clinic.
5. Isaiah 53:5, NKJV
6. Pamela Vredevelt and Kathryn Rodriguez, *Surviving the Secret,* expanded edition (Old Tappan, NJ: Fleming H. Revell, 1992).

Chapter 3: The Dysfunctional Home

1. Helen M. Lynd, *On Shame and the Search for Identity* (n.p.: Harcourt Brace, 1970).
2. Stanton Peele, Ph.D., *Love and Addiction* (n.p.: Taplinger Publishing Co., 1975).

Chapter 4: Into the Fast Lane

1. Dr. David J. Juroe, *Money* (Old Tappan, NJ: Fleming H. Revell Co., n.d.).
2. "Compulsive Shopping," *Glamour* magazine (April 1986).
3. Ray J. Hodgson and Peter M. Miller, *Self-Watching: Addictions, Habits, Compulsions* (n.p.: Facts on File, Inc., 1983).
4. Colette Dowling, *The Cinderella Complex* (New York: Summit Books, 1981).
5. Nancy Friday, *My Mother/My Self* (n.p.: Delta, 1997).
6. Howard M. Halpern, *How to Break Your Addiction to a Person* (New York: Bantam Books, 1983).
7. Position Paper on Drug Policy, Physician Leadership on National Drug Policy (PLNDP), Brown University Center for Alcohol and Addiction Studies, 2000. Retrieved on August 31, 2002 from "America's Number One Health Problem," www.ncadd.org/facts/index.
8. B. Grant et al., "Prevalence of DSM-IV Alcohol Abuse and Dependence," *AHRW,*

295

Vol. 18, No. 3 (1994): 243, 245. Retrieved on August 31, 2002 from "Use of Alcohol and Other Drugs Among Women," www.ncadd.org/facts/index.

9. Theodore I. Rubin, M.D., *Compassion and Self-Hate* (n.p.: Touchstone Books, 1998).

CHAPTER 5: THE CULTIST

1. Sonya Friedman, Ph.D., *Men Are Just Desserts* (n.p.: Warner Books, 1994).
2. Karen Horney, M.D., *Feminine Psychology* (n.p.: W. W. Norton and Company, 1993).
3. "Anatomy of Ecstasy," *American Health* (January/February 1987).
4. M. Scott Peck, M.D., *The Road Less Traveled* (n.p.: Touchstone Books, 1998).
5. "The New Paganism," *Whistleblower Magazine* (August 1, 2002): retrieved August 31, 2002 from WorldNetDaily exclusive, http://wnd.com/news/article.asp?ARTI-CLE_ID=28468.
6. Ibid.
7. Dr. Michael Langone, editor of *Cultic Studies Journal,* retrieved from www.csj.org/infoserv_cult101/checklis.htm.
8. Derek Prince, *Blessings or Curses: You Can Choose* (Grand Rapids, MI: Chosen Books, 1990).

CHAPTER 6: WHY LIVE?

1. From a pamphlet by Children of Alcoholism Foundation, Inc., 200 Park Avenue, New York, NY 10166.
2. Ibid.
3. Janet G. Woititz, *Adult Children of Alcoholics* (Pompano Beach, FL: Health Communications, Inc., 1983).
4. Fast Stats, National Center for Health Statistics, retrieved August 31, 2002 from www.cdc.gov/nchs/fastats/suicide.htm.
5. Arthur Janov, *The Primal Scream* (n.p.: Dell Publishing Company, 1970).

CHAPTER 7: BREAKING THE CYCLE

1. Hodgson and *Miller, Self-Watching.*

CHAPTER 8: DO IT NOW

1. Theodore Rubin, *The Winner's Notebook* (n.p.: MacMillan Publishing Company, 1985).

CHAPTER 9: THE PAIN IN CHANGE

1. Mary Ellen Pinkham, *How to Stop the One You Love from Drinking* (n.p.: Putnam Pub. Group, 1989).
2. Edward M. Brecher and the editors of *Consumer Reports, The Consumers Union Report on Licit and Illicit Drugs,* chapter 25, "Nicotine as an addicting drug" (1972).
3. Rubin, *The Winner's Notebook.*
4. "Smoking in the Workplace Costs Employers Money," retrieved August 31, 2002 from http://ash.org/papers/h100.htm#HOW.

Notes

5. "Cigarette Smoking Statistics," retrieved August 31, 2002 from www.american-heart.org/presenter.jhtml?identifier=4559.
6. John M. Leighty, "Smoking: How to Wrap It Up," *Washington Post* (November 19, 1986).
7. Hodgson and *Miller, Self-Watching.*
8. Margaret Hamburg, M.D., "The Nature of Craving," *Vogue* (August 1986).
9. Peck, *The Road Less Traveled.*
10. Lewis B. Smedes, *Forgive and Forget* (New York: Pocket Books, 1986).
11. Peele, *Love and Addiction.*

CHAPTER 10: INTERVENTION

1. Pinkham, *How to Stop the One You Love from Drinking.*
2. Anderson A. Spickard, M.D. and Barbara R. Thompson, *Dying for a Drink* (Waco, TX: Word Books, 1985).
3. Betty Ford, *A Glad Awakening* (New York: Doubleday, 1987).

CHAPTER 11: FACING TRUTH

1. Betty Ford, *The Times of My Life* (n.p.: HarperCollins, 1978).
2. Some materials in this chapter are adapted from *Broken Promises, Mended Dreams* by Richard Meryman (Little, Brown & Co., 1984). The anonymous woman in this book was a composite of several women, including Sandra Simpson LeSourd.
3. Janov, *The Primal Scream.*
4. Robin Norwood, *Women Who Love Too Much* (New York: Pocket Books, 1991).
5. "Amazing Grace" by John Newton. Public domain.
6. Smedes, *Forgive and Forget.*

CHAPTER 12: ANGER AND MALE DEPENDENCY

1. Norwood, *Women Who Love Too Much.*
2. Friedman, *Men Are Just Desserts.*

CHAPTER 13: DECEPTION AND OTHER LITTLE MONSTERS

1. Erich Fromm, *The Anatomy of Human Destructiveness* (n.p.: Henry Holt, 1992).
2. From materials distributed by Rogers Memorial Hospital, Oconomowoc, Wisconsin.
3. Romans 7:15, NIV
4. 2 Corinthians 10:5, NIV
5. Norwood, *Women Who Love Too Much.*
6. Peele, *Love and Addiction.*

CHAPTER 15: HELP FOR THE COMPULSIVE WOMAN AND HER FAMILY

1. Statistics from the National Council on Alcoholism and Drug Dependence and The Comprehensive Assessment Treatment Outcomes Registry Data, in Ohio.
2. The Twelve Steps reprinted with permission of Alcoholics Anonymous World Services, Inc.
3. Holly G. Atkinson, M.D., M.S.J., *New Woman* (September 1988).

4. Charles W. Crewe, *A Look at Relapse* (Center City, MN: Hazelden Literature, 1974).
5. With the exception of "Club drugs," information in this section is taken from *USA Today* (September 16, 1987).
6. "Club Drugs: Health Hazards, Extent of Illicit Use," OHS, Inc. Retrieved from www.ohsinc.com/club_drugs.htm.
7. Christine Adams, "Parenting the Drug-affected Youth," *Marriage and Family Living* (March 1986).
8. From Narcotics Anonymous booklet, copyright © 1986 by World Service Office, Inc.
9. "What You Need to Know About Anorexia Nervosa and Bulimia," Anorexia Bulimia Nervosa Association, retrieved fromwww.span.com.au/anorexia/info.html.
10. Ibid.
11. "Survival Tips for Families," Bulimia Anorexia Nervosa Association (BANA), retrieved from www.bana.ca/survival.htm.
12. Copyright © Overeaters Anonymous. Used by permission.
13. Domestic Violence Information Manual, retrieved from www.wise.infoxchange.net.au/DVIM.DVIM1.htm. Domestic Violence Information Kit, third edition (Western Australia, Australia: Dept. of Community Services, 1992), 14–15.
14. "Violence Related Injuries Treated in Hospital Emergency Departments," U.S. Department of Justice, Bureau of Justice statistics, retrieved September 2, 2002 from www.ojp.usdoj.gov/bjs/abstract/vrithed.htm.
15. National Domestic Violence Hotline, retrieved from www.ojp.usdoj.gov/ovc/help/hotline/ndvhpage.htm.
16. "Bipolar Facts," *Symptoms, Diagnose, Treatment and Survival,* retrieved from www.bipolar-disorders.com.
17. National Mental Health Association statistics.
18. "Depression: Treat It," National Institute of Mental Health, accessed June 1999.
19. D. B. Kandel and M. Davies, "Epidemiology of Depressive Mood in Adolescents: An Empirical Study," *Archives of General Psychiatry* 39 (1982): 1205–1212.
20. National Institute of Mental Health. "Women Hold Up Half the Sky," Updated June 1999.
21. D. Siedman, "Postpartum Psychiatric Illness: The Role of the Pediatritian," *Pediatrics in Review* 19 (1998): 128–131.
22. National Institute of Mental Health, Unpublished Epidemiological Catchment Area Analysis (1999).
23. Ibid.
24. "Depression: Treat It," National Institute of Mental Health, accessed June 1999.
25. E. McGrath, G. P. Keita, B. R. Strickland and N. F. Russo, *Women and Depression: Risk Factors and Treatment Issues* (Washington, DC: American Psychological Association, 1990).
26. A. Rupp, E. Gause and D. Regier, "Research Policy Implications of Cost-of-Illness Studies for Mental Disorders," *British Journal of Psychiatry* 36 Suppl (1998): 19–25.
27. O'Hara, 1995; Troutman and Cutrona, 1990.
28. Postpartum Depression: Causes, Symptoms and Treatments, retrieved from www.post-partum-depression.com.

Notes

29. Diane S. Dew, *The Standard,* retrieved from http://dianedew.com/trauma.htm.
30. "Post-Abortion Stress Syndrome: Does It Affect You?", retrieved from www.after-abortion.com/quiz.html.
31. Information in this section was obtained from "Teen Depression: Prevention, Detection and Causes," retrieved from www.teen-depression.info.
32. "Anxiety Disorders," The National Institute of Mental Health, retrieved from www.nimh.nih.gov/anxiety/anxiety.cfm.
33. Information in this section was obtained from the National Institute of Mental Health, retrieved from www.nimh.nih.gov/publicat/ocd.cfm.
34. Information in this section was obtained "What Is PTSD?", The National Center for PTSD, retrieved from www.ncptsd.org/faq.html, and the National Institute of Mental Health.
35. Information in this section was obtained from the National Organization for Victims Assistance, retrieved from www.try-nova.org, and the APA Help Center, retrieved from http://helpng.apa.org/daily/traumaticstress.html.
36. "Perfectionism," Suny Potsdam Counseling Center, retrieved from www.potsdam.edu/COUN/brochures/perfectionism.html.
37. Information in this section was obtained from the American Academy of Pediatrics, retrieved from www.aap.org.
38. Information in this section was obtained from Dr. Terry Neher, retrieved from http://209.180.175.75/becalmd/test/ADHA.htm.
39. Information in this section was obtained from The Stanton Peele Addiction Website, retrieved from www.peele.net/faq/tv.html.
40. John M. Grohol, Psy.D., "How Much is Too Much When Spending Time Online?", Center for Online Addiction, retrieved from http://psychcentral.com/netaddiction. Also from Dr. Kimberly Young, "Is the Internet Addictive, or Are Addicts Using the Internet?"
41. Information in this section was obtained from John Suler, Ph.D., retrieved from www.planetpsych.com/zPsychology101/cyber_addiction.htm.
42. Lori Valigra, "Study: Internet sex can be harmful," PsycPort news story, retrieved from www.psycport.com/news/19990328/18/comtex-00398W3f922663708.html.
43. Ibid.
44. Ibid.
45. Geneen Roth, *Breaking Free from Compulsive Eating* (New York: BobsMerril Co., Inc., 1984).
46. Problem Gambling Is a Women's Health Issue, Profile of Women Gamblers Highlights from the Connecticut Council on Problem Gambling 1998 Helpline Summary, retrieved from www.ccpg.org/resources/women_1998.asp.
47. Ibid.
48. Ibid.
49. Ibid.
50. National Council on Problem Gambling 10 Questions About Gambling Behavior, retrieved September 2, 2002 from http://www.ncpgambling.org/10questions.htm.
51. "The Addiction of the Millennium," retrieved from www.800gambler.org/mill.html.
52. Buy and Hold, a Division of Freedom Investments, retrieved from www.buyand-hold.com/bh/en/retirement/retirement_perspective.

53. "Nationwide Survey: Nearly One in Five at Missions Say Gambling a Factor in Their Homelessness," Statistics and Studies: 1998 Gambling and Homelessness Survey, Association of Gospel Rescue Missions, retrieved from www.agrm.org/news/gambling.html.

54. Women & Problem Gambling, retrieved from www.cobra-net.com/peardonvillegamb/adol.htm.

55. Jeffrey L. Derevensky, Ph.D. and Rina Gupta, Ph.D., "Youth Gambling: A Clinical and Research Perspective," *The Electronic Journal of Gambling Issues,* retrieved from www.camh.net/egambling/issue2/feature.

56. Norwood, *Women Who Love Too Much.*

57. Lois Leiderman Davitz and Joel Davitz, *Living in Sync: Men and Women in Love* (New York: Bergh Publishing, Inc., 1986).

58. Medical Information of The Cleveland Clinic, retrieved on July 29, 2002 from http://aolsvc.health.webmd.aol.com/content/article/2953.534.

59. From the booklet "From Shame to Grace."

60. Kimberly Daniels, *From a Mess to a Miracle* (Lake Mary, FL: Creation House Press, 2002).

61. Ibid.

62. Sandra LeSourd, "My Maker Is My Husband," *SpiritLed Woman* (December/January 2002): 22–24.

63. Jeannette Howard, Out of Egypt: *Leaving Lesbianism Behind* (Crowborough, England: Regeneration Books and Monarch Publications, 1991, 1997). Excerpt retrieved from www.narth.com/docs/egypt.html.

64. Ibid.

65. Adapted from Christina Anderson, "Pornography—Girl's Perspective," *Soul Purpose* magazine (SP 12) (Summer 2002): retrieved from www.soulpurpose.co.nz/mag/2002/12summer/12_2002_pfemale_01.shtml.

66. Portia Nelson, "Autobiography in Five Short Chapters," retrieved from www.no-porn.com/index.html.

67. Anonymous, "Do women struggle with pornography addiction?", retrieved from www.voy.com/39404/10.html.

68. Patrick Carnes, Ph.D., *Don't Call It Love* (New York: Bantam Books, 1992).

69. The author gratefully acknowledges the research done by several on the subject of women and sexual addictions (including pornography and masturbation): Noryne Mascarella; Patrick Carnes, Ph.D., David L. Delmonico, Ph.D. and Elizabeth Griffin, M.A., *In the Shadows of the Net: Breaking Free of Compulsive Online Sexual Behavior* (n.p.: Hazelton Information Education, 2001); Carnes, *Don't Call It Love;* Jennifer Schneider, M.D., Ph.D. and Robert Weiss, M.S.W., *Cybersex Exposed* (n.p.: Hazelton Information Education, 2001); Douglas Weiss, Ph.D., *She Has a Secret* (n.p.: Discovery Press, 2000).

70. *Diagnostic and Statistical Manual of Mental Disorders,* 4th edition (DSM-IV) (1994); Pamela K. Sutherland, "Sexual Abuse by Therapists, Physicians, Attorneys, and Other Professionals"; Joel Friedman and Marcia Mobilia Boumil, *Betrayal of Trust: Sex and Power in Professional Relationships* (n.p.: Bergin & Garvey, 1995), 109–113; *Breach of Trust: Sexual Exploitation by Health Care Professionals and Clergy,* John Gonsiorek, editor (n.p.: Sage Publications, 1995), 82.

71. Friedman and Boumil, *Betrayal of Trust: Sex and Power in Professional Relationships,* introduction.

72. Gary Richard Schoener, "Assessment & Rehabilitation of Psychotherapists Who Violate Boundaries With Clients."

73. Friedman and Boumil, *Betrayal of Trust: Sex and Power in Professional Relationships,* 10.

74. Ibid.

75. Steven B. Bisbang, Linda M. Jorgenson, Pamela K. Sutherland, "Sexual Abuse by Professionals: A Legal Guide", section 6-6(b) "Third Parties as Secondary Victims", which references: Jeanette Milgrom, "Secondary Victim of Sexual Exploitation by Counselors and Therapists: Some Observations"; *Breach of Trust: Sexual Exploitation by Health Care Professionals and Clergy,* 112.

76. Rev. Dr. Paul Chaim Schneck, "Child Pornography and the Gospel," retrieved from www.faithandaction.org.

77. Retrieved from www.siawso.org/effects.htm.

78. Retrieved from www.incestabuse.about.com/library/weekly/aa090197.htm.

79. Counseling for Loss & Life Changes, retrieved from www.counselingforloss.com/question.htm.

80. Jerry Deffenbacher, Ph.D. and Charles Spielberger, Ph.D., retrieved from www.angerproject.com and www.apa.org/pubinfo/anger.html.

81. Thomas P. Hollander, Ph.D., Anger Management in Sobriety, retrieved from www.shpm.com/articles/atd/anger.html.

82. Jerry Deffenbacher, Ph.D. and Charles Spielberger, Ph.D., retrieved from www.angerproject.com and www.apa.org/pubinfo/anger.html. Also, The Counseling Center for Human Development, retrieved from http://usweb.usf.edu/counsel/self-hlp/anger.htm.

83. From "Suicide—It Doesn't Have to Happen," by Edwin S. Schneidman, Ph.D. and Philip Mandelkorn. Prepared by the American Association of Suicidology in cooperation with MSD Health Information Services.

84. Information in this section was obtained from the National Strategy for Suicide Prevention (NSSP) A Collaborative Effort of SAMSHA, CDC, NIH, HRSA, www.mentalhealth.org.

85. Teresa Neumann, The Health List (August 16, 2002): e-mail newsletter dated August 23, 2002.

86. Ibid.

87. Ibid.

88. Frank B. Minirth, et al., *The Workaholic and His Family* (Grand Rapids, MI: Baker Book House, 1981).

Chapter 16: Help for Families and Friends

1. From booklet about Families in Crisis, 7320 Ohms Lane, Edina, Minnesota 55435.

To Contact the author:

SANDY LESOURD
"The Listening Heart" Ministries
P.O. Box 3808
Stowe, VT 05672
armdword@aol.com